This Book Donated To
The Everett Public Library
By Everett's
KRKO Radio 1380 AM
(425) 304-1381 phone (425) 304-1382 fax
www.krko1380.com

110630604

PIONEERS OF
WONDER

This Book Donated To
The Everett Public Library
By Everett's
KRKO Radio 1380 AM
(425) 304-1381 phone (425) 304-1382 fax
www.krko1380.com

Eric Leif Davin

PIONEERS OF WONDER

Conversations

with the

Founders of

Science Fiction

Prometheus Books

59 John Glenn Drive
Amherst, New York 14228-2197

Published 1999 by Prometheus Books

Pioneers of Wonder: Conversations with the Founders of Science Fiction. Copyright © 1999 by Eric Leif Davin. All rights reserved, except for first North American serial rights only (see below). No part of this publication may be reproduced, stored in a retrieval system, or transmitted in any form or by any means, electronic, mechanical, photocopying, recording, or otherwise, without prior written permission of the publisher, except in the case of brief quotations embodied in critical articles and reviews.

"The Age of Wonder" first appeared in *Fantasy Commentator* 37 (1987).
"The Silberkleit Years and the Birth of Comic Books" first appeared in *Fantasy Commentator* 39 (1989).
"Stanley G. Weinbaum and Black Margot" first appeared as "Remembering Stanley G. Weinbaum" in *Fantasy Commentator* 42 (1991).
"From Wisconsin to Mars" first appeared as "Pioneer in the Age of Wonder" in *Fantasy Commentator* 38 (1988).
"Teenage Author" first appeared as "The Optimistic Pessimist" in *Fantasy Commentator* 39 (1989).
"The Science and Science Fiction of R. F. Starzl" first appeared as "Remembering R. F. Starzl" in *Fantasy Commentator* 47–48 (1995).
"The Birth of Science Fiction Books" first appeared as "Pioneer Publisher" in *Fantasy Commentator* 45–46 (1993–94).
"From Print to Screen" first appeared as "Long Distance Runner" in *Out of James' Attic* (August 1997).

Inquiries should be addressed to
Prometheus Books, 59 John Glenn Drive, Amherst, New York 14228–2197.
VOICE: 716–691–0133, ext. 207. FAX: 716–564–2711.
WWW.PROMETHEUSBOOKS.COM

03 02 01 00 99   5 4 3 2 1

Library of Congress Cataloging-in-Publication Data

Davin, Eric Leif.
    Pioneers of wonder : conversations with the founders of science fiction / Eric Leif Davin.
        p.   cm.
    Includes index.
    ISBN 1–57392–702–3 (alk. paper)
    1. Science fiction, American—History and criticism—Theory, etc. 2. Authors, American—20th century—Interviews. 3. Science fiction—Authorship. I. Title.
PS374.S35D36   1999
813'.0876209—dc21   99–37717
                                                                                          CIP

Printed in the United States of America on acid-free paper

For

Sam Moskowitz

A. Langley Searles

Lloyd Biggle Jr.

The Science Fiction Oral History Association

and

all the Pioneers

This Book Donated To
The Everett Public Library
By Everett's
KRKO Radio 1380 AM
(425) 304-1381 phone (425) 304-1382 fax
www.krko1380.com

Acknowledgments

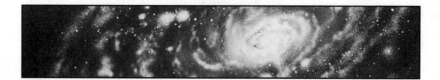

THIS BOOK WOULD NOT EXIST BUT FOR SAM MOSKOWITZ, who introduced me to A. Langley Searles, editor-publisher of *Fantasy Commentator*, now over a half-century old—science fiction's best-kept secret and the fanzine most deserving of a Hugo. In turn, Langley suggested a number of the subjects and caught many of my factual errors before they appeared in print, thus making me seem more knowledgeable than I am. Norm Metcalf was also invaluable in pointing out factual errors before they embarrassed me (although most of his source material is perpetually "in storage"). Lloyd Biggle Jr., founder of the Science Fiction Oral History Association, introduced me to Margaret Weinbaum Kay, who became a true, faithful, and supportive friend. I miss her. For their aid in preparing the index, thanks to fellow PARSEC members Anita Alverio, Dan Bloch, Barb Carlson, Ann Cecil, Kevin Hayes, John Schmid, Mary Tabasko, and Diane Turnshek. Thanks to Edgar Rice Burroughs for Dejah Thoris.

CONTENTS

FOREWORD

by Jack Williamson

ERIC LEIF DAVIN'S *PIONEERS OF WONDER* BRINGS BACK nostalgic recollections of the exciting sense of liberation I found in the early issues of Hugo Gernsback's *Amazing Stories* seventy years ago. His interviews and commentaries recall my own "Age of Wonder," beginning when that historic magazine lifted me out of the tedium of toil on a hardscrabble sandhill farm in eastern New Mexico, into dazzling infinities of future time and cosmic space.

My first few years had been spent close to the Stone Age. Until the Mexican Revolution of 1910, we lived in a grass-roofed house on a ranch high in the Sierra Madre of Sonora, a long day's ride beyond the end of any road for wheels, as my frontier mother used to say. Back in Texas and eastern New Mexico, we were almost as isolated. I grew up unaware of the great classics of Verne and Wells and the more recent imaginative work of such popular magazine writers as A. Merritt and Edgar Rice Burroughs, all of which filled the early issues of

9

Amazing. The magazine opened my mind to the domains of the imagination that have since filled my life.

Science fiction under any name, or more commonly under none at all, has been around almost forever. In the course I teach at Eastern New Mexico University with Dr. Patrice Caldwell, we once began with Homer's *Odyssey,* on the theory that it served as science fiction to the ancient Greeks. I used to include Jonathan Swift's *Gulliver* on the reading list. It's great science fiction, even though Swift was writing not to praise science but to ridicule the pioneer scientists of the Royal Society.

Verne and Wells were the great pioneers of the last century. Verne's "extraordinary voyages" were set largely in his own place and time. Wells, with his "scientific romances," became the chief creator of modern science fiction. The crucial event was his year as a student of Thomas Henry Huxley, Darwin's great champion. The concept of evolutionary change led to his "discovery of the future," to quote the title of his little primer for students of times to come. In *The Time Machine* in 1895 and the novels and short stories that followed in the next few years, he introduced most of the major themes of the genre.

But, though "wonder" was already as old as the human imagination, it was left for Hugo Gernsback to give it a local habitation and a name. "Scientifiction" was his label for my first story, published in 1928, the year before he lost control of *Amazing* and coined the term "science fiction" to designate the contents of the new *Science Wonder Stories.* That coinage has spread around the world, too often collapsed into "sci-fi," but still a synonym for "wonder."

Though Wells and others had foreseen the limits of progress and the dark side of technology, most of us waited with more hope than fear for the promised wonders to come. I remember with excitement the first car I saw, the first airplane, the first radio I heard. Gernsback could still beckon us toward a technological paradise where nothing would be impossible.

By the 1940s, however, technology had begun to show a

darker face. I remember the moment in 1945 when another weatherman on the South Pacific island where I was stationed told me about the A-Bomb. The mushroom cloud over Hiroshima marked a watershed in science fiction and our whole psychology. I remember the smog when I got back to Los Angeles after the war. The wonders were coming, not always so wonderful. I wrote *The Humanoids*. Though I still call myself a desperate optimist, the eager anticipation we found in those early issues of *Amazing* and *Wonder* and *Astounding* has faded and crumbled with the rough pulp paper they were printed on. The future looks darker.

A "Sense of Wonder" remains at the heart of science fiction, however vastly dimmed from what it was to me and the first generation of science fiction readers in that half-forgotten age before computers and TV and the Internet, before the atom, before space flight, back when maps still offered blank spaces for whatever lost races or new wonders we might imagine. I don't think anyone today can quite comprehend what the "Sense of Wonder" was to us, there and then—but in *Pioneers of Wonder*, Eric Leif Davin comes as close as possible as he takes us back to meet the creators of that "wonderful" new genre that has since grown to become a significant element of our cultural history.

Introduction

GENESIS OF WONDER

Hugo Gernsback, "Sense of Wonder," and the Birth of Science Fiction

I T WAS ANOTHER WORLD. IT WAS ANOTHER TIME. IT WAS THE Age of Wonder. It was a time of science fiction before there *was* science fiction—for the writers and editors of this Age were the ones who brought science fiction into existence as a distinct literary genre.

There had been, of course, writers and stories long before which historians and critics could later point to as "science fiction," though the concept did not exist at the time. Mythic adventures are as old as the *Epic of Gilgamesh* and the *Odyssey*. Writers of fantastic fiction—such as Cyrano de Bergerac, Edgar Allan Poe, Jules Verne, and H. G. Wells—spun stories which would later be seen as precursors. But these were myths, "utopian romances," "extraordinary voyages," or "scientific romances"—not "science fiction."[1]

The term itself was coined by Hugo Gernsback, thus literally "the father of science fiction," in the first issue of his magazine

Science Wonder Stories (June 1929).[2] The *fact* of science fiction as a separate and distinct literary genre was also the work of Gernsback when he brought it into existence with the publication of *Amazing Stories* (April 1926), the world's first *all* science fiction magazine. The general fiction magazines had always published some fantasy and "scientific romances," but now such fiction had a home in its own specialty magazine. In that very first issue Gernsback published stories by such science fiction forerunners as Poe, Verne, and Wells. Before long, however, he had writers who wrote specifically for him and for the editors of imitator magazines also demanding *only* science fiction. In creating a magazine where only a certain kind of fiction—*science* fiction—could be found, and by encouraging and creating a community of writers and readers who wrote and read *only* that kind of fiction, Gernsback thus brought about the birth of a self-conscious new literary genre.

This genre was primarily an American literary phenomenon until after World War II, although some British authors, such as John Beynon Harris ("John Wyndham") and Eric Frank Russell, contributed and there were a handful of small British magazines. It was also a genre of magazine short stories or serials: The specialist pulp magazines of the 1930s were not only the incubators and shapers of this new genre, they were also the only places it could be found. Book publication—at first by specialty amateur presses—also did not become a real possibility until after World War II and, despite an explosion of paperbacks in the 1950s, it was only after *1970* that the book become the primary medium of publication and influence.

Some have decried the resulting "ghettoization" of science fiction inside these magazines, but Lester Del Rey contends that science fiction wouldn't have existed at all but for this literary segregation into specialist magazines. "To develop," he argues, "science fiction had to remove itself from the usual critics who viewed it from the perspective of [the] mainstream, and who judged its worth largely on its mainstream values. As part of that mainstream, it would never have had the freedom to make the choices it did—many of them quite possibly wrong, but necessary for its development." Gernsback's naming and segregation of the literature was thus what actually brought about the birth of the literature.

> It was only when science fiction stood on its own feet, catering to its own special readers, that there was an opportunity to grow and shape itself. It was only in its own magazine that it had a chance to attract the writers who would never have the courage to dare a market like *Argosy*, where they would be competing with the best pulp writers of the day. . . . Critics and many writers now may cry large tears over the long period when science fiction was in "the ghetto" . . . but without that fact of being apart from other fields, it would have remained just a special case of some other kind of fiction.[3]

Del Rey identified five stages of literary development for the new genre, each consisting of twelve years, in which "the basic nature of the fiction, the type of magazines, the writers, and even the fan activities, all seem to change markedly from period to period."[4] Starting with the most recent stage and working backward, he said we are presently in the fifth stage, which began in 1974 and is still in the process of evolution. During this period science fiction (SF) has become big business in books, movies, and television, with a convention every week. We don't yet know where this stage is headed.

The fourth stage, from 1962 to 1973, coincided with the sixties and is termed "The Age of Rebellion." Attempting to blaze new paths into the unknown, "New Wave" writers challenged all the preconceptions of the genre. SF entered the schools and became "academic," there was an explosion of anthologies, and attendance at the World SF Convention passed the 2,000 mark.

The third stage, from 1950 to 1961, was "The Age of Acceptance," when the "mundane" world laughed a little less at science fiction. Two new SF magazines, *Galaxy* (1950) and *The Maga-*

zine of Fantasy and Science Fiction (1949) were born and began to chart departures from "hardware" SF. Indeed, there was a deluge of SF magazines flooding the newsstands and paperbacks began their invasion.

The second stage was John W. Campbell's era, "The Golden Age," from 1938 to 1949, when his magazine, *Astounding,* dominated the field and brought a new maturity to it. This period witnessed the first World SF Convention, saw atomic energy move from science fiction to science fact, and was shaped by new writers such as Robert A. Heinlein, Isaac Asimov, and Theodore Sturgeon.

The first stage, which Del Rey called, "The Age of Wonder," was from 1926 to 1937 and witnessed the birth of science fiction and science fiction fandom. This Age of Wonder belonged to "Uncle Hugo" Gernsback and his magazines. The most significant aspect of this age, Del Rey argued, was the rapidity of its evolution, which could not have happened without the existence of the new specialist magazines.

> Previously, for those capable of discovering them, there had been scattered stories that might be called science fiction, printed as books with no distinguishing label to set them apart from other, more conventional novels, or appearing as shorter works that were buried among conventional stories in general magazines. But to the reader who desired such literature, science fiction could only be found by a great deal of time and patience spent in browsing through material that did not interest him.
>
> The appearance of magazines wholly devoted to this literature brought it within the immediate reach of any reader who cared to look over the magazine racks. And many who had not known of their desire for such stories discovered them through the gaudy covers that caught their attention.
>
> Writers also found a ready market to which they could direct their writing. . . . In a sense, this was a program of inbreeding—a method often used by plant and animal breeders to speed development. A single interest was gathered in one

place, and those possessing it were exposed to each other. Each writer was constantly exposed to the work of every other one. Many ideas were tossed into the hamper, and some of them were quickly seized on by other writers for further development. Other ideas were quickly abandoned—losing their novelty or proving unsuitable for other reasons.

This was a form of feedback among writers, and it proved very influential on the field. There was also a strong feedback between writers and readers, both through the letter columns and through personal contacts. There was no long wait for critical comments that seldom came from established critics and reviewers. As soon as a story appeared, enthusiastic comments —both pro and con—began to flood into the editor's office. The magazines were a sort of link that made the connection between writer and reader (who might well be another writer).

It was as if the first life had crawled out of the sea of normal fiction and found a whole continent waiting to be taken over by science fiction that must adapt to fill all the ecological niches. . . . It was a time for enthusiasts to take over a field. Readers and writers became almost fanatic. And the result was the fastest evolution that ever affected any type of literature. . . . Rather than a ghetto, the magazines were a hot-house, encouraging the rapid growth and evolution of this type of fiction. And by 1937, science fiction was firmly established as a successful branch of commercial literature.[5]

Some look back upon the early examples of this new branch of commercial literature as thinly disguised science lectures. Indeed, like Wells, Gernsback shared in the typically Victorian enthusiasm for scientific progress, an enthusiasm which also caused cities of this age to build museums of science and technology which almost resembled places of worship. In fact, Gernsback probably had no intention of creating a new literary genre when he launched *Amazing Stories;* perhaps he was not even aware that he had done so. He was always a proselytizer for science and, as an entrepreneurial publisher, no doubt saw

Amazing Stories as a way of combining his zeal to spread the scientific gospel with his desire to make a buck. The stories he encouraged and published, therefore, usually had a didactic air to them which later generations found obtrusive and objectionable. But, perhaps unintentionally, they also had about them a sense of wonder which enthralled the largely adolescent readership. For this readership, the new literary genre brought a shock of mind-expanding revelation as the stories presented an infinity of previously unimagined possibilities far beyond the mundane world. Gernsback and his principal artist, Frank Paul, "showed us other worlds," recalled Jack Williamson, a young reader at the time. "The cities of the future, mysterious new machines, spaceships, alien monsters, the landscapes of Mars."[6]

Indeed, there *was* much to wonder about in these early stories, and the novelty of some of the ideas is perhaps difficult for us to recapture in our more jaded times. Many of the ideas that are now the SF traditions were then introduced. Not only did space flight become the central science fictional motif because of its repeated appearance in Gernsback's magazines, but the galaxy became our home. Today, for instance, virtually no science fiction story or film takes place in our boring backyard of the solar system. Interstellar space is the setting or background for adventures such as *Star Trek, Star Wars, Alien, Contact,* or *Men in Black.* Science fiction, it seems, *means* interstellar adventure.

But this was not the case before August 1928. That month, Gernsback's *Amazing Stories* published the first installment of the three-part serial by Edward E. Smith and Lee Hawkins Garby, "The Skylark of Space." This story became the first great classic of American science fiction by making interstellar travel—voyages between the *stars*—the central experience. The "space opera" adventure recounted therein covered mind-boggling distances beyond the solar system, vast distances previously unimagined by readers. Such interstellar adventures quickly became familiar in science fiction, as galactic empires toppled like houses of cards and worlds were destroyed like playthings.[7]

Today, organ transplantations—hearts, lungs, livers, spleens, whatever—are medical commonplaces. Science fiction readers learned about it long ago, however, in W. Alexander's "New Stomachs for Old" (*Amazing Stories,* February 1927), which introduced the idea. In the May 1927 *Amazing,* Ben Prout came up with the idea of using supersonic weapons as a means of defense. The consequences of firing a bullet on the Moon were first explored in Charles Cloukey's "Sub-Satellite" (*Amazing Stories,* March 1928). Philip Francis Nowlan introduced Anthony "Buck" Rogers in the August 1928 *Amazing Stories* with "Armageddon—2419 A.D." David H. Keller, a medical doctor, explored gender roles and relations in "The Psychophonic Nurse" (*Amazing Stories,* November 1928), wherein the emancipated women of the future turn their children over to robot nannies to raise. M. F. Rupert, a female writer, also explored gender roles in "Via the Hewitt Ray" (*Wonder Stories Quarterly,* Spring 1930). In the story, Lucille Hewitt enters the fourth dimension, where she discovers a world run by women after they had defeated men during the "Sex War Epoch." One of the women tells her, "For untold centuries, [men] had kept women subjugated and we finally got our revenge."

In Laurence Manning's "The Man Who Awoke" (*Wonder Stories,* March 1933) another socioeconomic problem is explored. Norman Winters awakes from suspended animation 2,000 years in the future. There he finds a civilization based on strict recycling of scarce natural resources after twentieth-century humanity, during "The Age of Waste," had poisoned, polluted, and plundered the Earth. The concept of "ecology" was thus introduced to a Depression-era America, which still ravaged the environment and thought natural resources would last forever. Isaac Asimov wrote in 1974:

> In the 1970s everyone is aware of, and achingly involved in, the energy crisis. Manning was aware of it forty years ago, and because he was, I was, and so, I'm sure, were many thoughtful

young science fiction readers. ... It was a funny kind of escape literature that had the youngsters who read it concerned about the consequences of the waste of fossil fuels forty years before all the self-styled normal and sensible human beings felt it necessary to become interested.[8]

In his "The Living Galaxy" (*Wonder Stories,* September 1934) Manning also introduced the idea of "generation ships," huge starships which take millions of years to reach other star systems, travelling, as physics demands, at less-than-light speed. In the process, generations of humans on board are born, live their lives, and die. This innovative concept was quickly picked up by Murray Leinster in "Proxima Centauri" (*Astounding Stories,* March 1935) and, most memorably, in Robert A. Heinlein's "Universe" (*Astounding Science Fiction*, May 1941).

Meanwhile, in July 1934, Stanley G. Weinbaum published "A Martian Odyssey" in Gernsback's *Wonder Stories,* introducing a novel idea about extraterrestrial aliens: They were not only truly "alien," instead of being cardboard figures or humans with extra arms—they were also friendly! Raymond Z. Gallun's "Old Faithful," written earlier but published later (*Astounding Stories,* December 1934), presented the same concept. Together, these stories broke an almost forty-year-old mind-set dating back to H. G. Wells's 1898 story "The War of the Worlds," in which aliens were invariably hostile and bent on the destruction of Earth. It was a paradigm shift to imagine we might actually be able to live in friendship with whatever life there might be out there. What a *wonderful* idea!

Gernsback's magazines, of course, did not have a monopoly on the "Sense of Wonder." As suggested by the Gallun story just mentioned, the pre-Campbell *Astounding* also contributed its share of "wonderful" ideas. For example, current scientific speculation at the end of the twentieth century has it that a gigantic black hole sits at the center of our galaxy, from which an unimaginably huge stream of antimatter spews out. Antimatter is the opposite of the everyday matter all around us. Thus, for instance, the positron is the positively charged "twin" of the negatively charged electron. When matter and antimatter come into contact, exploding radiation is the result. This arcane idea was first theorized by the physicist Paul Dirac in 1928. In 1932, Dirac's theory was given credence with the actual discovery of the positron. Then in 1955, antiprotons as well as antineutrons were produced in particle accelerators. In the meantime, however, chemist John D. Clark brought the idea to the rest of us with "Minus Planet" (*Astounding Stories,* April 1937), the first story featuring the theorized antimatter now accepted as fact.

A year later, in April 1938 (when Tremaine was still editorial director), *Astounding* presented another novel idea. With Lester Del Rey's "The Faithful," we have the extinction of humanity and its replacement by other mammals, in this case dogs. In "Sideways in Time" (*Astounding Stories,* June 1934), Murray Leinster described parallel time tracks, alternate "presents," resulting from decisions that could have gone either way. Thus, the past, like the present, is seen as highly contingent, not preordained. The past did not *have* to be the way it turned out—and, in another "present," wasn't at all! Something to think about, indeed!

Some have characterized the "Sense of Wonder" these stories inspired as simply the "Gosh! Wow!" enthusiasm of a twelve-year-old discovering that a larger world exists beyond the confines of the solipsistic self. However, Sam Moskowitz, who first used this phrase to describe early science fiction, meant something more by it. In the September 1955 issue of *Inside,* Moskowitz published "The Strange Business Attitude of the Science Fiction Industry," an attack on the three leading science fiction magazines of the day. By then there were thirty science fiction magazines on the market, but the leaders were John W. Campbell's *Astounding Science Fiction* (which had popularized the phrase "science fiction" by incorporating it into its title in 1938), Anthony Boucher's *Magazine of Fantasy and Science*

Fiction, and Horace L. Gold's *Galaxy.* Moskowitz charged them all with losing the "Sense of Wonder," which was the hallmark of early science fiction in their desire to force the field to "grow up." The resulting fiction, he claimed, was "overrefined" and "oversophisticated." It lacked the ability to wonder at the mysteries of the cosmos, without which the human soul was barren. Moskowitz turned to psychologist Rollo May, in his book *Man's Search for Himself,* for a definition of what he meant:

> Wonder is the opposite of cynicism and boredom; it indicates that a person has a heightened aliveness, is interested, expectant, responsive. It is essentially an "opening" attitude—an awareness that there is more to life than one has yet fathomed, an expectation of new vistas in life to be explored, as well as new profundities to be plumbed.[9]

Albert Einstein echoed this sentiment when he said, "One of the most beautiful things we can experience is the mysterious. It is the source of all true science and art. He who can no longer pause to wonder is as good as dead."[10] Indeed, proclaimed René Descartes in 1649, wonder is "the first of all passions."

This lack of cynicism and boredom with the universe, this "Sense of Wonder" about cosmic mysteries, was having a "Second Genesis" in the 1950s, even as Moskowitz wrote, when the science fiction film emerged as a distinct—and, again, distinctly American—genre unto itself. The films of that era were mostly crude, low-budget presentations, but they also exhibited the same exuberant vitality first manifested by their literary progenitors, the specialty pulp magazines of the 1930s.

Today, one could certainly argue that the science fiction film has burst the genre boundaries to emerge from the B-movie ghetto into the mainstream. The biggest box-office blockbusters of today are almost *all* science fiction films, while science fiction television shows, such as the various *Star Trek* series, are among the most profitable on the small screen, and not just on the cable Sci-Fi

Channel. The two "children of wonder" who are primarily responsible for this are those postwar baby boomers George Lucas and Steven Spielberg, who together demolished the ghetto walls in 1977 with *Star Wars* and *Close Encounters of the Third Kind.*

Literary science fiction, however, has not yet become mainstream. While some science fiction authors, such as Ursula LeGuin and Octavia Butler, are respected beyond the pale and "mundane" writers, such as Margaret Atwood and Joyce Carol Oates, have ventured behind the ghetto walls, literary science fiction yet retains its distinct genre identity.

This identity has sometimes been compared with that of another literary genre, detective fiction. Indeed, one often finds that the readership and authorship of both genres overlap. Besides being an influential science fiction editor, for example, Anthony Boucher was also well-known as a writer and an editor of detective fiction, with annual conventions—Bouchercons— being named in his honor. Some science fiction authors who have straddled the genres include Fredric Brown, John D. Mac-Donald, Kate Wilhelm, and, more recently, Karen Rose Cercone. This overlap is understandable in that a major element of science fiction's appeal has always been the solution of a technical problem. Both genres have as their foundations a shared worldview that the universe is both rational and comprehensible by the human mind. The attainment of knowledge, therefore, is the key to the denouement in both detective fiction and much of science fiction. In this, they share a common origin in the Enlightenment, which viewed rationality—reason—as the noblest attribute of the human mind. Before the Age of Wonder, then, there was the Age of Reason, an age which declared that the cosmos was a mystery, mostly unknown—*but knowable.*

Primitive societies are omniscient societies. Everything is known to them, as their myths tell them everything from how the world and humans were created to the origin of fire to how the leopard got its spots. And not only is everything known, but they also know how everything works—*through magic,* by which the future can be foretold and even the gods may be cajoled and manipulated. This presumed omniscience is perhaps the greatest intellectual obstacle to a civilized society, for it tells the primitive that everything is already known; there is nothing more to discover, there is nothing more to wonder about. Pure, acknowledged, defended *ignorance* is one of the greatest human achievements, for it *insists* that much—perhaps most—of the universe is unknown. But, over time, it is *knowable.* Insisting that we don't (yet) know is the mark of the scientific mindset and is what makes possible the continued and searching curiosity and *wonder* at the universe. Wonder at the profundities yet to be plumbed is the sign of the human mind's emergence from the darkness of savage omniscience. Wonder at the unknown is, indeed, what makes possible all human progress. And science fiction is the distinctive literature of that worldview.

For a literary genre with roots in the Age of Reason, it may be surprising to realize how close we yet remain to the genesis of the Age of Wonder. Though it seems like ancient history, there are still among us those who pioneered this distinctive genre back in the late 1920s and early 1930s—though they become fewer with each passing day. Indeed, since I began this project, several of these "Pioneers of Wonder" have died. At times I've felt like Margaret Mead during her doctoral research in Samoa. In her autobiography, *Blackberry Winter,* Mead recounted how each morning when she awoke she told herself, "The last oldster who knows the meaning of this particular ritual will die before sunset—and I have to get to him first!" So, too, with these pioneers. Each sunset has found fewer of them among us. When I began, C. L. Moore, Desmond Hall, Margaret St. Clair, Leslie F. Stone, and E. Hoffmann Price were still alive. The sun set on them before I reached them. Some that I *did* reach in time— David Lasser, Ray Gallun, Margaret Weinbaum Kay—have since seen their last sunset. Before this first generation of science fiction pioneers passed entirely from our presence, I wanted to reach them, to find out from their own lips, or the lips of those who knew them and their work most intimately, what it was like to be present at the Creation. I should have begun sooner—but I wasn't entirely too late. What you hold here, then, is the unique testimony of some of the founders of science fiction. From them we can glean a small idea of how it was that a new literary genre was born.

NOTES

1. Sam Moskowitz, among many others, would take issue with me on this point, arguing that science fiction was truly born in mythology, ancient travel tales, and Greek literature. See his "Voyagers Through Eternity: A History of Science-Fiction from the Beginnings to H. G. Wells," Part I, *Fantasy Commentator* (Winter 1981), which opens with Homer.

2. Sam Moskowitz, who was primarily responsible for crediting Gernsback with this neologism, also pointed out its sole previous use. In chapter 10 of his 1851 collection of essays, *A Little Earnest Book Upon a Great Old Subject*, British author William Wilson used the phrase to describe a book under review. However, the phrase did not enter the language and was soon forgotten. With Gernsback's coinage we have an instance of independent invention. See Sam Moskowitz, "Voyagers Through Eternity," *Fantasy Commentator* 39 (1989): 218.

3. Lester Del Rey, *The World of Science Fiction: 1926-1976, The History of a Subculture* (New York: Ballantine Books: 1979), pp. 35, 36.

4. Ibid., p. 38.

5. Ibid., pp. 81–82, 88.

6. Jack Williamson, "Introduction," *Amazing Science Fiction Anthology: The Wonder Years, 1926–1935,* edited by Martin H. Greenberg (Lake Geneva, Wisc.: TSR, Inc.: 1987), p. 7.

7. Purists may point to several possible precursors, such as Robert W. Cole's *The Struggle for Empire* (London: E. Stock, 1900), or J. Schlossel's "The Second Swarm" in the Spring 1928 *Amazing Stories Quarterly,* but "Skylark" was the breakthrough.

8. Isaac Asimov, ed., *Before the Golden Age: A Science Fiction Anthology of the 1930s* (New York: Doubleday & Co., 1974), p. 373.

9. Quoted by Moskowitz in "Five Steps to Science Fiction Sanity," *Extrapolation* 27, no. 4, p. 286.

10. Quoted as the frontispiece in *Pause To Wonder: Stories of the Marvelous, Mysterious, and Strange,* edited by Marjorie Fischer and Rolfe Humphries (New York: Julian Messner, Inc., 1944).

1.

THE AGE OF WONDER

Gernsback, David Lasser, and *Wonder Stories*

HUGO GERNSBACK PUBLISHED THE WORLD'S FIRST science fiction magazine. And the second. And the third. And the fourth. In doing so he launched an era, a pre-Campbellian Age of Wonder, the knowledge of which seems virtually forgotten.[1]

For three years, starting in April 1926, this immigrant from Luxembourg had the world of magazine science fiction to himself as editor and publisher of *Amazing Stories*. That first science fiction magazine, however, was only one product of the Experimenter Publishing Company, Gernsback's New York–based publishing empire. Others included *Science and Invention*, *Radio News*, the presciently titled *Television*, and *Your Body*, an attractive health publication, which competed successfully with Bernarr Macfadden's well-known *Physical Culture*. Of these, *Your Body* would prove to be the catalyst for Gernsback's inaugurating *Science Wonder Stories*, the world's second science fiction magazine, in June 1929.[2]

By early 1929, the Experimenter Publishing Company had

mushroomed into a profitable million-dollar enterprise, which apparently greatly disturbed rival publishing czar Macfadden. As has been documented, *Amazing Stories* alone was selling 100,000 copies per month, with some individual issues soaring to 200,000.[3] The magazine's estimated gross annual income from sales and advertising was $185,000, with a net operating profit of $55,000.

And, in that pre-Depression era, Gernsback and his staff were paid well. Hugo himself got a weekly salary of $1,045 (which he sometimes didn't bother to collect); his brother Sydney Gernsback, the company's treasurer, received $750 a week; and T. O'Conor Sloane, *Amazing*'s associate editor (who handled the actual editorial chores), was paid $225. Like virtually all other pulp publishers of that time, Gernsback usually paid authors only half a cent per word—and only upon publication. (He continued this practice with all his succeeding magazines.) In the 1920s, when he was flush, this policy created few complaints. Authors eventually did get paid—and, besides, there was nowhere else for his "science fiction" authors to go.

Later, during the Great Depression, the science fiction pulps, and Gernsback in particular, earned a reputation for under- or nonpayment of authors. Horace L. Gold, a veteran of the era, once described payment rates as "microscopic fractions of a cent per word, payable upon lawsuit."[4] Indeed, Gernsback himself came to be seen as the primary culprit responsible for this system, a perhaps undeserved reputation which yet lingers.

Donald A. Wollheim recalled that when he sold his first story, "The Man from Ariel," to Gernsback's *Wonder Stories* in 1934, he was owed $10—which never came. Wollheim wrote several other *Wonder Stories* authors and discovered that they, too, had not been paid. He combined with them to hire a lawyer and sue for payment. Gernsback settled out of court with the group for $75, of which the lawyer got $10. In 1935, Wollheim submitted a second story, "The Space Lens," to *Wonder Stories* under the pseudonym of Millard Verne Gordon. It was accepted and published, but never paid for.

Jack Williamson had similar problems. In early 1932, Williamson received $50 as partial payment for "The Moon Era," which appeared in the February 1932 issue of *Wonder Stories*. It took two years and the threat of a lawsuit to obtain the rest. For his part, Gernsback claimed financial distress resulting from the Depression. In reply to Williamson's importuning letters, Gernsback begged for patience. On January 21, 1933, for instance, he wrote Williamson that a "serious disaster" had befallen him when the Eastern Distributing Corporation, which distributed his magazines, went bankrupt, causing him to lose "a vast sum of money" and "raising the deuce with our finances."[5]

Yet it does appear that when Gernsback had money, those connected with his organization also had money—even his authors. At the time his Experimenter Publishing Company went into suspiciously forced bankruptcy in 1929, legal documents revealed that payment was outstanding for only four stories, all of them recently acquired.[6]

That bankruptcy itself makes an interesting story. According to Gernsback, Macfadden had offered to purchase his flourishing publications on three occasions, but he had spurned all the offers. In retaliation, claimed Gernsback, Macfadden conspired to force him into bankruptcy and acquired his company through third parties. On February 20, 1929, three creditors, none of whom were owed more than $2,100, simultaneously sued Gernsback for payment. According to New York business law at the time, such simultaneous action could automatically force bankruptcy proceedings to be initiated. Eventually, Gernsback's publishing empire and his radio station were sold; his creditors, he said, received $1.08 for every dollar they were owed.[7] The April 1929 *Amazing Stories* was the last issue published under Gernsback's aegis.

He quickly struck back by founding the Stellar Publishing Corporation and solicited orders for a new magazine, probably from *Amazing*'s list of subscribers, although Gernsback denied this source during the bankruptcy proceedings. Over eight thousand orders flooded in and, within a month, Gernsback's second publishing fiefdom was born. In June 1929, he produced the world's second science fiction magazine, *Science Wonder Stories*. It had a "bedsheet" format (8.5" × 11"), ninety-six pages, and sold for a quarter, more expensive than most smaller-sized pulp magazines at that time. The first issue initiated a serial, "The Reign of the Ray" by Fletcher Pratt and Irwin Lester (the latter simply a pseudonym for the popular Fletcher Pratt).[8] In that first issue's editorial, Gernsback coined the term "science fiction" to describe the contents.

In July 1929, he began the world's *third* science fiction magazine, *Air Wonder Stories*; and in October—the same month the stock market crashed—there appeared the first issue of *Science Wonder Quarterly* (which, with its summer 1930 issue became *Wonder Stories Quarterly*).

Gernsback had always agreed with Emerson that "men love to wonder, and that is the seed of our science." Indeed, it was through wonder, Gernsback felt, that his readers would be led to science. His policy had always emphasized the didactic aspects of science fiction. His first editorial in the old *Amazing* had declared, "Not only do these amazing tales make tremendously interesting reading, they are also always instructive. They supply knowledge that we might not otherwise obtain—and they supply it in very palatable form." *Science Wonder Stories* was to be no different. All stories, trumpeted Gernsback, would be judged by an editorial board composed of "an array of authorities and educators."

He took with him into his new venture many loyal retainers, including his brother Sydney (who remained treasurer), Irving Mannheimer (who became secretary), and Frank R. Paul, "The Father of Science Fiction Illustration," an Austrian artist who had painted all of *Amazing*'s covers and who would paint all but three covers for *Science Wonder Stories* and *Wonder Stories* as well.[9] But for managing editor, Gernsback selected a newcomer to his team. At *Amazing*, it had been his habit to set policies, write the editorials, and generally have the last word, but at the same time, to leave most of the day-to-day work of running the magazine to his associate editor, seventy-seven-year-old T. O'Conor Sloane. This now became the task of twenty-seven-year-old David Lasser.

Lasser was born in Baltimore on March 20, 1902, the son of Louis and Lena Lasser, Russian Jewish immigrants. To support his wife and five children, his father operated a tailor shop. At the age of fourteen, after only half a year of attendance, Lasser dropped out of high school to work as a bank messenger. "We were a very poor family," he told me, "and I thought I ought to help out." When America entered World War I, one of his brothers was drafted and another, serving in the National Guard, was activated for overseas duty. David wanted to get in as well, so he lied about his age and enlisted in February 1918. He was shipped to France, gassed during the Argonne offensive a few months before the Armistice, and hospitalized for about five months. In February 1919, Sergeant David Lasser was discharged—and was still only sixteen years old!

He then discovered that the government had a college scholarship fund for disabled veterans, which not only paid tuition fees, but also provided a modest living stipend. Despite never having finished high school, he talked his way into the Massachusetts Institute of Technology in 1920, and graduated in 1924.

For the next five years, Lasser worked at a series of what he called "dead-end jobs." First he was an engineer in Newark, then an insurance agent, and in 1927 he became a technical writer for the New York Edison Company. In 1929, he was fired by New York Edison for protesting the dismissal of several employees in an economy move. It was then that he applied to Gernsback for the managing editor's position and was hired.

During his first year with Stellar Publishing, Lasser juggled the editorial donkey work of both *Air* and *Science Wonder Stories* before they were combined into one magazine titled simply *Wonder Stories* in June 1930. He also edited the quarterlies and the last three issues of *Amazing Detective Tales* (August to October 1930) to be published by Gernsback. The latter, begun in January

1930 as *Scientific Detective Monthly*, attracted neither science fiction nor detective readers, and Lasser was unable to save it from financial failure. It was sold and shortly thereafter died.

On April 4, 1930, meantime, Lasser gathered a group of his New York–area writers together at the apartment of G. Edward Pendray and his wife and formed the American Interplanetary Society to educate the public about the feasibility and desirability of space travel. T. O'Conor Sloane had always laughed at the idea of space exploration, and in a 1929 editorial even declared that space travel could never be achieved. Lasser, on the other hand, was a true believer, and saw his affiliation with *Wonder Stories* as a springboard for spending the faith. The writers elected Lasser as president, Fletcher Pratt as librarian, Laurence Manning as treasurer, and *Wonder Stories* associate editor Charles P. Mason as secretary. G. Edward Pendray, then a reporter for the *New York Herald-Tribune* and one of Lasser's writers under the *nom de plume* "Gawain Edwards," was elected vice-president of the society. From 1932 to 1936 Pendray was an editor at the Milk Research Council, which let him use his own office for the society's business. After he left the council he became a top consultant at Westinghouse Corp., where he coined the term "time capsule" for the container that Westinghouse buried at the 1939 New York World's Fair.

Pendray became the second president of the American Interplanetary Society when Lasser resigned in April 1932, at the society's third annual meeting. Because of his activities in and on behalf of the organization, Pendray would go on to become "the most widely-known and read American authority on rocketry and space flight, other than [Robert] Goddard."[10] After Pendray's elevation, Nat Schachner, an attorney, another cofounder, and another of Lasser's stable of writers, then filled the vacant position of vice-president. Schachner next followed Pendray into the president's chair, with Laurence Manning filling the vacant vice-presidency. Manning, in his turn, next became the society's president, on April 6, 1934. At that same meeting, the society would change its name to the American Rocket Society.[11]

In the June 1930 *Wonder Stories*, the Interplanetary Society announced its existence and goals, and encouraged the formation of chapters throughout the country. Soon, even people such as Jack Williamson in faraway New Mexico, R. F. Starzl in Le Mars, Iowa, and Robert A. Heinlein, an ensign on the *USS Lexington* then in the South Pacific, were joining. That same month the society published the first issue of its mimeographed *Bulletin of the American Interplanetary Society*. Edited by Lasser, it became the offset-printed *Astronautics* in May 1932, with Lasser remaining as editor until at least April 1933. That first issue reported that Charles P. Mason had been charged with the task of making a survey of the "entire field of information relating to interplanetary travel," and it published Fletcher Pratt's paper "The Universal Background of Interplanetary Travel," which he had read at the society's meeting on May 2. Future issues would publish similar articles, as well as reports from German Willy Ley about the progress of German-rocket-society experiments by Wernher von Braun and others with actual rocket flight. Willy Ley had been put in touch with the American group by member R. F. Starzl, who'd sent Ley the first issue of *Science Wonder Stories* (Fall 1929), thus converting him instantly to science fiction.[12] It was his contacts with the British and American rocket societies which would later make it possible for Ley to escape Nazi Germany and emigrate to America before the war. Ley would later become a prolific contributor of science articles to the science fiction magazines of the 1950s.

Meetings of the society were held in the American Museum of Natural History, made possible through the intercession of society member Dr. Clyde Fisher, who served on the museum's staff. They met with immediate success. One of the society's biggest events was held on the night of January 27, 1931, when over twenty-five hundred people gathered to hear an address by Robert Esnault-Pelterie, a French "astronaut," on the "unborn science of cosmic flight called astronautics,"[13] a word invented in 1927 by the Belgian proto-science-fiction novelist J. J. Rosny, *aine* (the elder), a pseudonym of Joseph-Henri-Honore Boex.[14] In addition, the society presented two free screenings of *The Girl in the Moon,* a film by German rocket scientist Dr. Hermann Oberth. A police captain and ten patrolmen augmented the museum's own guards (thirty-two additional ones hired for the event) to insure that the crowd did not destroy the museum in a much-feared "riot." The museum had already experienced an unruly crowd when Albert Einstein spoke there in 1929. The large audience which turned out at that time did considerable damage in what came to be called "the Einstein riot." The museum feared that the visit of this French "astronaut" might be a repeat. "Riot Guard Joins 2,500 at Film Flight to Moon," screamed the headline in the *New York Herald-Tribune* the next day. "Police Stand By in Museum Lest Rocket Trip Thrill Revive Einstein Episode." The paper then went on to report that "Captain Mead and ten policemen, reinforced by the private garrison of the American Museum of Natural History, guarded the museum against a possible repetition of the 'Einstein riot' of 1929 last night when a free motion picture and a free lecture on the subject of rocket flight to the moon were presented by the American Interplanetary Society. There was no riot, but it was necessary to put on the show twice to satisfy the lovers of free science who turned out to the number of 2,500."[15] Indeed, the room's capacity was a thousand, so the second thousand-plus stood in line outside for two hours waiting for the second showing.

Lasser and his colleagues were "astounded" by the turnout. They'd expected a small crowd and planned to have only one screening of the film. "It demonstrated," Lasser told me, "that in spite of the Great Depression (or perhaps because of it), there was that intense interest in travelling into space."[16] Given the usual scorn to which space travel was then subjected, this episode seems hard to believe; but the massive turnout and the previous "Einstein riot" suggest that there may indeed have been a huge population hungry for such ideas in the 1930s.[17]

At a meeting of the society on April 3, 1931, Lasser called for "an international interplanetary commission to act as a central agency for all information on the development of rocket vehicles and to build the first ship for extraterrestrial navigation." But, "before that dream can be realized," he explained, "there must be a long period of experimentation. First, the scientists must achieve construction of a meteorological rocket . . . then develop rocket planes for transoceanic service and gradually work out a type that will be capable of a trip far out into interplanetary space."[18] At the meeting of October 22, 1931, Lasser prophesied "war by rocket." The rocket, he predicted, "will serve as a terrible engine of destruction in future conflicts." Future war "would change from battles of armies to duels between long-distance engines of destruction."[19]

Yet, despite the society's efforts at realistic projection and seeming popular success, it also met with ridicule and resistance. Raymond Z. Gallun, an author and another true believer, recalls that "in those early days, the whole subject of space travel, to most persons, was about as reasonable and productive as making mud pies."[20] Even as late as 1949, Dr. Isaac Asimov offered his resignation to the dean of the Boston University School of Medicine—to spare that worthy institution the shame of association with a writer of space stories—when he learned that his publishers had listed his university affiliation on the back cover of his first novel, *Pebble in the Sky.* (The dean refused it.)[21]

To further their proselytizing work, Lasser felt a book was needed to explain in accessible language the realistic potential of the rocket as a vehicle for space exploration. He had already published several articles about space travel in such magazines as *Scientific American, Nature,* and Gernsback's *Everyday Science and Mechanics,* as well as the *New York Herald-Tribune.* Using these as a basis, in 1931 he wrote *The Conquest of Space,* the first book in the English language on astronautics. No publisher would touch the manuscript, so Lasser, Pendray, and Schachner pooled their resources to come up with $12,000, enough to self-publish and distribute perhaps 500 copies. The great bulk of this money seems to have come from Schachner, and the publishing headquarters of the press the writers set up was at his law office.[22]

The book was favorably received, with sometime SF writer Waldemar Kaempffert, also the science editor of the *New York Times*, commenting that "the book cannot but capture the imagination of a reader interested in science. After the capture he will find that he has unconsciously absorbed many principles of elementary physics and thus considerably added to his stock of useful knowledge."[23]

Meanwhile, society members were conducting a series of rocket experiments which paralleled those of the Germans. On May 14, 1933, they finally succeeded in launching a rocket. It rose for 250 feet before its oxygen tank exploded. It was considered a great success. At the same time, Laurence Manning, a nurseryman and head of the society's Committee on Biological Research, had been leading America's first experiments in subjecting living subjects to the increased pressure rocket thrust would exert. In 1931—unknown to them at the time, but predating Wernher von Braun's similar experiments in Germany by a year—the society subjected white mice to 80 g of pressure in a centrifuge. These experiments served to pull in more technically minded members, while the ongoing public relations work increased overall membership. By 1932, according to the society's journal, the American Interplanetary Society boasted members in twenty-one states and nine foreign countries, including England, France, Germany, and the Soviet Union. Because of Lasser's book, the society's ancillary rocket experiments, and its public educational work, historian Frank H. Winter has observed that "more than any other nation, America traces its astronautical roots to a science fiction fatherhood."[24]

In 1932, a British edition of Lasser's book, perhaps five thousand copies, was published by London's Hurst & Blackett, a firm which specialized in romance, mystery, and adventure novels. The royalties from this edition probably saved Schachner, financial backer of the American edition, from a major loss. In any case, it was this edition which captured the imagination of seventeen-year-old Arthur C. Clarke, transforming him forever into a fervent champion of "hard-core" science fiction. "Although there was already considerable German and Russian literature on the subject," he remembers,

> *The Conquest of Space* was the very first book in the English language to discuss the possibility of flight to the Moon and planets and to describe the experiments and dreams (mostly the latter) of the early rocket pioneers. Only a few hundred copies of the British edition were sold, but chance brought one of these to a bookstore a few yards from my birthplace . . . and so I learned, for the first time, that space travel was not merely fiction. *One day it could really happen.*[25]

Lasser was also aware of and concerned about other developments around him in Depression-era New York. The massive unemployment he saw everywhere moved him to join the Socialist Party. He voted for the Socialist presidential candidate, Norman Thomas, in both 1932 and 1936, before finally leaving the party in 1938.

In 1932 and 1933, Lasser also flirted briefly with the Technocracy movement, which preached that engineers and scientists were the only people who could pull the country out of the Depression. He edited the only two issues that were produced of its journal, *Technocracy Review,* both published by his boss, Hugo Gernsback, who was perhaps also briefly smitten with Technocracy. Gernsback, for example, wrote an editorial in the March 1933 *Wonder Stories* on the "Wonders of Technocracy," though he hedged at the end by declaring, "Whether this will work out or whether Technocracy is only a theoretical idea, only the future can tell." He also published a series of articles on the movement in his associated magazine, *Everyday Science and Mechanics.* Lasser meanwhile published in *Wonder* a three-part series of Technocracy-oriented stories, "The Revolt of the Technocrat," written by Nat Schachner. Sam Moskowitz says these were commissioned by Lasser and perhaps based on ideas furnished by him.[26] This flirtation with Technocracy did not continue in the pages of *Wonder* after Lasser left.

Also while editor of *Wonder Stories* and president of the Interplanetary Society, Lasser formed another organization, the Lower West Side Unemployed League, and began leading it in demonstrations for jobs. It was this activity that led to Lasser's leaving Gernsback; the last issue of *Wonder Stories* that he edited was the one for October 1933. Throwing himself full-time into organizing the unemployed, Lasser became head of the Workers' Alliance of America, a nationwide agitational organization which became the major representative of the unemployed and of WPA workers during the Great Depression. As such, he played a significant role in our labor history.[27]

But his role in science fiction history is just as significant. Coming after the founding of *Amazing Stories* and before the Campbellian "Golden Age," Lasser and the *Wonder Stories* interregnum tend to be overlooked and neglected by both fans and science fiction historians. Yet in many ways, this middle "Age of Wonder" was extremely formative for the still-evolving genre, as Lasser sought to bring a certain maturity to the literature.

For those first years of the Depression, *Wonder Stories* was the dominant magazine in its field, well ahead of *Amazing* and *Astounding* (which was launched in January 1930). Under Lasser's editorship, the *Wonder Stories* family of magazines published the first stories of John Beynon Harris (later known as "John Wyndham"), Clifford D. Simak, Raymond Z. Gallun, Frank K. Kelly, P. Schuyler Miller, Leslie F. Stone, Raymond A. Palmer, Laurence Manning, Nat Schachner, and "Gawain Edwards."[28] Other well-known authors who appeared in the magazine regularly were Edmond Hamilton, Manly Wade Wellman, Clark Ashton Smith, Jack Williamson, Fletcher Pratt, mathematician Eric Temple Bell (who wrote under the name of "John Taine"), Stanton Coblentz, and David H. Keller.

One indication of the magazine's popularity among readers during the Lasser years came when Raymond Palmer (later editor of *Amazing*), as chairman of the Jules Verne Prize committee, awarded the first such prize (a precursor of the fan-voted

"Hugo") to Edmond Hamilton's "The Island of Unreason," from the May 1933 *Wonder Stories*, as the best story of 1933.[29] Hamilton's story beat out such worthy competition as C. L. Moore's "Shambleau," Laurence Manning's "The Man Who Awoke," Donald Wandrei's "A Race Through Time," and David H. Keller's "Unto Us a Child Is Born."

Another such indicator was the more-than-normal frenzy of fan correspondence in the magazine's letters department. Particularly vocal fans who communicated regularly included Bob Tucker, Forrest J. Ackerman, Raymond Palmer, and Donald Wollheim. Because these letters included the addresses, the writers were able to contact each other readily; this, along with the constant and various promotions, encouraged fan activity to energetically blossom.

A typical promotion was the contest announced in the February 1930 issue of *Air Wonder Stories*, which offered a hundred dollars in gold to the reader who came up with the best slogan to typify the magazine's contents. British fan John Beynon Harris ("John Wyndham") won with the alliterative phrase "Future Flying Fiction."

Another such contest, with a top award of $500, was featured in the spring 1930 *Science Wonder Quarterly*, which asked fans to answer the question "What I Have Done to Spread Science Fiction." Third place here went to New York fan Allen Glasser for founding a fan club called the Scienceers and publishing its newsletter, *The Planet*—the world's second science fiction fanzine. Second place was taken by an Indiana printer named Conrad H. Ruppert, who suggested a week of nationally coordinated fan activities to be called "Science Fiction Week." This was an idea that Gernsback particularly liked and so, in the May *Science Wonder Stories*, he suggested that March 31–April 7, 1930, be set aside for such a week. But first place in the contest went to Chicago fan Raymond Palmer for starting the Science Correspondence Club.

Under the stimulation of these promotions and contests, fan clubs and fan magazines proliferated. Ruppert, for instance, shortly began to publish the nonfiction fanzine *Science Fiction Digest* (the first magazine with "science fiction" in its title), which by 1933 was the foremost fan magazine, thanks to Ruppert's printing press. The shape of "First Fandom" began to emerge.

Wonder Stories also exercised a decided influence on the evolution of science fiction as a genre during these years. Before *Astounding* appeared in 1930, Lasser, through the various magazines he edited, was responsible for well over half of all the science fiction being published. Even after *Astounding*'s appearance and the merging of the two *Wonder* titles, Lasser was still choosing a substantial fraction of it. Indeed, given the anemic performance of *Amazing* under the octogenarian Sloane, who didn't believe in science fiction, and the pathetic performance of *Astounding* during its first few years, Lasser was the dominant force in shaping the direction of the field.

He was working in unknown terrain. The genre had just been invented; as such, there was no depth of talent to the field, which is why Gernsback had been initially forced to rely upon reprints of such writers as Edgar Allan Poe, Jules Verne, and H. G. Wells. Mainstream writers with literary skills disdained the new genre, especially since one could only find it in the pulp magazines, rags which had the reputation for publishing only "lurid stuff for semi-literates on cheap pulpwood paper." Thus, the writers who rallied to the genre were new, untried novices; indeed, they were, in many cases, just enthusiastic teenagers. Their writing talents were in many cases rudimentary at best. But these were the writers that Lasser had to work with. In doing so, he helped shape that first generation of science fiction writers, creating a pool of talent where none had previously existed. Magazines such as *Wonder Stories*, said Isaac Asimov, became "a forcing ground in which many youngsters sharpened their talents, when otherwise they would never have entered writing at all, or would have written something other than s.f."[30]

Regarding the stories then appearing in the SF pulps, Arthur C. Clarke recalls, "Of course the literary standards were usually abysmal—but the stories brimmed with ideas and amply evoked that sense of wonder that is, or should be, one of the goals of the best science fiction."[31] Lasser, though, wasn't satisfied with merely evoking a "Sense of Wonder." He wanted to improve low literary standards and, just as importantly, inject an element of scientific realism into the wild and fantastic fiction then common. He wrote to Jack Williamson, stating:

> Our policy is aimed more at the realistic than at the fantastic in science fiction. We find that our readers have wearied a little of unbelievable monsters, unbelievable situations and feats of the imagination that never could become reality. We want imagination used, but we want the author to back it up with a convincing background, so that the reader will find that these things could be true.
>
> We are placing as much emphasis on plot as we are on science ideas, and we feel that if you take even scientific ideas that have been worked out a number of times and have an original plot, that is, an original set of characters and an original set of experiences that you carry them through, that good stories can be written.[32]

Brian Aldiss has complained that "Gernsback was utterly without any literary understanding," and that all he wanted in stories he published was a diagram.[33] This may have been because English was not Gernsback's mother tongue, and Sloane just didn't care. The result was often leaden prose disguising a science lecture. But Lasser, like Aldiss, was concerned about the lack of literacy and a willingness to accept diagrammatically proficient but pseudoscientific gibberish. Nor was he content merely to state his policy. He also attempted to shape and mold the field by working closely with authors, suggesting ideas, commenting on drafts, and even collaborating, as he did with David H. Keller on "The Time Projector" (*Wonder Stories*, July 1931), a tale of a computer-generated prediction of World War II. This editorial stance was apparently at variance with the previous ones of Gernsback and Sloane, who simply either accepted or rejected submitted stories. In fact, it may well mark the very first editorial intervention in the creative process in the field, something for which Campbell later became famous.

Illustrative of this approach is Lasser's correspondence with Jack Williamson concerning his novelette, "Red Slag of Mars" (*Wonder Stories Quarterly,* spring 1932). The plot originated from an "Interplanetary Plot Contest" the magazine had sponsored; readers were awarded prizes for the best plots, which were then to be worked into publishable stories by the magazine's stable of writers. Lasser sent one of the winning plots, contributed by Lawrence Schwartzman, to Williamson to see if he would be interested in wrestling it into shape. Lasser wrote:

> Admittedly this plot is very amateurish and would have to be revised considerably to make a worthwhile story. So long as you maintain some relationship with the original plot, you have perfect freedom to write your story as you please. What appealed to me in this plot was the idea of the lost race of Martians, and I think you could very well construct your story about that, even neglecting your other characters of the plot. You might, for instance, have the cloud that our author speaks of sweep over the solar system. When the cloud has passed on, the entire Martian race with which we had been in communication has vanished. The story could be the working out of the mystery of the lost race.[34]

Williamson worked up a synopsis and sent it to Lasser, who replied,

> I believe if the story is well written, it will be acceptable. I would caution you, however, to be sure to make the incident connected with the Martians convincing and plausible.
>
> For example, you speak of the earth-men deciphering the Martian inscriptions. Now, you must be sure and make it convincing how they did it; for they have absolutely no method of approach to a written language of another world.

Similarly, in recounting the professor's contacting the Martians, you must be very careful to make that convincing too; for, here again, you have the impact of two races who have absolutely nothing in common.[35]

Despite Lasser's attempts to nurture his writers and improve the scientific and literary quality of their work, *Wonder Stories* began to flounder financially as the Depression ground on. *Air Wonder Stories* had always attracted fewer readers than its sister magazine and had been merged with it after eleven issues. In November 1930, *Wonder Stories* contracted to the smaller dimensions of a pulp magazine, but returned to the larger bedsheet size twelve issues later. In 1932, it dropped its price from a quarter to 15 cents, below even *Astounding*'s 20-cent price. However, this only exacerbated the magazine's cash flow problem without significantly increasing circulation. *Wonder Stories Quarterly* was discontinued after its January 1933 number; a 50-cent cover price was just too steep for the kids of the Depression, and halving the price came too late to save it. Perhaps the only consolation was that there was less competition, as that March saw the demise of *Astounding* due to the same financial pressures.

In the wake of the Eastern Distributing Company bankruptcy —a "misfortune," Gernsback wrote Williamson, "which left us holding the bag"—*Wonder Stories* missed two issues in the middle of 1933. With the November 1933 number it regained its monthly status, but only by dropping again to pulp size (this time permanently); by financially reorganizing Stellar Publishing as Continental Publications, Inc., in December; and by firing Lasser after the October issue, a move he interpreted as at least in part dictated by economy.

To replace Lasser, Gernsback brought in seventeen-year-old Charles Derwin Hornig—the first and perhaps most unexpected of the fan-to-editor transformations later common in science fiction. Hornig was a New Jersey fan who had launched a fanzine called *The Fantasy Fan* in September of that year. He sent a copy to the editor of every professional SF magazine, and one reached Gernsback just as he was firing Lasser. So, two months after starting his own fanzine, Hornig found himself a professional editor.

Hornig immediately announced a "new story" policy. Coincidentally, *Astounding* appeared back on the stands that October under a new publisher, Street and Smith, also with a new "thought variant" story policy. Both policies were intended to bury the old stereotypes of pulp science fiction forever. In the meantime, *Wonder*'s promotion of fan activities became even more energetic, and would soon result in the formation of the Science Fiction League, the first (and last) fan club "empire."

Nevertheless, the finances of the magazine continued to decline. Authors went unpaid (except upon lawsuit) throughout 1934 and 1935. In November 1935, *Wonder Stories* went bimonthly. In April 1936, Gernsback wrote an editorial denouncing the criminal acts of distributors who were robbing the magazine of revenue by selling coverless copies and returning the covers for credit on "unsold" copies. That summer, Hugo Gernsback abandoned the science fiction field and sold the magazine to Standard Magazines, which renamed it *Thrilling Wonder Stories* with the August issue and installed Leo Margulies from its own stable of editors as the new editor. Under this masthead, it survived for another two decades and even attained comfortable profitability for a while after World War II during the great SF boom, before ceasing publication with its Winter 1955 issue.

But the glow of that first Age of Wonder was never recaptured. For those in First Fandom, who were present before what Asimov called "the Coming of Campbell" in 1937 (which ushered in the "Golden Age"), nothing replaced those early years of magic.

Captivated by the garish primary colors of a Frank Paul cover, the nine-year-old Asimov picked up his first science fiction magazine in August 1929; it was the third number of *Science Wonder Stories*. The first serial he "slavered joyously over" was Edmond Hamilton's "Cities in the Air," in *Air Wonder Stories* (November–December 1929). The first short story to lodge itself firmly in his memory was Hamilton's "The Man Who Evolved" (*Wonder Stories*, April 1931). "Those stories were dear to me because they aroused my enthusiasm, gave me the joy of life at a time and in a place and under conditions when not terribly many joys existed," recalled Asimov. "They helped shape me and even educate me, and I am filled with gratitude to those stories and to the men who wrote them."[36]

Raymond Z. Gallun was also first snared by a Frank Paul cover, the one on the fourth number of *Amazing Stories* (July 1926). It illustrated Curt Siodmak's story "The Eggs from Lake Tanganyika." Gallun bought it, devoured the stories, and was enthralled. "That early stuff of the 1930s, though perhaps crude, conveyed a certain consistent feeling," he later said.

> In those days there were so many things that, though speculated about as future developments, were still generally considered impossible. So, to read of and imagine doing what can't be done, seeing what never has been seen, touching the perhaps eternally too distant and strange, had an inevitable enchantment. Therein, I think, we reach the central keynote of the science fiction of then. . . . the word for it is *wonder.*[37]

A CONVERSATION WITH DAVID LASSER

T. O'Conor Sloane, Hugo Gernsback's first editor, passed away in 1940. Gernsback himself died in 1967. David Lasser was thus the oldest living science fiction editor when I interviewed him on April 6, 1986. At the time, he was eighty-four years old. It is through the memory of Lasser, then, that we can reach back furthest into the past—almost sixty years at that time—to unveil the dim beginnings of that new literature known as "science fiction" during the pioneering Age of Wonder. David Lasser died a decade later, on May 5, 1996, at the age of ninety-four.

ERIC LEIF DAVIN: *Why did you want to go to MIT in 1920?*

DAVID LASSER: Well, I'd just been discharged from the army and I wanted to find something with a scientific background. Engineering was beginning to bloom and I thought it would provide me with an interesting, useful, and profitable career. MIT had a new program called "Engineering Administration." It was a combination of engineering and business administration. It sounded interesting, because I didn't want to be just a plain engineer.

But with only half a year of high school, how did you gain admission?

I said I would go to night school and summer school to make up what I had lost. I had to use an awful lot of persuasion, but they took me on a trial basis. To illustrate what I was up against, half the students at MIT had not only been graduated from high school, but also from prep schools like Exeter and Andover. So, here was I, without even a high school education.

In our first geometry class the instructor said, "Now, we'll review. Will someone tell us what a function is?" A function, you see, is the relationship between mathematical quantities. So, bright David Lasser put up his hand and said, "A function is some kind of social event." The whole class roared with laughter. It shows how ignorant I was at the time. But it worked out and I was graduated with my class in 1924.

What did you do after you were graduated?

Until I joined *Science Wonder Stories* in 1929 I had a couple of dead-end jobs. I just couldn't find myself. I had no particular background or influence or even direction. So, when I saw an advertisement in the *New York Times* that Gernsback was looking for an editor, I thought, "Well, I'll look into this and see what it is."

I had absolutely no experience in running a magazine, but when I met with Gernsback he was attracted by my MIT degree. He and his brother were Germans and were attracted by good education. My degree sold them, even though I was a complete novice as an editor. As far as science fiction was concerned, I'd read H. G. Wells and a couple of others, but otherwise I was a complete novice in science fiction as well. Anyway, Gernsback hired me at a salary of about $70 a week, and that was a lot of money in those days.[38]

Since you were such a complete novice, why did you think you were qualified to edit a science fiction magazine?

I was willing to try new things. I find in life that one should try things and not be repelled by seeming obstacles. That's why I'd applied to MIT. If you apply yourself and you have intelligence and the will and imagination, you can usually work it out.

What kind of person was Hugo Gernsback?

He was a very cultured and well-educated man. I think he had some inventions to his credit. Both he and his brother, who was his partner, were fine people.

Now, you always have problems, differences of opinion, in any work situation. For example, once I was on the job and began to look into the stories that were being submitted, I was dismayed by the low quality of many that Gernsback had already accepted. Gernsback had been accepting stories himself until I was hired. I thought that some of these were pretty terrible from both a literary and a scientific standpoint. So, I immediately had a long talk with Gernsback about this. I told him if *Wonder Stories* was to amount to anything, we had to do better.

At that time, *Amazing Stories* was our big competitor. I said to Gernsback that if we wanted to compete with *Amazing* we had to lift the quality of the stories. We needed more imagination in the stories, we needed a sound scientific basis, and, since these were appealing mainly to young people, there should also be a socially useful theme to inspire the readers.

Gernsback agreed with this, so I was given a free hand. Therefore, I examined the stories that were submitted quite rigidly and rejected a great many, even from authors who had previously been accepted.

How much editorial control did you actually have?

I had 90 percent control over what appeared in the magazines. The Gernsback brothers wanted final review of what I had accepted; after all, they were the publishers. But they were involved in a lot of other things and pretty much left me alone to run the magazines. It went to the whole question of what stories to accept or not accept.

Did Gernsback have any kind of an editorial board of experts that evaluated the stories?

No, it was just me.

I understand it was his policy at Amazing *to leave much of the day-to-day operation of the magazine to his managing editor. Was that true at* Wonder?

Yes, insofar as the editorial aspects were concerned. The business aspects were handled by other people. There were a lot of mundane details to take care of. When I started, I had no assistant. I was the entire editorial staff. There was a secretary, but that was it.

At the same time you were editing Science Wonder Stories, *you were also editing other Gernsback magazines, including* Air Wonder Stories.

Yes, *Air Wonder Stories* took a lot of time. Since it was a drain on my time and energy to be editing so many different magazines, he finally hired an editorial assistant for me. This was Charles P. Mason. He remained on the payroll until Gernsback sold *Wonder* in 1936.

But I was a young man then. I was twenty-seven when I took the job, and young men have lots of energy. It was also an enjoyable job. I liked what I was doing. It was an imaginative field that opened up a vast number of new aspects of life. There was no limit on your imagination. You could become immersed in stories of the future, and I found it fitted well with my temperament.

Gernsback once said that his ideal formula for a "scientifiction" story was 75 percent literature and 25 percent science. What were your criteria?

Well, you had to have a good story which would stand up. The science formed the background. But if the story itself wasn't any good, then the science part was useless. Let's assume there's a new development in science, say in radio. I would think about the development and say, "Now, I wonder if this could be made into a story?" Once I had an idea, I'd write to a particular writer I thought could handle it and present my idea; if he could write a good story around it, we'd be willing to accept it.

Do you remember any writers in particular?

No, my memory is poor, very poor, in that area.

What if I mention some names? Do you remember Fletcher Pratt?

Oh, yes, sure, sure. Of course I remember him. He became the librarian of the Interplanetary Society. He was a little fellow with heavy glasses and had a fine mind. We worked together quite well. I liked his stories.

How about Laurence Manning?

Oh, yes, sure. We were very good friends. Manning was a very fine-looking person—tall, well-proportioned. He had a very agreeable, charming, outgoing manner. He wrote good stories, also, and he was a very imaginative fellow. We published a lot of his stories. He became treasurer of the Interplanetary Society.

How about Jack Williamson?

Only very vaguely. I don't think we ever met.

Here's a name I'm sure you'll recall. How about David H. Keller?

Oh, sure. He was a medical doctor, a very scholarly person. He was very genial, full of humor. I really liked him.

It's good of you to spur my memory with these names. They come back as if out of the blue when you mention them. These are all people I had a personal association with, as you can see.

You worked particularly closely with Dr. Keller, didn't you? You published a long story with him, "The Time Projector."

That's right. "The Time Projector" was based on a machine which could take all the facts governing a given situation, analyze them, and project its future development. In other words, it was a master computer, but we didn't have anything like that at the time. In the story, the scientist who developed the Time Projector discovered there would be a great war which would decimate the earth. We were talking about a computer extrapolation of World War II. But the hero reckoned without the feelings of ordinary people faced with disaster. They got together and killed the scientist.

How did you come to collaborate with Dr. Keller on that story?

It was my suggestion that we collaborate. It was my story idea and he was interested in it. He had the skill to do it right.

I liked his stories; they were very—*human*. Some science fiction writers are *in*human in their approach. They can't deal with people. Keller had a feeling for people; he knew how to portray them and their reactions. I liked that approach.

All the covers of Wonder Stories *were painted by Frank Paul . . .*

Yes, that's right! I liked his work. We often worked together in that I would suggest an idea for a painting and he would suggest ideas also. He was quite talented. I met Frank Paul many times, but I just can't recall what he was like as a person. This was almost sixty years ago!

What was your impression of the science fiction field at that time—the first years of the thirties?

It was an *emerging* field, still trying to find itself without much of an historical basis, not much tradition. A lot of the stories had a flimsy basis, both scientifically and literarily. I can't speak for *Amazing* at the time, but as far as *Wonder Stories* was concerned, the standards weren't very high.

But I felt at the time that science fiction could—and *should*—become an important field of literature. As science took over more and more of our lives, the *meaning* of science, the future of science, how science would affect our lives, would become extremely important. And there were cases where science fiction stories stimulated inventions and scientific development. I'm thinking here of the satellite communications system proposed by Arthur C. Clarke before it ever became a reality.

Was the low quality of stories because the science fiction writers of that era just weren't that good, or was it because Gernsback was willing to settle for anything that came his way?

Gernsback just wasn't willing to devote the time and energy necessary to develop good writers. As I said, he had many other interests, and he just wasn't willing to spend the time on it. And if the publisher doesn't care, then the writers won't care.

I tried to combat this tendency on the basis of specific instances. I would get a story and I'd say, "Well, this story has possibilities, but it's not developed." So, I'd send it back to the author and tell him what I thought about it and suggest revisions. I tried to be not merely critical, but also cooperative with the writers in a positive sense. Gernsback wasn't willing to invest time to do that. There were some authors who didn't like their stories being rejected, and the idea that they had to do much more research or work on them. But, on the whole, it worked out. I think my approach was helpful to them—and to the field.

Gernsback also had a reputation for not paying writers. Was that a problem while you were his editor?

We used to have fights about that. I believe he felt—maybe because of his German background—that the very fact that the authors were published should have been compensation enough. But I felt that if you wanted to encourage these writers to devote the time and energy and imagination needed for better stories, they should be properly compensated.

I can't remember how much I knew at the time about the financial situation of the magazines—if they were making money, how much, and so on. But Gernsback was certainly *proud* that he was the publisher of the magazine.

How did you come to write The Conquest of Space*?*

Many of the stories we published dealt with space travel. I felt that most of them were very poorly done. They were unconvincing as to the method of getting into space and what happened in space.

So, I researched the problem. I spent evenings poring through technical journals and scientific books and became familiar with rockets. The rocket, I discovered, could not only operate where there was no air, but could operate *best* where there was no air.

And, like a clap of lightning, it suddenly struck me that here was the instrument which could conquer space. So, I gathered together a group of writers, some of those you mentioned, and I told them about my research. I told them we ought to do something about this to make people more aware. They agreed, and we formed the American Interplanetary Society in March 1930.

I then concluded that we needed a book which would explain in realistic, accurate, but understandable scientific terms how space could be conquered and what the conquering of space would mean for humanity. So, I wrote the book.

When I tried to find a publisher, most didn't think it was a viable idea. One publisher told me, "If you write this as fiction, I'll publish it, but not if you treat it as something real." Moreover, it was 1931, in the midst of the Great Depression, and fewer books were being published and bought.

How did you finally find a publisher?

We didn't. We published it ourselves. The writers and I put up the money. Most of the writers had full-time jobs and did their science fiction writing on the side, so they had incomes. We got a printer, called ourselves the Penguin Press, and distributed it.

The book didn't sell very well; I may have earned about $50 on it. It went out of print after that initial print run.

But, a year later, in 1932, we managed to get it published in Britain. Arthur C. Clarke has written in articles and told me that when he was a boy in England, he bought it, read it, and it was my book which convinced him to go into science and science fiction writing.

Ten years later, in 1941, on the floor of the United States Congress, I was denounced by a Congressman—and I'm quoting here—as "a crackpot with mental delusions that we can travel to the moon!" And the entire U.S. House of Representatives roared with laughter at the idea.[39]

How did you come to be denounced as a crackpot on the floor of the House of Representatives?

Well, I'd been in the Workers' Alliance, you know. President Roosevelt had asked me to take a post where I would help return the jobless to private industry. I'd suggested to him that a Job Corps training program be established, and he liked the idea. He proposed it to Congress and asked me to come aboard as a consultant. You see, in the ten years of the Depression, there were millions of young people who had never *had* a job; they had no skills, no training. My view was that they needed training so they would be qualified for jobs.

However, since I'd led many delegations of the Workers' Alliance to Congress to chide members for not giving more help to the unemployed, some of them were getting back at me. It was a way of ridiculing me by ridiculing my ideas. Moreover, I was also called a radical for my Workers' Alliance affiliation, even though I had resigned in protest against the efforts of the Communists to gain control.

But, in any case, in 1981, fifty years after the book came out, the American Institute of Aeronautics and Astronautics (AIAA) had a celebration of the fiftieth anniversary of the Interplanetary

Society and the book's publication. The Interplanetary Society later changed its name to the American Rocket Society, which then finally became the American Institute of Aeronautics and Astronautics, which is still in existence.

In a big celebration in Los Angeles, the AIAA honored me as the founder of the Institute, and gave me a plaque as its first president. Last year I was invited to Stockholm for the International Astronautical Federation meeting, and this year they invited me to the first meeting of all the former presidents of the AIAA for the end of April. But, after recently having undergone a heart operation, I reluctantly had to decline.

Still, it's interesting to realize that our little group of science fiction writers from *Wonder Stories* actually founded that prestigious organization. That's an amazing and concrete example of science fiction's having a great influence on the development of space exploration.

What kind of activities did you want to promote when you and the writers founded the Interplanetary Society?

We wanted to stimulate interest in space exploration as a real possibility. We encouraged the formation of chapters around the country to propagandize the idea, and we carried out experiments to develop the then-primitive and unpredictable rocket. We used the magazine as a vehicle for obtaining recruits. There were quite a number who were interested. It was a going concern.

Did Gernsback approve of using the magazine in this fashion?

Oh, yes! He observed how it would help the magazine. It was a reciprocal thing. He was for anything which would help the magazine and advance science.

The Interplanetary Society was the seed. The seed sprouted, but it didn't fully bloom at the time because the Depression was in full force. People were interested in simply staying alive and not going out into space, so we were swimming against the tide. And the Depression went on and on until the war came in 1941.

Around that time the New York Times *ran an editorial chiding Robert Goddard, the rocket pioneer, for wasting his college's money on rocket experiments.*

That's right. I was in communication with Goddard at that time. He approved of what we were doing, but didn't want to join us.[40] He was getting a stipend of $25,000 a year from the Guggenheim Foundation to send rockets up a couple of miles to sample the upper levels of the atmosphere. The purpose was to help develop rockets for reporting on the weather. He felt that if he joined us he might lose his stipend for associating with those crazy science fiction people. I just can't tell you how difficult it was to convince people we could actually travel into space!

What later happened with the Society?

Well, although it was started by science fiction writers, a new group of scientists and engineers started coming in who were mainly interested in the development of the rocket, not simply travelling into space. That was too far-fetched for them. They felt the very name, Interplanetary Society, was a hindrance and invited ridicule. So, they changed it to the American Rocket Society. Eventually, it became the American Institute of Aeronautics and Astronautics, but I'd left the society before that.

There were a lot of unemployed in the Greenwich Village neighborhood where I lived. I'd say that 80 percent of the mostly Italian residents were out of work. They were in a really desperate situation. I felt a responsibility to do something about it. So, I formed a little group of these people from the neighborhood to represent them at City Hall. That grew into a city-wide unemployed organization. We used to go down and meet with Mayor LaGuardia and agitate for jobs or relief. Stories about us began to appear in the papers. In 1935 it grew into a national organization, the Workers' Alliance, with me as president.

How did Gernsback feel about your activities?

[Laughter.] He didn't like them! I don't blame him. I don't think he was politically opposed, though I never knew his political views. But I was spending time away from the job. These demonstrations and meetings with Mayor LaGuardia were during the day when I should have been at my desk at *Wonder Stories*. So, one day he called me into his office and said, "If you like working with the unemployed so much, I suggest you go and join them." And he fired me.

But I think he had an additional reason. The magazine was in trouble financially. By then I knew that kids just didn't have the money to buy the magazine. Gernsback had to cut costs where he could. So, after he fired me, he hired a young kid to replace me at half my salary. That was a big savings for him.

While I could understand Gernsback's view, I felt the most important question before us was not travelling into space but saving the country—if it could be saved—from this dreadful plague of unemployment. We never had anything like it before or after, with a quarter of the entire workforce out of work. I think it was 18 million at the time. Before 1933, when Roosevelt took office, there was just nothing for them. Hoover was President, and he and Congress were opposed to assistance. They thought it would all just go away. But the breadlines were everywhere. People had been dispossessed, thrown out of their homes. The farmers were going bankrupt. Banks were closing. The country was really in terrible shape. I felt that this was the important question of the moment and space would have to wait. I think I did the right thing, but I paid heavily for it.

Was it a natural progression for you to go from science fiction to agitating for the unemployed?

It was the Depression and what it did to my mind—especially in those four years before Roosevelt came in—in those four horrible years I was going through a mental revolution. There were so many horrible things that happened. For example, the stock market had gone up and up in the late twenties. After the crash of 1929, many stocks went down to about 10 percent of their previous value. Then stories of terrible market manipulations were revealed. I felt we needed a political change. Not a revolutionary change, but a peaceful change to bring us up to what a lot of other countries were doing for their citizens.

In some accounts I've read, you're called a Socialist. Were you?

Yes, I joined the Socialist Party in '31 or '32 while I was still editor at *Wonder Stories*. I remained in it for four or five years. Then I felt that, while the Socialists were people who had dreams of what they *might* do, it was Roosevelt who was really doing things. So I became a Roosevelt supporter.

And yet, you were very critical of Roosevelt up until 1936, weren't you?

Yes, there was an early period when he hadn't found himself. He came from a patrician family and may not have been aware of what was happening in the country. But I think our Workers' Alliance may have had some effect on him. I used to get in to see him or Mrs. Roosevelt, either alone or with a delegation, and I pleaded the cause of the unemployed long and hard. Being a great, shrewd politician, he didn't want to commit himself to things he couldn't carry out. But by 1936, with the New Deal laws, the unions had built themselves up and became a great political force for him. So there developed the kind of atmosphere in which he could move.

You left the Workers' Alliance in 1940. Did you work with the job training program you mentioned earlier?

No, Congress blocked my appointment. Those Congressmen who opposed me had written into the job training law a statement that said, "No part of these funds shall be paid to David Lasser." It's significant that after I had been kept out of that program, many Congressmen may have been ashamed of what they had done. A year later a separate resolution was introduced to repeal that action against me, and it passed without dissent. In any case, it was illegal—contrary to our Constitution, which prohibits legislation against a specific individual.

So, I had a period of unemployment myself. Then, when the war came, I was asked to join the War Production Board. I remained with them until the end of the war. Then Averell Harriman, Secretary of Commerce, asked me to join his staff. When the Marshall Plan was launched to rebuild Europe, Harriman was named to head it in Paris. He asked me to join him to work on the serious problem of the Communist-influenced European labor movement, which was hostile to the Plan.

However, the same Congressmen who'd blocked me on the other position now arose to oppose me again. They'd written into the law a section on eligibility of employees, and claimed I came under the heading of people who were not allowed to work. I appealed and proved that all charges against me of Communism were wrong. But, with the exception of Harriman, the officials in the organization were too timid to oppose these political forces, and I was again blocked.[41]

In 1950 you became Chief Economist for the International Union of Electrical Workers. Where did you receive your economic training for that position?

At MIT, as part of my original training. I worked with the IUE until I retired in 1968.

What have you been doing since your retirement?

All during those years I'd been brooding over the injustices done me by twice preventing me from taking important government posts with the charge that I was a Communist. No proof had ever been offered and, in fact, I had proved over and over again that I had been a loyal American. So, when I retired, I was determined to correct those injustices. While my sophisticated Washington friends warned me it was impossible, I persisted. These efforts finally paid off. Eventually, I received a letter from President Carter, dated April 2, 1980, clearing me and adding, "Your loyal and valuable service to this country in both public and private sectors has won you many friends and admirers."

Then I turned my mind to a consideration of the status of mankind, not only on earth but in this universe, and its origin. I wrote a long poem about it entitled, "Some Say Creation Came . . ." I decided to write a book on our origins and real meaning, dwelling on the possibility that our universe is only a part of a larger and vaster body and that, in turn, part of a still larger one, like a series of balls each encased in a larger one, going on to infinity. But then, in my research over several years, I discovered many distinguished university professors were publishing books with similar themes. I asked myself what I could contribute in the face of that. So, I abandoned the book project.

Then the State Department asked me to undertake a series of visits to a number of European and Asian countries to present the truthful picture of the American labor movement, in order to counter the efforts of the Communists to win over these countless millions of working people.

Finally, in 1982, at the age of eighty, I asked myself what I would do with the rest of my life. I recalled that in 1970 I'd started and abandoned a science fiction novel entitled "Big Joey." It dealt with a crisis in the affairs of mankind that required complete unity of purpose and action of all countries to save us. The question was whether we possessed the vision, wisdom, and courage to meet this challenge. I reread what I'd written and, with the state of the world even more dangerous than in 1970, decided to return to the project with a broader outlook and, perhaps, more skill. It's now progressed to the point where I'm looking for an agent.

Is there anything else you'd like to say?

I think it's significant and perhaps symbolic that, after sixty years and at the age of eighty-four, I return to science fiction as a means of expressing some of my deepest feelings and make, perhaps, my final contribution. Happily, I still have my mental and, thanks to a recent operation, my physical faculties. I believe they will remain with me until I complete this task to my satisfaction.

In any case, I have put aside all other activities to concentrate on finishing my book. I hope it will make a contribution to our dangerous and unstable world.[42]

A CONVERSATION WITH CHARLES D. HORNIG

To replace Lasser as managing editor of *Wonder Stories,* Hugo Gernsback brought in seventeen-year-old Charles D. Hornig. The choice of someone so young and inexperienced astounded many in the science fiction community, not least among them Hornig himself. Sam Moskowitz speculated that "Gernsback had to gamble on a kid like Hornig because he was in no position to hire a top man, not just because of money, but because his reputation as a payer and employer had sunk so low that qualified men avoided him."[43] That may be. However, it was a brand-new literary genre! In a field as newly created as science fiction, only seven years old, one might legitimately ask, "Where were there surplus qualified editors?" Lasser himself, who turned out to be a superb editor, knew nothing of science fiction or editing when he was hired. Arguably, Hornig, when hired, was much better qualified than Lasser, despite his youth, as he was far more familiar with the field and was already editing his own magazine.

Still, it is true that the financial condition of Gernsback's publishing empire had continued to worsen. Horace L. Gold remembers visiting the 98 Park Place offices of *Wonder Stories* around this time. "Park Place was once like London's Fleet Street," he recalled. "But it was run down when Gernsback was there. His office was a stinking, awful, shabby place."[44] Isaac Asimov recalled that *Wonder* and *Amazing* "were declining steadily in 1934, and neither was received regularly at my father's newsstand."[45]

As to story manuscripts, Hornig told me that, because of the finances, "we had the bottom of the pile."[46] Even so, observed Moskowitz, of the stories *Wonder* published,

> partially because of their very clean-cut presentation, they read very original and interesting at the time. Every now and then he would have an issue quite as good as *Astounding*. His comment now lays greater importance on Gernsback's searching out foreign translations. He needed them to try to get better quality material, as well as something novel. Unfortunately, they were not as swift-paced as American material and did not have the same acceptance.[47]

Then, late in 1935, both *Wonder* and *Amazing* went bimonthly. "During 1936 those doddering ancients . . . continued to weave downhill," said Asimov. *"Wonder Stories* was so poorly distributed that . . . I hardly ever saw it. The March-April 1936 issue was its last. It was dead."[48] Gernsback sold *Wonder Stories* to Beacon/Standard Publications, which published a number of magazines under the editorial supervision of Leo Margulies. In August it returned as *Thrilling Wonder Stories* with Mort Weisinger, an in-house editor from the company, as editor. But it was no longer Hugo Gernsback's magazine. After seventy-eight issues—twelve as *Science Wonder—Wonder Stories* was gone.[49]

Gernsback briefly and unsuccessfully returned to the field in the 1950s as the publisher of *Science Fiction Plus,* with Sam Moskowitz as editor. At that time, however, Gernsback's editorial practice seems to have been dramatically different from his style at *Wonder Stories,* and this deserves brief mention. Lasser and Hornig stated independently that Gernsback essentially adopted a "hands off" editorial policy. According to them, except for personal friends (such as Laurence Manning or David H. Keller, who was also a business associate), Gernsback never communicated with any authors concerning editorial (as opposed to financial) matters. Nor did he have anything to say to either of them concerning stories. Both were given a free hand in running the magazine, and what appeared (or didn't appear) in *Wonder Stories* was solely the result of their own decisions. The editorial *laissez-faire* appears to also represent a sharp break from Gernsback's early practice at *Amazing.* Moskowitz said, for example, that he possessed extensive correspondence between Gernsback and Edgar Rice Burroughs (among others) concerning requested changes in some of Burrough's stories which appeared in *Amazing.* In addition, Moskowitz's own experience under Gernsback was quite different:

> As editor of *Science Fiction Plus*, every story I thought was good had to be approved by Gernsback and also by his son Harvey. There were many stories the two of us thought were bad which he accepted over our disapproval. He was constantly demanding rewrites, and usually not for the better! . . . I couldn't even get an illustration printed without Gernsback's approval (and we sometimes ran five to a story), and he was constantly having the artist redraw them.[50]

It would seem, then, that Lasser and Hornig enjoyed a moratorium from Gernsback's original and later "hands on" approach to editing and publishing. What might explain their editorial freedom—a freedom to essentially shape the new field as they wished? Moskowitz suggested that Gernsback's financial condition might have been the determining factor. In the early days at *Amazing,* Gernsback dominated the field and could demand anything he wanted from authors, who had few alternatives. And, recalled Moskowitz,

> When I went to work for him, he was paying three cents a word on acceptance [very favorable rates and terms] and his rates for illustrations were at least as good as any of them, so he threw his weight around.
>
> The possibility exists that since Gernsback was paying very little at *Wonder Stories,* and very late, he was in no position to be fussy. He might have been grateful for anything Hornig could get into the magazine under such conditions, and the reason he did not correspond with authors was that they would ask him for money he owed them. *I think that is the answer.*[51]

Hugo Gernsback has acquired an enduring and unenviable reputation, especially among the veterans of First Fandom, as a penny-pinching skinflint. But perhaps this odium is not fully deserved. It now appears that he never really recovered from the *Amazing* debacle. *Wonder Stories* was in straitened finances from the beginning, and remained so until its death. A recent examination of Laurence Manning's papers shows that even he was not being paid at the end.[52] Additionally, Hornig states (*vide infra*) that employees at *Wonder* frequently missed paydays simply because Gernsback didn't have enough money in the bank to cover their salary checks.

Certainly Manning, *Wonder's* most frequently published author and a well-liked close friend of Gernsback's, would have been paid if Gernsback had the ability to pay. Likewise, there is no reason to believe he would have risked not paying his editors and his office staff if he could have at all done so. But if he couldn't afford to pay his writers, at least they didn't hear from him demanding endless revisions. And if he couldn't afford to pay his editors and office staff, at least he could give them a free hand. It was the best trade-off Gernsback was able to offer.

The following conversation with Charles D. Hornig took place on August 2, 1986. He was seventy years old at the time. In August of 1997, I spoke with Hornig again. Although only semi-mobile, his health was still good and, at age eighty-one, he could now claim the title of science fiction's most senior editor.

ERIC LEIF DAVIN: *How did you become a science fiction fan?*

CHARLES D. HORNIG: The same way a lot of fans did, by discovering science fiction. It was by chance. I remember the date: August 12, 1930. I was fourteen years old, and usually every day during the summer my mother gave me a quarter to go to the movies.

But I'd already seen every movie in town, so I walked into this drugstore which had a newsrack. I saw this magazine cover which showed the Chrysler Building being uprooted in flames. That was very exciting. It was the September 1930 *Amazing Stories.* I bought it out of curiosity and walked across the street to the library and began reading it. Within minutes, though, the librarian threw me out. *"You can't bring that kind of trash in here!"* she yelled. So I took it home and read it. And I was hooked. It had an installment of "Skylark Three" by E.E. Smith and a number of other good stories. It was like an LSD experience, a sort of opening up of my mind, a feeling of awe and wonder—*it was fantastic!*

I soon discovered *Wonder Stories* and a few months later *Astounding* and then *Weird Tales.* Soon I was collecting all four. I'd save up my nickels until I had quarters and I'd buy every one I could. That went on for two or three years. Then I thought I'd start a fan magazine. I'd have had no idea what a fan magazine was except that I'd been buying back numbers of magazines from a man named Carl Swanson in Washburn, North Dakota. He sent me fliers of other fan activities and one of them was a copy of *The Time Traveller,* an early science fiction fan magazine. I said, "Gee, I ought to be able to do something like this!" I got in touch with publishers and writers in New York, like Julius Schwartz and Mort Weisinger and a few others, and I began meeting with them regularly. They encouraged me to put out a fan magazine. So I did. I got it printed rather than mimeographed and called it *The Fantasy Fan.* It ran for eighteen issues.

The way I got with *Wonder Stories* was by sending a copy of the first issue to Hugo Gernsback, as well as every other editor and fan I knew, in order to build up a subscription list. It just happened that at that time he was becoming dissatisfied with David Lasser, whom I learned all about only through you.

So I received a telegram from Gernsback—I lived in Elizabeth, New Jersey, about fourteen miles outside of New York, and didn't have a telephone—saying he had an interesting proposition for me if I'd come over and see him. I had no idea what it could be about. This was in July 1933, and I was working full time for a lawyer typing briefs for five dollars a week while his secretary was on vacation. I took a day off, went into New York, and met Gernsback.

Can you describe that meeting?

Well, Gernsback looked a little disappointed when he first saw me. He expected someone a little older. Even so, I looked older than I was. I had to assure him I was seventeen before he'd believe it. I just sat there dazed. I couldn't believe I was talking to the great Hugo Gernsback! He was my hero, "The Father of Science Fiction." It was like a dream.

And, despite my age, he wanted to hire me! I think he felt that because I was a superenthusiastic fan, completely addicted to science fiction, any story I liked would also be liked by other fans, most of whom were boys about my age. It seemed to work out. Of course, I knew nothing about literature, but that didn't matter; science fiction wasn't literature. A good story was one that stirred the imagination and created a true "Sense of Wonder."

I think the other reason Gernsback wanted me was because he could save money. I didn't know it at the time, but I later learned that David Lasser, whom I was replacing, was paid $75 a week.[53] When it came to finances, Gernsback said, "Well, what do you think your starting salary should be, in the light of your extreme youth and inexperience?" I very meekly said, "Well, $25 a week?" And he said, "Let's just say $20 to start."

I know now, of course, that if I'd asked for $35 or $40, I might have gotten $30 or $35, but I was happy to be hired and would have worked for nothing if he'd asked me to. I learned from you that Gernsback later boasted to Lasser that he'd hired a replacement for half of what he'd been paying Lasser. I wish that had been true, because then I'd have been making $37.50 a week! But I guess even Gernsback was ashamed to admit he was really paying me less than a third of what he paid Lasser. Still, in those days $20 a week was lots of money for a seventeen-year-old boy when men with families were sometimes lucky to make $15.

Then he gave me the manuscript of a novel, a translation of something German—I forget the name of it. He said, "Take this home over the weekend and edit it." He also gave me a mimeographed list of proofreader's marks. I was to return on Monday with the edited manuscript and my parents' permission. Then I left. Before I went home, though, I took the subway to the Bronx to tell Julius Schwartz about it. He couldn't believe it, either!

My parents were delighted to have me working. That was the depth of the Depression and we had very little money. I still had a year and a half of high school to finish, but I did that by going to night school for the next four years. I went to work as editor of *Wonder Stories* on August 7, 1933—almost fifty-three years ago to the day!

How did your parents feel about your science fiction interests before this?

They seemed to be indifferent. But my mother loved to brag. After I became editor of *Wonder Stories*, she'd go around saying I was editing the *Saturday Evening Post*. She exaggerated a bit! Although she didn't understand what was going on, she was supportive. And I was earning $20 a week and paid for my room and board, so that was a help.

Would you talk about your working relationship with Gernsback? For instance, how much control did you actually have over what appeared in the magazine?

I had total control over what appeared in the magazine. The one thing we all liked about Gernsback and which kept us with him, despite his poor rate of pay and his employees having to hold paychecks for weeks upon weeks at a time, was that he gave everyone a free hand. He was good to work for in that way. He didn't stop you from doing anything. He didn't criticize your work unless there was something really wrong. So I was totally free to reject or accept stories. Of course, he never saw the rejected stories, but in the two and a half years I worked for him, he never once disagreed with me over a story I accepted.

The practice was for me to read all the stories which came in. Maybe one out of twenty was worth considering. If I wanted to accept any story I wrote an evaluation on a special cover sheet which was then attached to the manuscript. I described what I liked about the story and why I wanted to use it. This was passed on to Gernsback, and he'd send it back with an "OK" on it. That's all he ever did. So far as I know, he never contacted authors in any way, except his friends, like Laurence Manning or David Keller. He gave me free rein. I wrote to all writers criticizing their manuscripts, suggesting revisions, whatever. Also, I wrote all the editorials, handled "The Reader Speaks" letters section, wrote all the blurbs and captions, and chose the work of all artists except for Frank Paul.

There's only one story during my tenure that Gernsback ever paid any special attention to. That was "A Martian Odyssey" by Stanley Weinbaum, which was a real find. Now, *that* story *was* literature—it was really well-written. It had personalities, characterization. Perhaps for the first time it showed an alien creature on another planet from a favorable viewpoint, as something other than a horrible monster. This character Tweel was something cute, sort of like "E.T."

I was very excited by this story and I wrote a very enthusiastic note to Gernsback on the cover sheet. He paid close attention to it and agreed about its quality. In fact, he wrote the blurb for it himself, which is the only time I can ever remember his writing the blurb for a story. He knew it was a good one.[54]

Now, Julius Schwartz, who was an agent at the time, thought he stole Weinbaum away from me and *Wonder Stories*.[55] You see, Weinbaum lived in Milwaukee and Schwartz told me he wanted to let Ralph Milne Farley and other Milwaukee writers know they had a fellow science fiction writer in town, so he asked for Weinbaum's address. But the real reason he wanted it was to become his agent and take his stories to other, higher-paying markets.

Well, that may be true, but I wasn't at all unhappy to give him Weinbaum's address, because I was a fan before I was an editor. I wanted the writers to get a break. If Weinbaum could get a cent or a cent and a half a word from *Astounding* instead of having to sue Gernsback for half a cent, more power to him! So I was happy to see Weinbaum sell to *Astounding*, although I did get a few Weinbaum stories before Schwartz took him elsewhere.

Did Gernsback ever write comments on stories which he would pass on to you for forwarding to the authors?

No, he never did that. He never had anything to do with any of the stories except for that one Weinbaum story. Once in a while

Gernsback would give me a story he had selected, but it was always something from Germany which had been translated by Fletcher Pratt. There were two or three novels like that. Evidently, he got them at a very low rate, or maybe free—I don't know. They were never very good from our American standpoint—very heavily scientific, dry and boring, as far as I could tell. But I had to print them because Gernsback personally selected them.[56]

What was your personal relationship to Gernsback?

It was mostly formal. I never knew him on a personal basis. After all, he was old enough to be my father, and I was in awe of him. Oh, he would sent me postcards from Europe when he went on vacation, things like that. But I and everyone else on the staff always called him "Mr. H." This was in contrast to "Mr. S.," his brother Sydney, although I didn't see Sydney very much.

But Gernsback was always friendly. I can't remember him ever being angry or critical about anything I did.[57] Now, if I asked for a raise, he was very hesitant about it. But I seldom asked for a raise.

Did you ever get one?

After I'd been editor for six months I learned what Lasser had been getting, so I wrote Gernsback a long letter in which I said I thought I'd proven myself and should be getting $50 a week. He called me into his office and said, "This is ridiculous!" and we both laughed about it. Then he gave me a five dollar raise, so I was getting $25 a week. I eventually wound up with $27.50; that's the highest I ever got.

But remember, this would be like $300 today. For a young man, what I earned was not bad money. I lived handsomely on my wages. I was taking weekend trips to Pittsburgh and Norfolk and Boston on buses and trains, as well as a vacation to California. At the same time I was contributing to my family, so I was doing okay.

What was it like in the office?

I worked in a very small, dingy, smoky office. I'm now allergic to cigarette smoke and I think one of the reasons is working in that very tiny office with C. P. Mason puffing away on his pipe and a guy named Kraus[58] smoking a cigar and a secretary who smoked cigarettes. Luckily, we were there only about six months before we moved to larger quarters.

Did Gernsback also smoke?

Not that I know of. I never saw him smoke.

Did people around the office ever talk about David Lasser?

I heard very little about him except that he was so involved with his socialist activity that he wasn't paying enough attention to his work at *Wonder Stories*, so Gernsback let him go. No one said much of anything else. Now, I did get the impression—I don't know how—that he was in the Socialist Labor Party. I was surprised to learn from you that he was actually in the Norman Thomas Socialist Party, which is what I was in. But I never met Lasser in the party.

When did you join the Socialist Party?

I joined in 1940 or '41, but I eventually dropped out. There was a lot of bickering going on and I didn't feel it was doing much good. There were two factions at each other's throats all the time. They weren't accomplishing anything, so I got out. But I always voted for Norman Thomas. I always went to his lectures and talks, and I liked him very much. I also got to know his brother Evan quite well.

Evan Thomas was a doctor, and he provided the blood test that my wife, Florence, and I had to take to get married. Before we were married Florence was his secretary. Evan Thomas was at that time executive secretary of the War Resisters League and a leading pacifist of the Forties. My son is named after him.

A few years ago, after the Freedom of Information Act was passed, I wrote for a copy of my FBI file. Of course, what they send you is so full of blackouts I don't know where anyone got the idea there was any "freedom of information." But one thing that got through the censors was a report that I'd married the *daughter* of Norman Thomas! The closest I got to that was to marry the secretary of his *brother.* The FBI had so many things wrong it'd be laughable if it wasn't so tragic.

I'd like to come back to this, but first I'd like to clear up a few things about Wonder Stories. *For instance, what was the "New Story" policy you announced with the very first issue that came out under your editorship?*

It was just a matter of personal prejudice in stories. I preferred what would now be considered a very old-fashioned type of science fiction. I wanted stories that were really plausible and logical and based on known facts. A story had to be *possible.* I wrote authors very long letters when I rejected stories, telling them exactly *why.* For instance, one author had a story about a tree given some sort of growth hormone so it never stopped growing. It became thousands of times larger than the earth. "Where did the tree get all that building material?" I asked him. Things like that I rejected.

How did this type of story differ from what had been published under Lasser?

Well, a lot of the "New Story" policy was just propaganda. That is, if I liked the story and it was scientifically plausible, I looked for new ways to present old themes. Of course, there was no way I could really make any demands. I had to take what I could get, and I got last choice because Gernsback paid the least and the latest. That made things really difficult. Still, I got quite a few good stories simply because the field was so small at that time. Even if *Astounding* rejected a story, it might still be good and I might eventually get it.

But I think propagandizing for new stories did encourage people like Otto Binder to produce this sort of story, and so changed the field a little. Binder was one of my favorite writers, not only because he was good, but because he also took suggestions. If I had an idea for a story that I personally couldn't write, he would work it into one. I couldn't get others to do that. I can't remember any particular ideas I gave him, but we printed quite a few of Binder's stories.

How would you describe the science fiction field at that time?

Very exciting. It wasn't accepted as good literature, of course. The term "science fiction" appeared nowhere except in the field itself. No one else knew what science fiction was. Perhaps, at most, there were fifty thousand people in the *entire world* who indulged in it at that time. The circulations of the magazines ran to no more than twenty, thirty, or forty thousand copies. It was a very limited field.

Also, the idea of travelling to the Moon was considered crazy. My sisters would ridicule it, and so did almost everyone else. There were few females in the field. We had a couple of female writers, Leslie F. Stone and Amelia Reynolds Long, but very few female fans. There was Virginia Kidd, who became a well-known agent. Later on Judith Merril came along. It was mostly boys in their mid- and late-teens. That was fandom.

Oh, there might have been a few oddball adults. They tell me Ethel Barrymore used to read science fiction in the thirties. I imagine a number of other adults also read it, but kept it a dirty little secret because it wasn't respectable literature. Only a kid would admit to reading science fiction.

What did you think of the quality of the writing?

Well, at seventeen years of age I was not a great literary critic. I didn't even know what literature *was,* except in school they forced us to read Dickens and stuff like that. Looking back, I'd say that science fiction then was a very low grade of literature. It wasn't literature at all, except for a few writers! Basically, the technique for writing science fiction did not include great literary ability. Characters weren't developed. The emphasis was all on science and amazement and the "Sense of Wonder." But, then, youngsters weren't too concerned with psychology and character development, anyway.

So, you primarily looked for that "Sense of Wonder"?

That was the main thing. The idea that you should really be amazed at what was happening in the story—that it would just grab your mind and open up mental vistas for you, as it did for me in the first place. The idea of time travel and alternate worlds just blew my mind, as I think they did for a lot of others. It was the ideas which carried the stories. Of course, there had to be *some* writing ability, but it didn't have to be really literary, like you find, say, in the *New Yorker.*

Besides propagandizing the "New Story" policy, did you try anything else to shape the field?

I had an article in *Author and Journalist* entitled "How to Write Science Fiction,"[59] which was rather presumptive of me. I wrote it when I was seventeen, but I was eighteen when it appeared. At that time people in the office didn't know how young I actually was; they thought I was at least in my twenties. But when this article appeared, the magazine said I was seventeen. Then people began calling me "The Boy Wonder." I told them, "Oh, no. That was long ago. I'm an old man now—I'm eighteen!"

But, in that article, I told people how to write science fiction. It all had to do with this emphasis on science I mentioned previously.

How would you or the writers find these "amazing" ideas?

A lot of them came from the scientific news of the day. A lot of things were happening. In 1930, for instance, the planet Pluto was discovered. That started a whole series of stories about Pluto. Writers got ideas from the sensational science news in the *American Weekly,* which appeared in Hearst newspapers on Sundays.

They'd also take ideas from each other a lot. For instance, H.G. Wells wrote stories with ideas which would still have been considered new in the thirties. If you remember his story "The New Accelerator," he had a way to speed up your metabolism so much you could move too fast for people to see you. So, a new story could be worked out of something like that.[60]

You mentioned earlier that Otto Binder was one of your favorite authors. Who else did you like?

Laurence Manning. Manning actually got three-fourth cents per word because he was a friend of Gernsback's, and he was one of the better writers. Dr. David Keller I liked very much. I liked Raymond Z. Gallun. Ed Hamilton, of course. And Jack Williamson was one of my favorites.

Did you ever meet any of these authors?

Yes, I met Jack Williamson several times. He gave the impression of being a New Mexican cowboy, which was actually what he was! He had a Western drawl and he walked and acted and looked just like a cowboy. You'd never think he could sit down and write his wonderful stuff.[61]

Dr. Keller was a great guy. I visited his home a couple of times in Pennsylvania, where he was the supervisor of a mental hospital.

He also came into the New York office frequently because he was the editor of Gernsback's *Sexology* magazine. That was the first serious magazine about sex, a scientific magazine which discussed sexual matters that were greatly taboo at the time.

Dr. Keller was a better writer than many, but his manuscripts were terrible to edit because he typed them himself and they were horrible. Not only was he a poor typist—corrections all over—but his grammar was poor, his punctuation was all wrong, and he couldn't spell. They took a lot of editing. But once you cleaned them up, you had good stories.[62]

Did you meet Laurence Manning?

Several times. He came into the office because he was a friend of Gernsback's. Once in a while we'd have an office party and he'd be there. He was a quiet, mild man, very good-looking.[63]

You mentioned Fletcher Pratt as a translator of German stories. . . .

Right. He was also a very quiet, unassuming middle-aged man. I think he smoked a pipe. An ordinary-looking man— nothing special about his looks.

Wasn't he also a historian?

That's right. He was a military historian. He'd done a lot of work in that field, but I didn't read it because I wasn't interested in it.[64]

Did you ever meet Leslie F. Stone?

Yes, once. It was an interesting adventure. It was over the Labor Day weekend of 1935. I had an old jalopy, a 1926 Chrysler. Julie Schwartz and I decided to take a trip around for several days visiting fans and writers within a few miles of New York. So we drove to Pennsylvania and stayed overnight with Lloyd Eshbach in Reading.[65] Then we went on to visit William Crawford, who later became known as the father of small press science fiction publishing. Then we went on to Ohio and West Virginia.

On the way back we stopped in Washington, D.C. Leslie Stone was living there with her husband. We spent a long Sunday afternoon and evening with them, talking until about two o'clock in the morning. Unfortunately, I can't remember anything about the conversation. But she was very pleasant, a good-looking young woman. She was an exceptionally good writer, too.[66]

I was also probably the first one in the field to meet C. L. Moore. Catherine was already writing for *Weird Tales*. She knew quite a bit about science fiction, but she wrote a very distinctive type of story that was more fantasy than science fiction. She lived in Indianapolis at the time, working as the secretary to the vice-president of the Fletcher Trust Co. When I drove across the country in 1936, after *Wonder Stories* folded, I dropped in on her at work. We went out for lunch together and had a very nice talk. She was an attractive young woman, very beautiful, very pleasant. She told me she wanted to go to California, also—and she eventually did, and married Henry Kuttner.[67]

Did you ever meet Amelia Reynolds Long?

Yes, on the trip with Julius Schwartz in 1935. After stopping at Eshbach's, we went on to Harrisburg, where she lived. On seeing her, we were really shocked. This was 1935, but when she opened the door to greet us she was dressed as if it were 1865! She wore high buttoned shoes and very old-fashioned clothing. She wasn't an old woman, only about 30 or 35, but you'd swear you were back in the days of Lincoln.

She also had very shifty eyes. She wouldn't look straight at you. Quite a weird character! We had only a brief conversation at the door, because she didn't invite us in. We weren't expected, and I think she was embarrassed because we just dropped in. She was a strange one![68]

How about Clark Ashton Smith?

Oh, yes. Another strange one. He was quite a good friend of mine, although I met him in person only once, on a trip back from California in 1938. He helped me start *The Fantasy Fan.* I obtained the addresses of a number of writers somewhere, perhaps from Forrest Ackerman. So I wrote to Smith, [H. P.] Lovecraft, [August] Derleth, and a number of others. All of them sent me manuscripts to publish, free of charge, in *The Fantasy Fan.* Unfortunately, these are now in the common domain because I didn't copyright anything. Derleth later used a lot of these stories in his Arkham House books.

Anyway, Smith lived near Auburn, California. That's about thirty miles east of Sacramento. He met me at the hotel bus station and drove me to his isolated cabin. He lived way out of town on top of a mountain in a tiny cabin all by himself. He had decorated the place in the fashion of his writings. For instance, he had a rock garden in which every single rock was a gargoyle, which he had sculpted. He was also a good painter, and his weird paintings were hanging all over the walls. It was all very bizarre. Smith was probably Lovecraft's best friend, although they never met.[69]

I understand Lovecraft was also pretty weird.

Yes, he was. He was a recluse. He was very tall and thin. He didn't dress in an old-fashioned style, but very plainly. He looked like an undertaker, with a very somber appearance, but he was actually very good-natured. I met Lovecraft a number of times, but the only time I remember well was in 1935, two years before he died. He was about forty-four then, and was living with his aunt in her house right off the Brown University campus in Providence.

Lovecraft despised anything modern. He never went into

downtown Providence. Hated it. He took me on a guided tour of Providence and showed me sights that hadn't changed for three hundred years—mostly graveyards. He loved them. Except for cars parked in the distance, you could easily imagine it being 1635 instead of 1935. He could also pronounce words which no one else could, like "Cthulhu," or whatever that strange god of his was. You'd choke trying to pronounce that word the way he did. It started way down in the bottom of his throat.

Could you pronounce it the way Lovecraft did?

[Laughter.] No, I'd choke right here if I tried! But we had quite a correspondence between us. Years later, when I was hard up, I sold my correspondence to somebody in Texas.

Did you ever meet Raymond Z. Gallun?

No, I never met him, although he was one of my favorite writers and I've been reading his stuff for over half a century.[70]

Didn't you meet Isaac Asimov around that time also?

As a matter of fact, I did, but I didn't realize it. He was in the Futurians,[71] or on the edge of that group, and lived on Long Island at the time. I was reading one of his anthologies a few years back. He had little blurbs before each story telling how the story came about. In one of these he said, "Charles D. Hornig is the only science fiction notable who has absolutely no talent." I got a kick out of that, so I wrote to him and said, "I come to New York frequently and I'd like to meet you. I don't think we've ever met." (He'd also written in that blurb that he'd never met me.) So, on my next trip to New York, I went to his apartment near Central Park. He greeted me and said, "You know, I discovered that we *did* meet, back around 1939[72] when you were out in Brooklyn. I found it in one of my old diaries."

Then he showed me these voluminous diaries he's been keeping since the early 1930s, and said he was going to use them to write his autobiography, which he's since done. Asimov can tell you on which day thirty years ago he had a flat tire! I don't think anyone could stand to read them unless they were dyed-in-the-wool fans of his. Just too much trivial detail. But neither of us recalled that 1939 meeting. Except for his diaries, we'd never have known it.

So we had a very nice afternoon and he showed me his collection of Asimov books, big cupboards filled with them in every language in the world. Asimov has a tremendous ego, but he deserves it because he's a genius. He's got a brain that absorbs everything. He can write a book a week—as fast as he can type. He has no secretary. He has no agent. He does everything himself. He just recently got a word processor. And, despite doing everything himself, he's now put out three hundred books. It's just amazing.

As a result of that meeting, I wrote an article called "The Greatest Non-Talent in Science Fiction," which was published in *Galileo* in 1979. It was sort of tongue-in-cheek, demonstrating how I was the greatest non-talent. There was a bit of autobiography, but basically I advised science fiction writers who didn't have a great deal of talent how to succeed in the field.

Was there anyone you didn't hit it off with?

The one author I had unpleasant experiences with, unwittingly, was probably the greatest editor in science fiction—John W. Campbell Jr. Campbell was a very popular writer when I was still fourteen or fifteen. He'd written stories which had appeared in *Wonder Stories, Amazing Stories Quarterly,* and so on.

One day about 1934 Campbell walked into my office. He'd not joined *Astounding* yet and was still just a writer. He brought with him a great pile of short stories which he told me I could publish. But, he said, "I have to have a cent a word for them." Now, this was double our going rate, so I said, "Well, I'll have to talk to Gernsback about that, because he doesn't generally pay that much." And Campbell said, "Well, you let me know. If you pay a cent a word, you can have them."

I read them immediately and *none* of them was any good. Evidently, he was trying to pawn off on me stuff he'd written as a child or a young man, things he'd had in a drawer for ten or fifteen years that no one else would buy. Probably he thought, "What does this kid know about anything? He'll be glad to publish anything by John W. Campbell!" But I just couldn't do it. I passed them on to Gernsback and told him, "I'm sorry, but I don't think any of these are worth publishing, and anyway, he wants a cent a word." Gernsback agreed.

So I called Campbell and I rejected them. After that, I never got along with Campbell. At conventions he would purposely snub me. Campbell was a great one for hating people. Then again, I was "inferior" to him. I didn't know science properly and I couldn't write for *Astounding,* so I wasn't worth much in his eyes.

But I humbled myself enough once to ask Campbell for a job. Years after I'd left *Wonder Stories,* I tried again to get back into science fiction, so I wrote to him asking for a job at *Astounding,* when he was then editing. He replied, asking me to come in and see him. I went and he told me personally, "No." I think he only wanted to see me crawl. But that was the only unpleasant relationship I had with any of the authors.

What about Frank Paul?

He was probably the most likable person in the field. He was full of sun and laughter and smiled all the time—always pleasant and cooperative. I was fascinated watching him work as he painted covers for *Wonder Stories.* The art studio was in another room. First we were at 98 Park Place behind the Woolworth Building, and then, in about April of 1934, we moved to 99 Hudson Street, about a mile uptown.

Paul did most of his painting and black-and-white art work

right there in that studio. I'd make suggestions and he'd paint some of them. Usually what he did was read the story—he liked science fiction—and he'd get ideas from the story. Generally, his own suggestion for an illustration would be the best.

Paul had other clients as well, and another office somewhere else in downtown New York. One day in 1936 I visited his other office and found he was painting something really odd. "What's that?" I asked. "That's a cross-section of the New York subway," he said. "There's going to be a new magazine out called *Life* and they want to run this." So, even after *Wonder* folded, he did all right.[73]

So most of the ideas for Paul's paintings he thought of himself?

Yes, although if I had an idea I *really* thought was good, Paul would generally go along with it. He'd take ideas from anyone, but generally his own were the best. We had a lot of other artists as well. Them I told specifically what I wanted and they'd just go home and do it. These were all interiors, because Paul did all the covers.

If you remember Paul's work, a lot of his characters, even for the 1930s, looked old-fashioned or European. They were wearing knickers, for one thing. Even then, only little boys wore knickers—we didn't wear long pants till we were about fifteen or sixteen then. Paul was weak on painting people. But he was great on the weird stuff and the machinery.

What was the state of fandom at that time?

There was a lot more enthusiasm, and it dealt with science fiction, *the stories,* more than it does now. Now, it's personalities. You go to a convention today and you hardly hear anything about science fiction. In those days it was the stories, the ideas. We felt exclusive because we were an outcast society. We were on the outskirts of civilization. People didn't like or accept our literature, so there was a lot of camaraderie which you don't see today. We all had friends and relatives who laughed at us, at science fiction, so we sought each other out for companionship.

Or course, there were also a lot fewer of us. For instance, the first World Science Fiction Convention in New York in 1939 had only about two hundred or two hundred fifty attendees, and we thought that was a big deal!

Didn't you organize the Science Fiction League while at Wonder Stories?

Right, and that was the first real organization of fandom. It was Gernsback's idea, but I did all the organizing. Gernsback had already established a Radio League to support his radio magazine and he thought a science fiction league, composed of officially chartered local clubs, would be good for the magazine. So he told me to set it up. I really enjoyed the work. We chartered chapters, sent out membership certificates, which were beautiful scrolls, and the idea really took off. The league got a lot of isolated fans in touch with each other, and local chapters just seemed to mushroom all over the country.

But some fans didn't like the idea that it was sponsored by and designed to support a commercial magazine. So, they splintered off from the league [the Futurians, for example] and things grew in that direction, too. We had chapters all over the world. It went very well for a couple of years until *Wonder Stories* folded. After that, the league folded—but the fans kept on. And, at least in inspiration, all the fan organizations of today can really be traced back to that beginning.

Sometimes there's a more direct connection. For instance, the Los Angeles Science Fiction League, which I helped organize in 1934 and which had Forrest Ackerman and Ray Bradbury as members, became the Los Angeles Science Fantasy Society, which is still in existence today, half a century later! It's probably the longest-running organization of science fiction fans anywhere.

So we had a pretty good time in fandom. I even had a reconciliation with Leo Margulies, who died in 1975. You know the
story of how I left *Wonder Stories,* don't you?

Tell me.

Well, Gernsback finally ran out of money and sold *Wonder* to
Beacon Magazines in early 1936. Our last issue was dated April
and their first one was dated August. But they changed the name
to *Thrilling Wonder Stories.* Beacon had a lot of other magazines
which all had the word "thrilling" on them—*Thrilling Detective,
Thrilling Western,* and so on. They had about six editors working
under Leo Margulies, who was editorial director of the house. In
fact, one of those editors was my friend, Mort Weisinger, an original fan along with Julie Schwartz. Mort had started working for
Margulies in January or so of 1936. So when Gernsback sold
Wonder to Ned Pines, the publisher of Beacon magazines, he
said to me, "Maybe you can get with Beacon."

I called up Margulies and told him I'd been editing for two
and a half years and would like to join his staff. He said, "That
sounds great. I'll have to talk it over with Pines. Call me back
Monday."

So I figured I'd be hired. I didn't know how I'd do there,
because you had to do a lot more than just science fiction; you
had to read detective stories, westerns, a lot of other things. But,
with the purchase of *Wonder,* they needed a specialist in science
fiction. Then, over the weekend, I began thinking, "Mort
Weisinger is working for Margulies and *he* knows science fiction. Maybe I'm not needed after all."

Then, on Monday, Margulies said, "I'm sorry, but we can't
use you here." He seemed rather abrupt. I asked, "What did Mort
have to do with it?"

He said, "None of your business, son!" and hung up.

I guess I wasn't supposed to have asked about that. But I figured Mort had probably said, "What do you need Hornig for? I

know science fiction." And, in fact, he did become the editor of *Thrilling Wonder.*

Three years later, at the 1939 World Convention, I finally got a chance to talk to Margulies again, this time on a friendly basis. He was a nice guy if you could get to know him.

Had Gernsback given you much warning that the magazine was folding?

No, but I gradually got the idea. For instance, two months before the end I got a request from Finland from a publisher who wanted to reprint some of our stories. I went to Mannheimer, our business manager, and asked him if it was alright. He said, "Yeah, I guess so."

Then I tried to make a pun, saying, "Well, I guess this'll be the *Finnish* of *Wonder Stories!*"

Mannheimer said, "You *bet* it's the finish!"

That was my first warning. Two months later Gernsback sold out. I left in February 1936.

What did you do next?

I couldn't find another opening in the field, so I sort of went off in other directions. I bought a large-sized paperback entitled *100 Ways to Make a Living.* In the thirties everybody wanted desperately to make a living, so it was a good seller. I thought I ought to be able to find one way that worked out of a hundred. The book had pictures and descriptions of all kinds—you could invent your own chemical formulae, invent products to sell, and whatnot.

One way was putting out special editions of small-town newspapers. It told you how to put out commemorative editions. I got three or four papers temporarily interested, then they dropped the idea.

Or you could be a representative for European corporations.

So I called myself "Hornig Consolidated Service" and, at age nineteen, wrote to several English corporations saying, "I want to be your American representative." They all wrote back and asked for a list of companies I already represented. So that didn't work out. Another way was public typing, taking a typewriter out on the street and typing letters for passersby. Well, I could type and I figured I could make some money at that, since it was what I'd been doing before I started working for Gernsback. And it was the only thing I really did make money at! Then I found out that this book I was following was yet another one of Gernsback's ideas! He was the publisher!

So I took off for California. I spent about four weeks in Los Angeles, met a number of L.A. fans, and became good friends with Forrest Ackerman. He was still living with his grandparents at the time. Even then he had the largest science fiction collection I'd ever seen, although it didn't fill three garages and seven rooms, as it does today. He'd been collecting since he was ten and had everything in the field up to that time.[74]

But you just couldn't find a job out there unless you were a native Californian, so I returned to New York. In the fall of 1936 I finally got a bookkeeping job with a photoengraving company uptown. That lasted for a year and a half, but they were paying only $18 a week. I decided that wasn't enough, so I went back to California—and so on and so on.

During the war you were a Conscientious Objector. Did you belong to a pacifist church?

No, it was just the way I personally felt when I became certain we were going to get into that war. I wasn't going to be part of it. I wasn't going to kill anybody. Since that seemed to be the main occupation of an army, I wasn't going to serve. But I'd never even heard of the term "Conscientious Objector." I had no idea there was a recognized position, or that there was this draft status you could request. I thought they'd probably just take me out and shoot me when it came time to register for the draft. I didn't know anything!

I thought of escaping to the South Seas—that seemed far enough away from the war. The place I picked was an obscure little island no one had ever heard of called New Caledonia; I figured no one would ever find that place. Of course, to show you what I knew of things, that island became a major battlefield of the Pacific War, so it's just as well I never made it.[75]

But by the time I registered for the draft, which I did in Elizabeth, New Jersey, in 1940 [the same year he joined the Socialist Party], I'd become more knowledgeable. I registered as a Conscientious Objector. But Elizabeth was very conservative politically, and I decided my local board wasn't likely to classify me as a Conscientious Objector because I wasn't a Quaker or a Mennonite or a Brethren or a member of any other peace church. I decided to go to Los Angeles, where I felt I'd have a better chance. My draft registration was transferred there and I did, indeed, get a C.O. status.

Then I was drafted for civilian alternative service and sent to Cascade Locks, a Civilian Public Service Camp in Columbia Gorge, Oregon, a beautiful place. It was an old Civilian Conservation Corps camp and was run pretty much like the C.C.C. We worked for the Forest Service putting out forest fires, maintaining forest trails, that sort of thing. I enjoyed it very much and made a lot of friends among the other C.O.s. It was the first community I'd ever really belonged to. We've kept in touch and, in fact, I just got back from a camp reunion.

This was in 1942 and our most prominent camper was the movie star Lew Ayres. He was with us for about seven weeks before he succeeded in getting his 1AO status changed so that he could choose his own corps when joining the army. He wanted the medical corps and eventually got it. Ginger Rogers was a big star then and I couldn't help but think every time I passed Ayres in his bunk—*that man was married to Ginger Rogers!*[76]

I really hated to leave Cascade Locks, but I decided I just

couldn't stand the regimentation any more. It was run like a prison. They told us we had no rights any more, only privileges—which they then took away. After they cancelled all our furloughs, I decided that I'd rather be in an honest prison than in a hypocritical prison. So, after a year, I just walked away one day and never went back. I knew the FBI would come for me, but in the meantime I had a few months of freedom. I went back to New York and I married Florence.

Then the FBI arrested me and sent me back to Oregon, which had jurisdiction over my "crime." I was tried and sentenced in October 1943 to three years in prison. I served a year at McNeil Island, a federal prison in the state of Washington, and then I was paroled to work in a Seattle hospital. My daughter was born while I was in prison. I have two children and four grandchildren.

Actually, McNeil Island had an absolutely beautiful setting. We had the sun rising behind Mt. Rainier in one direction and setting behind the Olympics in the other. It was an absolutely marvellous place to spend a year if you had to be in prison—certainly better than New Caledonia would have been!

What have you been doing since World War II?

Well, I did a lot more *before* World War II than I've done since. In Seattle I caught pneumonia and they agreed to transfer me to Los Angeles, a more clement climate. We were in L.A. for about three years, working for various hospitals. Then I worked for the Hospital Service of Southern California. Blue Cross started in 1944 and this was one of the first Blue Cross plans in the country. In 1948 I was replaced at that job by IBM computers.

My wife and I are both pacifists and we saw an ad in *Fellowship,* put out by the Fellowship of Reconciliation, the leading Christian pacifist organization of the day. The Fellowship was looking for an office manager and a secretary for A. J. Muste, who was then the most prominent pacifist. We thought we'd fill the bill. We wrote them and they accepted us. So we moved back East and lived around New York and New Jersey for three years.

We came back to California in 1952, moved into this place, and we've stayed here for the past thirty-four years. Most of that time I've worked preparing income tax returns. It seemed to be the most practical, because I work only fifteen weeks of the year and I don't have to work the rest of the time. I like that. Of course, I do a year's work in those fifteen weeks. I work twelve hours a day, seven days a week. But I'd rather do it that way.

Have you kept up with the science fiction field?

Not really, though I do read science fiction frequently. I read anthologies and I subscribe to *Analog*. I'm reading Asimov—he's my favorite author right now. But I don't really keep up with the field. They lost me back in the 1950s when there was such a proliferation of magazines. I just couldn't keep up. So I just pick at them here and there and occasionally I go to conventions.

Are there any you're looking forward to?

The next thing I'm looking forward to is Forrest Ackerman's seventieth birthday bash in L.A. He's having a big blow-out at the Biltmore Hotel, and he expects me down there for it in late November. We've known each other since we were teenagers, so I can't stand him up now!

NOTES

1. John W. Campbell, editor of *Astounding/Analog* from 1937 to 1971, was the hugely influential editor who is widely credited with making magazine science fiction "grow up."

2. I am not looking upon *Amazing Stories Quarterly* and *Amazing Stories Annual* as separate from *Amazing Stories*.

3. Sam Moskowitz, "Amazing Encounter," Part II, *Fantasy Review* 89 (March 1986): 9. I am grateful to Sam Moskowitz for his helpful comments on an early draft of this essay.

4. Quoted by James Blish, "Introduction—The Function of Science Fiction," in *The Light Fantastic: Science Fiction Classics from the Mainstream,* edited by Harry Harrison (New York: Charles Scribner's Sons, 1971), p. 7.

5. Jack Williamson has kindly made available copies of his correspondence from Hugo Gernsback and David Lasser.

6. Moskowitz, "Amazing Encounter," p. 9.

7. Ibid., p. 10. Actually, this represents the ratio of assets to disbursements at the time of the bankruptcy. Because of administration fees, creditors would have received slightly less, about 95 percent of their claims, according to an estimate published in the *New York Times,* April 3, 1929. But because of a New York State tax claim that was appealed all the way up to the Supreme Court, matters were not wound up until late 1935, by which time these fees had eaten up even more of the funds. The final figure was 85 cents on the dollar.

8. In a letter to me dated October 19, 1986, Sam Moskowitz commented that Fletcher Pratt "was never a good story teller" and that "his wife, Inga M. Stephens, collaborated with him for years on his early science fiction." This might be why Pratt collaborated with others so often, such as L. Sprague de Camp and fellow Interplanetary Society founder Laurence Manning.

9. Trained as an architect in Vienna and Paris, Paul began his collaboration with Gernsback in 1914. It would last until 1953, when Paul illustrated Gernsback's short-lived *Science Fiction Plus,* edited by Sam Moskowitz. In all, he painted over one hundred fifty covers for Gernsback. So pervasive was Paul's influence on the science fiction imagination that he was chosen as the guest of honor at the First World Science Fiction Convention in 1939. He died in 1963 at age seventy-nine.

10. Frank H. Winter, *Prelude to the Space Age—The Rocket Societies: 1924–1940* (Washington, D.C.: Smithsonian Institution Press, 1983), p. 24.

11. In 1963 the Rocket Society merged with the Institute of Aerospace Sciences to become the current American Institute of Aeronautics and Astronautics.

12. Mike Ashley in *Science Fiction, Fantasy, and Weird Fiction Magazines*, edited by Marshall B. Tymn and Mike Ashley (Westport, Conn.: Greenwood Press, 1985), p. 763.

13. *New York Herald-Tribune,* January 28, 1931.

14. On December 26, 1927, Rosny, Robert Esnault-Pelterie, and others met in a Paris apartment to form an organization to promote the idea of space flight. They decided to award a prize to those pioneering in rocket experimentation. "A word was needed to describe the subject of the prize. Rosny thought of *astronautics,* an almost literary invention, meaning 'navigating the stars.' Esnault-Pelterie inaugurated the word thereafter in his space travel talks and in print. It became the title of his most famous work, *L'Astronautique* (1930). Thus, by 1930, 'astronautics' was legitimized. It was both a new entry in the languages of the world and a body of literature on the ultimate realization of the still youthful science of space flight." Winter, *Prelude to the Space Age,* p. 25.

15. *New York Herald-Tribune,* January 28, 1931.

16. Letter to the author, April 28, 1986.

17. There is a humorous footnote to this episode. It seems that Esnault-Pelterie, the French "astronaut," was not able to attend the event. He sent the manuscript of his address on "astronautics," however, which was read to the audience by one of the society members, G. Edward Pendray. Pendray was a distinguished-looking individual and, unusual for the time, sported a Van Dyke beard. Despite the fact that Lasser explained that Pendray was merely reading Esnault-Pelterie's paper, Pendray recalled twenty-five years later that many in the audience still believed he was the astronaut. After the film ended, Pendray was besieged by autograph-seekers. He insisted that he was not the Frenchman; the throng insisted he was. He finally tired of explaining that he was *not* Esnault-Pelterie and began signing the Frenchman's name right and left, just so they would go away. "As a result of that night's work," said Pendray, "there are hundreds of copies of Esnault-Pelterie's signature in autograph collections today that couldn't be phonier." Winter, *Prelude to the Space Age,* p. 76.

18. *New York Times,* April 4, 1931, p. 28, col. 2.

19. *New York Times,* October 23, 1931, p. 26, col. 4.

20. Raymond Z. Gallun, *The Best of Raymond Z. Gallun* (New York: Ballantine Books, 1978), p. 326.

21. Isaac Asimov, *In Memory Yet Green* (New York: Doubleday, 1979), p. 573.

22. Sam Moskowitz, "The Science-Fiction of Nat Schachner," *Fantasy Commentator* 7, no. 3 (Spring 1992): 167. Moskowitz provides the five-hundred-copy figure as a reasonable guess. However, Frank H. Winter put the press run at five thousand copies. See Winter, *Prelude to the Space Age,* p. 80. Moskowitz points out that Schachner wrote an autobiographical sketch for the dustjacket of his 1946 book, *Alexander Hamilton,* in which he said, "In the mid-thirties [I] ventured into book publishing. Broke even and quit in time."

23. *New York Times Book Review,* January 10, 1932. The book was also favorably reviewed in *Books* (November 29, 1931), *The Saturday Review of Literature* (November 21, 1931), and *The Boston Transcript* (November 21, 1931). It was noted as well in the science fiction community with reviews in the November 1931 issues of *Wonder Stories* and Gernsback's *Everyday Science and Mechanics,* as well as by C. A. Brandt in *Amazing Stories* (November 1934). By then, however, it was long out of print.

24. Winter, *Prelude to the Space Age,* p. 25.

25. *New York Times Book Review,* March 6, 1983.

26. Sam Moskowitz, letter to the editor, *Fantasy Commentator* 6, no. 2 (Fall 1988): 138. In this same letter, Moskowitz says that Gernsback told him the publication of the two issues of *Technocracy Review* "was strictly Lasser's idea." See also Sam Moskowitz, "The Science-Fiction of Nat Schachner," *Fantasy Commentator* 7, no. 3 (Spring 1992): 177.

27. The Workers' Alliance was formed in 1935 by a merger of all Communist- and Socialist-led Unemployed Councils around the nation. The one substantial account of the Workers' Alliance is flawed by dealing only with the period after 1937. See Frances Fox Piven and Richard A. Cloward, *Poor People's Movements: Why They Succeed, How They Fail* (New York: Vintage Books, 1977), chapter 2. No institutional archives of the Workers' Alliance exists; however, we may be able to learn more about this huge, but now largely obscure, organization when the Federal Bureau of Investigation releases its large ten-thousand-document file on the organization, as well as its additional one-thousand-document file on David Lasser. The FBI was ordered to

release uncensored copies of its WAA file on August 1, 1995, by the U.S. Court of Appeals for the Third Circuit in the case, *Eric Davin* v. *Dept. of Justice, Federal Bureau of Investigation.*

Interestingly, when Mike Ashley was working on his forthcoming biography of Hugo Gernsback, he used the Freedom of Information Act to discover that the FBI also had a file on Gernsback!

28. G. Edward Pendray, aka "Gawain Edwards," *did* publish a science fiction *novel* earlier, however. This was *The Earth Tube* (New York: Appleton, 1929). His short fiction first appeared in *Science Wonder Stories.*

29. Not to be confused with the Jules Verne Prize, which was sponsored, starting in 1927, by the French magazine *Lectures pour Tous.* For details of this, see Raymond A. Palmer, "Spilling the Atoms," *Fantasy Magazine* 3, no. 1 (March 1934): 20.

30. Both quotes by Isaac Asimov, "Science Fiction Finds Its Voice," in *The Mammoth Book of Classic Science Fiction Short Novels of the 1930s,* edited by Isaac Asimov, Charles G. Waugh, and Martin H. Greenberg, (New York: Carroll & Graf, 1988), p. x.

31. *New York Times Book Review,* March 6, 1983.

32. Lasser to Jack Williamson, March 22, 1932.

33. Brian W. Aldiss, *Billion Year Spree* (New York: Schocken Books, 1973), p. 209.

34. Lasser to Williamson, December 24, 1931.

35. Lasser to Williamson, January 6, 1932.

36. Isaac Asimov, *Before the Golden Age* (Garden City, N.Y.: Doubleday, 1974), p. xiv.

37. Gallun, *The Best of Raymond Z. Gallun,* p. 328. Actually, the enchantment really did not end with the Age of Wonder. I, too, was snared by a cover on a newsstand. It was the March 1960 issue of *Astounding Science Fact & Fiction.* It featured a gigantic death's head looming over an elderly couple just beyond a huge fence of needles and test tubes. It illustrated the story "Immortality For Some" by Scottish science fiction writer J. T. McIntosh. Everything having to do with science then intrigued me and I thought I was buying a science fact magazine. I had no idea something known as "science fiction magazines" existed. Once I read it, I realized my mistake. But by then, it was too late. I was instantly hooked for life by an addiction more pow-

erful than crack cocaine. I immediately sent in a subscription to *Astounding* and began haunting the newsstands for every fantasy or science fiction magazine I could find. As it turned out, McIntosh's story was quite forgettable—but not so the other stories in that issue. And I have a framed full-color reproduction of that March 1960 cover hanging on my wall.

38. The record reveals his salary was actually $65, still a lot of money.

39. This statement was made by Democratic Representative Martin Dies of Texas. His Dies Committee was the major red-hunting body in Congress before Joseph McCarthy came along after the war. It was responsible for sending many to prison. Dies was later convicted of theft and sent to prison himself.

Republican Representative (later Senator) Everett Dirksen of Illinois led the fight against the WPA budget and introduced the amendment to bar payment of any funds to Lasser. Both Dies and Dirksen lived to witness Neil Armstrong's moon landing of July 20, 1969.

40. According to Frank H. Winter, Goddard *did* become a member of the society, while refusing to become "directly involved." See Winter, *Prelude to the Space Age,* p. 74.

41. Most of the one thousand documents in David Lasser's FBI file, which I obtained (with his permission) under the Freedom of Information Act, resulted from background investigations of his loyalty during this period. Even though he did fight Communist influence within the Workers' Alliance—his resignation in 1940 was to protest their increasing control of the organization—he was always suspect because he'd been a member of the Socialist Party and because he'd been president of a "Communist front" organization.

42. Lasser did finish his science fiction novel, but was unable to find a publisher before he died. I tried to convince him of the importance of writing an autobiography, but he wasn't interested. He was not interviewed by Piven and Cloward for their chapter on the Workers' Alliance in *Poor People's Movements.* This conversation, then, is as close as we came to Lasser's "autobiography."

43. Letter to author, August 14, 1986.

44. Conversation with author, August 21, 1986.

45. Asimov, *Before the Golden Age,* p. 578.

46. Letter to author, October 29, 1986.

47. Letter to author, November 10, 1986.

48. Asimov, *Before the Golden Age,* p. 728.

49. On July 6, 1939, just after the first World Science Fiction Convention, Charles Hornig, Forrest Ackerman, and some other fans dropped by Gernsback's office to visit. Gernsback emphasized to all of them that there was no money in science fiction! Excerpt from Charles Hornig's diary in the author's possession.

50. Letter to author, August 14, 1986.

51. Letter to author, August 14, 1986.

52. Letter to author, October 19, 1986.

53. As we have since discovered, Lasser was actually paid $65 per week. See note 36.

54. Gernsback also wrote the acceptance letter for "A Martian Odyssey" to Weinbaum.

55. Schwartz's own account of this appears in *After Ten Years: A Tribute to Stanley G. Weinbaum, 1902–1935,* collected by Gerry de la Ree and Sam Moskowitz (Westwood, N.J.: 1945), p. 15, and was summarized in Moskowitz's *Explorers of the Infinite* (Cleveland: World Publishing, Co., 1963), p. 300.

56. Gernsback paid a low flat rate for these stories, but in his letter to me of November 10, 1986, Moskowitz said that Gernsback told him he also paid Fletcher Pratt to translate them, so foreign reprints "frequently ended up costing him *more* than new stories." Moskowitz also believed Gernsback was responsible for the French and British novels that were sometimes serialized, which seems likely. These included *The Fall of the Eiffel Tower* by Charles de Richter, *The Green Man of Graypec* by Festus Pragnell, and *The Perfect World* by Benson Herbert.

57. "In contrast," remembered Moskowitz, "when I worked for Gernsback, he was often irritated and petulant (a good word to describe a frequent attitude of his) with the help." Letter to author, November 10, 1986.

58. This was Joseph Kraus, who had been with Gernsback since the 1920s and who, with C.P. Mason (who wrote under the pen-name of "Epaminondas T. Snooks"), edited Gernsback's *Everyday Science and Mechanics.*

59. "Novelty—The Essential of Science Fiction," *Author and Journalist* (July 1934): 11–13. Reviewed briefly by Raymond A. Palmer in *Fantasy Magazine* (September 1934): 36.

60. And often was—e.g., Stanton Coblentz's "Triple Geared," *Astounding Stories* (April 1935). The theme has even been used more recently: See John D. MacDonald's *The Girl, The Gold Watch, and Everything* (1981).

61. Born in Arizona Territory in 1908, Jack Williamson published his first story in 1928 and is still active in the field. His "Legion of Time," *Astounding* (1938), was an early and imaginative account of two alternative universes battling through time to deny each others' existence. He also had a dual career, teaching in the English department at Eastern New Mexico University beginning in 1956. In 1964 he earned a Ph.D. from the University of Colorado with a dissertation on H. G. Wells. Dr. Williamson retired in 1977. In 1984 he published his autobiography, *Wonder's Child: My Life in Science Fiction* (New York: Bluejay Books).

62. Dr. Keller was a psychiatrist who published much in his professional capacity. Active in fantasy and science fiction in the period 1928–1935, he was second only to Laurence Manning in number of stories (twelve) published in *Wonder Stories*. Although his work was misogynistic, it also sometimes presented a sociological perspective rare in the field at the time.

63. Manning published more stories (sixteen, including one in *Science Wonder Stories*) than any other author in *Wonder Stories*. His work was innovative in discussing ecological problems at an early date and his story "The Living Galaxy," *Wonder Stories* (September 1934), was the first presentation of the "generation starship" idea. See chapter 10 on Manning.

64. Pratt wrote a series of books on the Civil War, the Napoleonic Wars, a biography of James Madison, and a naval history. An example of Pratt's historical work is his excellent early history of World War II, *War for the World: A Chronicle of Our Fighting Forces in World War II* (New Haven: Yale University Press, 1950).

65. Both a writer and pioneer science fiction book publisher, Eshbach is still active in the field. See chapter 7.

66. Stone was married to writer William Silberberg. She was a

Lasser discovery for *Air Wonder Stories,* and her stories appeared mainly in *Wonder.* She essentially ceased writing after 1937.

67. Catherine L. Moore was one of the giants in science fiction, and her 1930s' Jirel of Joiry stories remain in print, early classics of the "Sword and Sorcery" subgenre (and unique for their female hero). She married science fiction writer Henry Kuttner in 1940 and most of her writing after that was in collaboration with him, sometimes under the name "Lewis Padgett." Her solo 1946 story, "Vintage Season," portrayed time travel to historical disasters as a tourist industry. It was made into an excellent, but obscure, Jeff Daniels film in 1992 entitled *Grand Tour: Disaster in Time.* It is available on video.

68. Long was briefly active in the late 1920s and early to mid-1930s. In 1963 Forrest J. Ackerman also visited her and found her still living alone in Harrisburg. "I guess she died a spinster," he recalled. "I have only the vaguest memory of her as being a kind of 50ish librarian type, a sort of Andre Norton of an earlier day." Forrest J. Ackerman, ed., *Gosh! Wow! (Sense of Wonder) Science Fiction* (New York: Bantam Books, 1982), p. 531. He included "Omega," her 1932 story of the end of the world from *Wonder Stories,* in this "Sense of Wonder" anthology.

69. The two shared interests and styles. Smith wrote more than one hundred short stories—some space opera, but mostly fantasy. His lapidarian style and outré imaginary worlds and alien cultures broadened the genre, helping it accept ideas which didn't concentrate so much on "hardware." He published mostly in *Weird Tales* and *Wonder Stories* between 1930–1936. After 1936 he ceased writing, but didn't die until 1961.

70. Along with Weinbaum, Gallun introduced the sympathetic alien to science fiction. Gallun, however, remembers dropping by the *Wonder Stories* office once and meeting Hornig. See chapter 4 on him herein.

71. Major fan club formed in opposition to Gernsback's Science Fiction League.

72. At the May 7 meeting of the Queens Science Fiction League in Astoria, New York.

73. This is part of a larger drawing Paul did of the United States entitled "What President Roosevelt Did to the Map of the U.S. in Four

Years with $6,500,000,000." It appeared in the January 4, 1937, issue of *Life*. Another of Paul's "outside" commissions was "Micromegas," the gigantic decoration for a pavilion at the 1939 World's Fair.

Hornig liked Paul's work so much that he chose Paul to paint all twelve covers of *Science Fiction,* the Silberkleit magazine he edited in the late thirties. Sam Moskowitz told me, the only time I met him, that he also liked to watch Paul paint covers while both worked for Gernsback in the fifties at *Science Fiction Plus.* Evidently, however, Gernsback did not share their enthusiasm for Paul's work. Moskowitz recalled that he was working late in the office one night when he heard a noise in the hall. He stepped out of his office to find the janitor struggling with armloads of Paul's cover paintings. "What are you doing with those?" Moskowitz asked. He was told that Gernsback had ordered him to toss out all the old paintings in Paul's studio, because they needed the room. Moskowitz was appalled and told the janitor to bring them into his office, that he would dispose of them. And so, Moskowitz acquired a priceless collection of Frank Paul artwork.

74. Ackerman's collection literally began at the beginning with the first issue of Gernsback's *Amazing Stories* (April 1926), to which he was an original subscriber. "I shall never forget that day," he said, "when I came home from grade school for lunch and forgot about eating as I held in my eager hands the first issue of Hugo Gernsback's new *scientifiction* periodical, which had arrived in the morning mail. . . . Because I had had confidence in Hugo Gernsback and had subscribed in advance to an unnamed magazine and an unknown quantity, it only cost me 12 and a half cents an issue and I was entitled to subscribe to it at that reduced rate for the rest of my life—or its life." Ackerman, ed., *Gosh! Wow! (Sense of Wonder) Science Fiction,* p. xi.

75. Actually, the Free French took New Caledonia away from the Vichy French and gave usage rights to the United States, but Hornig is right, in general, to say the South Pacific would not have been a good place to flee to.

76. After the war, Ayres starred in the classic 1953 film version of Curt Siodmak's most famous science fiction novel, *Donovan's Brain.* (See chapter 8 on Siodmak herein.) His leading lady was starlet Nancy Davis (later Nancy Reagan), and omnipresent SF fan Forrest Ackerman visited Ayres on the set, carrying copies of Gernsback's *Science*

Fiction Plus. However, Ayres was best known as the original Dr. Kildare in a series of nine MGM films, 1938–1942, and for starring in the Oscar-wining 1930 antiwar epic, *All Quiet on the Western Front.* According to the *New York Times,* January 1, 1997, "In a case of life imitating art, Mr. Ayres was a conscientious objector during World War II and for that reason became a Hollywood outcast. Before the war, he had been one of the most popular leading men in the movies. But, when he announced his pacifism, which had a religious basis, he was shunned by the studios, and in some cities exhibitors refused to show his movies. He said that to bear arms would cause him 'to live in a nightmare of hypocrisy.' After two months in a labor camp, he entered the Army as a noncombatant, serving for three and a half years in the Medical Corps and winning three battle stars."

Ayres managed to revive his career after the war and played a doctor opposite Olivia de Havilland in *The Dark Mirror*, directed by Curt's brother, Robert Siodmak. He received a 1948 Academy Award nomination for Best Actor in *Johnny Belinda* opposite Jane Wyman, who won the Oscar for Best Actress. Long a student of world religions, in 1955 he produced a five-part documentary entitled *Altars of the East.* In 1976 he produced *Altars of the West*, which won a Golden Globe Award for the Best Documentary of 1976. In later years he appeared in character roles in such Hollywood films as *Battle for the Planet of the Apes* and on television in the series *Battlestar Galactica.* He died December 29, 1996, at age eighty-eight.

2.

THE SILBERKLEIT YEARS AND THE BIRTH OF COMIC BOOKS

A Further Conversation with Charles D. Hornig

WHEN HUGO GERNSBACK SOLD HIS *WONDER STORIES* to Beacon/Standard after the March–April 1936 issue, it seemed to be the end of Gernsback's science fiction career and that of his editor, Charles D. Hornig. Such was not the case, however, and before the decade ended, both of them—as well as Frank Paul, Gernsback's preferred artist—were collaborating on yet another, and unprecedented, venture in science fiction publishing.

In the meantime, Hornig searched for another position in the field. After attempting unsuccessfully to go with *Wonder Stories* to its new publisher, he landed a job as science fiction editor for Louis Silberkleit, publisher of a string of pulps under the imprint of Blue Ribbon Magazines (later Double Action Magazines). Silberkleit (or "Louie the Lug," as the Futurians called him at the time[1]) was a friend of Gernsback's and, now that they were no longer competitors, Gernsback seemed willing to aid Silberkleit in breaking into the field. In 1936, when Gernsback left the field, there had been only three science fiction magazines. By 1940 there were thirteen, three of them Silberkleit's, including *Science Fiction, Future Fiction,* and *Science Fiction Quarterly.* Upon Gernsback's recommendation, Silberkleit hired Charles Hornig to edit these, and Gernsback himself wrote a full-page guest editorial in the first issue of *Science Fiction* (March 1939) to help launch the venture.

It was an appropriate gesture, for *Science Fiction* was the first professional SF magazine to adopt as its title the simple designation Gernsback himself had coined to describe the genre.[2] It was also appropriate that Gernsback's editor, Charles Hornig, should be the editor of this new contribution to the field and that Frank Paul, his artist, should paint the covers. Over a period of two and a half years, twelve issues of *Science Fiction* appeared. Although he began working on it in late 1938, Hornig was "officially" in charge of the magazine for two years, from its March 1939 debut to March 1941. Following Hornig's departure, Robert A. W. ("Doc") Lowndes replaced him as Silberkleit's science fiction editor and did some work on the final September 1941 issue of *Science Fiction*, after which it was ostensibly merged with its sister magazine, *Future Fiction*.[3]

Perhaps thinking the climate propitious, Silberkleit had introduced *Future Fiction,* under Hornig's editorial direction, in September 1939, with a November cover date.[4] Hornig edited four issues of it between then and November 1940. Then Lowndes took over with a fifth issued dated April 1941 and a sixth dated August 1941, after which it came out every two months. *Future Fiction* had a long run, producing sixty-five issues in two series, seventeen of them between November 1939 and July 1943, at which point—now called *Science Fiction Stories*—it went into hiatus due to wartime paper shortages. In 1950 it was revived with a May–June number under a minor title variant and ran for forty-eight issues until April 1960. Lowndes was responsible for the magazine's editorial direction from its April 1941 edition to its eventual demise.

In the summer of 1940 Silberkleit christened yet a third SF magazine, this one entitled *Science Fiction Quarterly*. Edited initially by Hornig, it ran for thirty-eight issues in two series, with ten appearing between its summer 1940 debut and spring 1943, when it went into wartime hibernation. Hornig edited only the first two issues, summer and fall 1940. Afterward, Lowndes would be credited as editor from spring 1941 until its termination with the fall 1958 edition.

When "Doc" Lowndes took over the Silberkleit SF magazines, they seemed to have become vehicles for his Futurian colleagues, including James Blish, Cyril Kornbluth, Donald Wollheim, and Damon Knight. At least in the beginning, however, "Louie the Lug" appears to have exercised more editorial control over Lowndes than he did over Hornig. While Hornig tells us in the following conversation that he was left to do as he pleased with the magazines, five of the seven stories Lowndes originally planned for his first issue of *Future Fiction* were vetoed by Silberkleit.[5]

Yet if the Silberkleit magazines under Lowndes eventually became regular outlets for the Futurian circle, the determining factor under Hornig's editorship may well have been Julius Schwartz. As Hornig explains below, he had little direct contact with most of the authors he published and relied upon Schwartz, who was agent for most of them, to supply him with a steady stream of material.

But Hugo Gernsback himself was not yet out of the picture. At the same time Hornig and Paul were working for Silberkleit, Gernsback recruited them to help him make his comeback to science fiction publishing—but in a newly invented medium. In April 1940, Gernsback created a science fiction comic book entitled *Superworld Comics*. With trademark covers by Paul and stories by Hornig, *Superworld* offered sixty-four pages of full-color action for ten cents. Writing under his pen name, "Derwin Lesser," Hornig created Hip Knox, a "super hypnotist," for the debut issue of *Superworld*. His other creations included Buzz Allen, the "Invisible Avenger," and Mitey Powers, interplanetary troubleshooter.

Comic strips had been a feature of newspapers ever since "The Yellow Kid" launched the genre in the 1890s. In addition, Winsor McCay's "Little Nemo in Slumberland" for the Hearst papers contained many fantastical elements as early as 1906. But these appeared only in newspapers, nowhere else. Then, in 1934, Eastern Color Printing launched an entirely new creation—the comic book. Eastern's *Famous Funnies* debuted in May 1934, with reprints from the newspapers of the most popular comic strips, including "Joe Palooka," "Tailspin Tommy," and others. Science fiction appeared in this new medium for the first time with the third issue of *Famous Funnies* (October 1934), when it began reprinting the Sunday "Buck Rogers" strips from 1933. "Buck Rogers," of course, had originally appeared as a story in Gernsback's *Amazing* (August 1928).

Comic books swiftly caught on as the fastest growing periodical medium in the country, with others quickly entering the fray. The second comic book to hit the stands was *New Fun Comics*, which appeared in February 1935. Its first three issues featured the adventures of "Don Drake on the Planet Saro," a blatant imitation of the popular "Flash Gordon" strip which had debuted in the newspapers in 1934. This was not only the first comic book to feature an original science fiction storyline, it was the first comic book with original art and stories *of any kind.* Thus, one might argue that the first "real" comic book was a science fiction comic book. Later in the year, *New Fun* featured another science fiction series, "Super Police 2023." In April 1936, David McKay Publishing launched a line of comic books with *King Comics,* which reprinted the Sunday comic strips of "Popeye," "Mandrake the Magician," and the original "Flash Gordon."

None of this was lost on the science fiction community. When Mort Weisinger took over newly named *Thrilling Wonder Stories* with the August 1936 issue, he introduced a science fiction comic strip called "Zarnak," which lasted for eight issues, a little more than a year. The artist for "Zarnak" was Max Plaisted, who also drew for the new *Startling Comics* and helped launch the "Space Rovers" series in *Exciting Comics* (May 1940) (both published by Weisinger's publisher, Ned Pines). Meanwhile, Edmond Hamilton's and Mort Weisinger's pulp magazine creation, "Captain Future," also appeared as the principal character in *Startling Comics.*

Between 1935 and 1940 the number of comic book titles mushroomed from three to one hundred fifty, published by over two dozen companies specializing in the new print medium. With this proliferation, the number of newspaper comic strips available for reprinting were soon depleted and the demand for original-art comics grew. Before long, science fiction writers were flooding into the new medium to fill its hunger for "product." Otto Binder (who, with his brother Earl, wrote under the name of "Eando Binder") created a time travel adventure series, "Mark Swift and His Time Retarder" (in obvious imitation of Tom Swift) for *Slam Bang Comics,* beginning in March 1939. It was illustrated by his brother Jack Binder, a sometime illustrator of Eando Binder SF stories in the magazines (e.g., "Queen of the Skies," *Astounding Stories* [November 1937]). The two brothers also collaborated on the popular "Captain Marvel" character, with Jack doing most of the illustration and Otto writing most of the adventures. Other science fiction writers who soon made appearances in the new comic books were Edmond Hamilton, Henry Kuttner, Manly Wade Wellman, Alfred Bester, and Theodore Sturgeon. Indeed, some, such as Otto Binder and Ed Hamilton, were soon making far more money writing science fiction for the comic books than they were writing it for the magazines. The prolific Binder, for instance, went on to write more than fifty thousand comic book scripts over the next thirty-five or more years. Binder, who died in 1975, was still producing comic scripts up to the end. His last scripts, which appeared 1976–78, were adaptations of Jules Verne and H. G. Wells to comic-book format for *Marvel Classic Comics.*[6]

What finally established comic books as a viable genre in

their own right was the now-famous *Action Comics* No. 1 of June 1938, which featured the first appearance of Jerome Siegel's and Joseph Shuster's character Superman. This superhero took off on his own in *Superman Quarterly Magazine,* which appeared in May 1939. Again, this was the work of the science fiction community.

Siegel and Shuster were Cleveland fans who had launched the fanzine *Science Fiction* in October 1932. From its second issue through its fifth (and last), *Science Fiction* carried cartoons drawn by Shuster. In a 1933 issue, Siegel (speaking of himself in the third person as "Bernard J. Kenton") said he "was at present working upon a scientific fiction cartoon strip with an artist of great renown." That artist was his pal Shuster and the strip was "Superman"—but it would not see print for another five years in *Action Comics.*

This migration of science fiction into the comic book medium soon attracted the interest of science fiction magazine publishers. In October 1939, Martin Goodman, publisher of *Marvel Science Stories,* produced the first issue of *Marvel Comics,* with a cover by Gernsback's favorite artist, Frank Paul. Marvel continues to this day as one of the major players in the comic book field. Soon thereafter, Ned Pines was heard from. Pines was the one who bought *Wonder Stories* from Gernsback and turned it into *Thrilling Wonder Stories* under the editorship of Mort Weisinger—and who also published the magazine *Startling Stories.* In February 1940, he launched *Thrilling Comics,* followed quickly by *Exciting Comics* (April 1940), and *Startling Comics* (June 1940).

But even in late 1939, despite the dozens of science fiction strips which were featured in the comic books, there was not yet a comic book devoted entirely to science fiction. Sensing an entrepreneurial possibility, Hugo Gernsback decided to enter the new field. Commissioning Frank Paul to do the artwork and recruiting his last editor, Charles Hornig, to do the writing, Gernsback launched what he planned to be the very first all-science fiction comic book: *Superworld Comics,* debuting in April 1940. Unfortunately, Fiction House beat him out of the gate with *Planet Comics,* which appeared in January 1940. *Planet Comics* went on to become the longest-lived science fiction comic of the 1940s and 1950s, producing seventy-three issues before it folded with its winter 1953 issue. Gernsback's *Superworld Comics,* meanwhile, lasted only three issues. Although Gernsback scheduled issues four and five for publication, poor sales forced him to cease publication with his August 1940 issue.

The next year, 1941, Mort Weisinger left the editorship of *Thrilling Wonder Stories* and *Startling Stories* to work for *Superman* comics, which was being published by his old literary agent partner, Julius Schwartz, as it would be for many years to come. Indeed, Schwartz went on to become perhaps better known in the comic book world than in the SF magazine world. In addition to *Superman,* Schwartz was also responsible for many other comic books, including *Strange Adventures,* the first all-science fiction comic to be launched by DC Comics in August 1950, and *Mystery in Space,* DC's second all-science fiction comic, launched in April 1951.

Thus, soon after the creation of comic books, there was already a close intermixing between them and the science fiction magazines of both story ideas and actual personnel. In a very real way, it was science fiction which gave birth to the comic book. By the early 1940s the merger was complete, as comic books became the new medium for science fiction.

The following conversation with Charles D. Hornig took place on January 16, 1988. Mr. Hornig was seventy-one years old at the time. In it, he discusses his participation with Gernsback on *Superworld Comics* and his years back in the world of science fiction as a magazine editor.

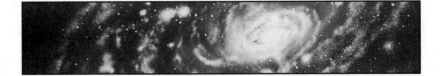

CHARLES D. HORNIG: Before we start, I just want to say I got a call from Forrest Ackerman yesterday to tell me Catherine Moore—C.L. Moore—died.[7] She had been in very bad shape. He called me because I guess I was the first one in science fiction circles to have met her. This was in 1936 in Indianapolis. She was secretary to the vice president of the Fletcher Trust Co.

ERIC LEIF DAVIN: *I remember your telling me about taking her out to lunch. You were on your way out to L.A. and stopped to look her up. Charlie, does it disturb you to learn of news like this?*

Well, I'm seventy-one now and have to expect it. A lot of these people were older than me. When I was seventeen I was meeting people who were already in their twenties and thirties and forties, so, of course, a great portion of them have gone by this time. I'm sometimes surprised I'm still here!

I didn't know her that intimately. But I was shocked, because I didn't know she had Alzheimer's disease. I remember her as she had been. She was a very beautiful young girl in 1936. Very well-dressed. She had a good job in Indianapolis and I never expected her to leave it for California, which she did in 1940 when she married Henry Kuttner.

Did you know Kuttner very well?

I knew him, but not well. He was always smoking these big cigars and I couldn't get too close to him because I couldn't stand the smoke. I was kind of surprised when he and Moore married because they didn't seem to be each other's type, but I guess I was wrong.

Why weren't they each other's type?

Oh, they were different personalities altogether. I wish I knew a movie star I could compare Kuttner to for you. He looked like he was drunk most of the time, but he wasn't. Oh, I guess he was sometimes. He was very friendly in a gruff way. He would've made a good stevedore or lumberjack.

Now, Catherine, on the other hand, was very ladylike, very petite, very pretty. Always dressed nicely. You wouldn't expect this delicate girl to marry a rough guy like Kuttner, but she did. They got along very well. I guess the fact that they were both science fiction writers is what did it for them.

But, of course, it surprised me when Leigh Brackett and Ed Hamilton got married, too, so maybe I'm not a good judge. I knew Hamilton quite well, Brackett less well. They were out in L.A. about the same time as me—in 1940, or thereabouts. They also had very different personalities. Brackett had a very mannish way about her. I didn't think she'd ever get married. Hamilton was very easygoing, soft-spoken, very friendly. He had a crooked nose which looked like it'd been broken. The two of them hit it off very well with each other, so what do I know?[8]

Well, that was all a long time ago. So, what can I do for you?

This seems to be an old subject, but I wonder if I might try to clarify some points concerning your editorial control under Gernsback before moving on to your work for Silberkleit. In Fantasy Commentator *no. 37, Sam Moskowitz suggested that you had less editorial control than you indicated. For instance, he said that while he worked for Gernsback in the fifties, Gernsback often wrote him memos asking for editorial changes in stories, which he then had to transmit to the authors. He thought this was probably the same policy Gernsback followed with you, indicating less editorial freedom than you implied. Was this true?*

No, that never happened. I wrote long letters myself to the authors about stories suggesting improvements. The authors usually wrote back that they appreciated the time I took with them. But this was at my own initiative. Gernsback was the overall editor of all the magazines, but he didn't put any editorial time in on them, so far as I can tell.[9] The only thing I ever remember Gernsback doing directly was securing the European, mostly German, novels. Evidently he got them dirt cheap or he wouldn't have used them. They were very long-winded and not very good, but I had to run them even though I didn't like them.

Gernsback let his people run their own show. That's what we all liked about him. We could pretty much do as we wanted and he never interfered. People in the science magazines, the radio magazines, they felt the same way. Some of them worked there with their paychecks piling up in their wallets because there was no money in the bank to redeem them. I asked, "Why do you keep working for him?" They said they liked to work for a man who gave them so much freedom. He was known, at least in my day, in the thirties, as a man who allowed other people to take charge.

So, if a story appeared in Wonder Stories, *such as the cover story by Joseph Kraus which Moskowitz mentioned, you would have chosen that story instead of Gernsback?*

Well, Kraus also was a Gernsback employee, so that may have been an exception to my overview. I remember Kraus very well, as we worked in the same office, but I don't remember any story by him. If he did write a story, it's possible he had Gernsback read it, but I'm not aware of it.[10]

The only person who really gave me any sort of editorial help was C. P. Mason, who used to help me a lot with the science question-and-answer department. I'd go to him for everything, because I didn't know much science and he knew everything. He was a genius. At that time he was probably about forty-six years old. To me he was an older man, since I was only seventeen or eighteen. We had a very good working relationship. Mason really deserves credit there, even though the department was officially my responsibility.

The only time Gernsback ever gave me any indication as to his preferences was when he made a comment once about my fanzine, *The Fantasy Fan.* It ran eighteen issues, but it might never have gotten off the ground if Gernsback had known about it. Well, he *did* know about the first issue, because that's how I got my job with him. I sent him a copy of the first issue at the same time he was letting David Lasser go and he needed a new editor, so he called me in. But, about the middle of 1935, he said to me one day, "Say, you're not still putting out that fan magazine, are you? Because I don't think you ought to be doing that if you're editor of *Wonder Stories.*"

Since I'd terminated the magazine about six months before, I said, "Oh, no, that's gone under." But, if he'd asked me that question in 1933, I would have had to close it down and it wouldn't have existed at all except for the first couple of issues. But I never gave him another copy of it and, evidently, he was so out of touch with the fan world that he never knew about it. Only after it was dead did he let me know that he didn't want me to publish it! That's the only time Gernsback ever indicated any kind of what might be called an editorial preference to me.

How did you become Louis Silberkleit's editor?

Well, I'd been kicking around looking for steady work after the sale of *Wonder Stories.* In late 1938 I'd just returned from L.A., where I'd been looking for work, and I got a message directly from Silberkleit. He said Hugo Gernsback recommended me as a good editor for a science fiction magazine he wanted to publish. So, I visited Silberkleit in his office and he agreed right away to hire me. I had the background with Gernsback and that was good enough for him, so I began working on the initial issue of his new magazine in October 1938. But if Gernsback hadn't put my name in there, I'd never have gotten the job, because there were a lot of others in New York who could have done it just as easily.

What was your working arrangement with Silberkleit?

Well, the major difference from *Wonder* was that I didn't have an office! I was essentially a freelance editor who just checked in once or twice a week with Silberkleit. I'd drop off manuscripts with the secretaries to be typeset, pick them up later to proof, lay out a dummy of the magazine at home, and drop the dummy off once a month for publication. I was paid $100 per issue, which given the fact that with three magazines there was usually one coming out every month, even with an erratic schedule I got about $100 a month. That was easy money—comparable to what I was making at Gernsback's—because I was free to do other things. For instance, at the same time I worked as a night auditor in the Plaza Hotel. So I was doing okay for those days.

Silberkleit had a chief editor in overall charge of his magazines. I can't remember his name, but I usually reported to him.[11] He sometimes looked over what I had, but he knew nothing about science fiction and trusted me to know what I was doing. I often changed the titles of stories. He once applauded one of those changes. I came up with "The God That Science Made," which he thought was great. I don't recall if he picked out the covers or not. I don't remember how that worked, as I had nothing to do with the artists. In a sense, it was a remote-controlled job.

Did writers send their stories to Silberkleit's office or to you?

I don't remember that I ever got any stories from Silberkleit. Nor did writers send their stories directly to me, because I didn't have an official editorial address. Instead, I relied heavily on Julie Schwartz, who was still an agent at that time. I depended on

Schwartz. Without him, I'd have had to do a lot more work. I'd have had to find writers myself. That would have been difficult, as we only paid a half cent a word. Also, it wasn't easy to get your pay, so we were not an attractive market for writers. I think other magazines also only paid a pretty standard half cent a word, but they'd pay more to special writers and *Astounding* always paid bonuses, so people liked to sell there first.

Julie, of course, placed his stories in the most profitable places, beginning with *Astounding, Amazing,* and so on down to us. Julie would have a pile of stories left over and I'd sift through them and pick out what I felt I could take. I couldn't take everything because some of them were pretty awful. So having only last choice from Julie's stable didn't give me many outstanding stories.

I noticed two authors who seemed to appear a lot in the magazines were Eando Binder and John Russell Fearn. Did their stories also come from Schwartz?

Well, Fearn's would have, as I had no contact with him personally. He was an Englishman, and I think he later edited a British science fiction magazine [Yes, *Vargo Statten Science Fiction Magazine*].

However, I was a close friend of Otto Binder's and he gave me stories directly—though Julie would have gotten credit for them, because he was Binder's agent. I guess Binder is now considered a hack, but he was a good science fiction writer in those days. Otto could be relied upon to write a story to order. If you had a great idea for a story, you gave it to him and he would write it. I liked that. That happened two or three times, but I can't recall which stories they were now. The Adam Link robot stories, of course, were entirely his.

Given the fact that you were at the end of the line, did you have enough editorial clout to request any revisions from authors?

Oh, yes, the same as I did at *Wonder.* Lots of the stories I wouldn't take as-is because they were lower than even my standards. But since the writers were glad to sell them at all, they were willing to make changes, although there weren't that many to be made.

Were there any memorable stories in the slush pile?

As far as I'm concerned, none of them were memorable. I don't remember a single one. Actually, I think I did better than I anticipated, given the circumstances. I got better stories than one might expect. But there was nothing exceptional.[12]

Did you try to accomplish any kind of editorial goal with these magazines? Did you try to shape the stories in any way?

I just wanted to get the best stories I could, though I knew I didn't have much of a chance. I knew I'd never get the best stories as long as I worked for Silberkleit—or even for Gernsback—because they wouldn't pay enough. So I knew I had to take the bottom of the pile and make do as best I could.

But that doesn't mean all the stories were bad. *Astounding* could use just so much material. They took the cream, but that didn't mean there weren't good stories below that level. Besides, tastes of editors vary. A perfectly good story just might not suit John Campbell or some other editor and I'd be able to pick it up.

But I never considered that *Future Fiction* was in the same league with Campbell's *Astounding.* There was just no way to compete with him or his magazine. You know, I always had great respect for John W. Campbell, not only as an editor, but as an educated and cultured individual. Personally, I never liked him; I thought he had an antagonistic personality. But I had great admiration for him. He inspired a lot of writers to become great and, without him, I don't think science fiction would have reached the heights it has. But our personalities just clashed.

. . . .

How did you and Silberkleit come to part ways?

Well, I worked on the magazines at home in New York all through 1939. Then in 1940 I went back to California. I was determined to be a Californian! L.A. was great in those days. There were no freeways, the air was clean, it was a beautiful place, a city of maybe about a million.

So, I told Silberkleit I wanted to live out there and edit the magazines from California. He said, okay, if it's possible. So Julie sent me stories in L.A., I'd select the ones I wanted, ship them to New York to be typeset, and I'd get big packages of proofs back from Silberkleit to dummy up. I made up the magazine and sent it back to New York. It seemed to work out pretty well all through 1940.

Near the end of 1940 I returned to New York and worked more closely with Silberkleit once more. Then, early in 1941, I decided to return to L.A. again. At that time he said to me, "Look, it's kind of cumbersome having to send you these things way out there. There's a lot of time-delay and I can't talk to you very well. If you want to go to L.A. we'll have to give this job to somebody else." I said, "Well, I'm really determined to go to L.A., so I guess you'll have to find a new editor." Now, I believe "Doc" Lowndes, who replaced me, thinks I was fired, but that's the way it actually worked out.[13]

But you were still working for Silberkleit when you collaborated on Gernsback's comic book, weren't you?

Yes, I guess that was about this time. Comic books were not yet all that popular and Gernsback wanted to try his hand at one. So, I wrote what we called "squinkas" for them. Manly Wade Wellman invented that term. He may have been the only one who ever used it, but that's where I heard it.

A "squinka" is the written continuity for a cartoon. In other words, I wrote the stories—terrible stories—for the three comics.

There might have been four "squinkas" per issue and Gernsback paid me $15 per "squinka." These outlandish tales were so bad, I didn't even use my own name. I used a pen name which I'd also used in *Wonder Stories* for "The Fatal Glance," my single story published there. This was "Derwin Lesser"—not to be confused with David Lasser—which was taken from my middle name and my mother's maiden name. They were awful stories, but they had the required science fictional slant. The comics are real rarities because they folded after only three issues.

I once discovered a copy of issue no. 2 many years ago in an Oakland comic book store. I brought it back to an SF con in Oakland many years later, sometime in the late seventies. I thought it'd be fun just to thrill some kid at the con by giving it to him and watching him go into ecstasy over it.

So, I took it to the con. The first thing that happened when I walked in was that I ran into Forrest Ackerman dressed in a suit and looking very dignified. I got to talking with him and a couple of others who were standing around and I said, "Look, Forrey, I have something strange here. It's the second issue of *Superworld Comics*. I'm going to give it away to some young fella just to watch him grovel on the floor."

Well, I'll be if Ackerman didn't fall to the floor and begin grovelling in his suit! He said, "Charlie! That's the one thing missing from my collection! I gotta have that second issue of *Superworld Comics*!" So I said, "Okay, you've earned it!" Then I gave it to him.

Did you go to many SF cons while working for Silberkleit?

Well, I tried to, just to keep abreast of what was happening in the field. I was at the First Worldcon in 1939, of course. I also travelled around a lot meeting SF people. I've always had wanderlust. Even as a child, I'd wander off as far as I could. As I got older and had more money to travel, I kept going further and further. In '35 I finally made it to California by train. That time I was in L.A. for only four days. Then, in '36 I spent four weeks in L.A. In '38 I was there for maybe five months. Finally, I got to live there for three years, from 1945 to 1948, after I married.

It was on one of those trips to California that I met C. L. Moore in Indianapolis. I met a lot of others the same way, people I'd never have met if I'd stayed home in New York. In 1934 Conrad Ruppert and I went out to Chicago on a package tour and met a lot of Midwest fans and writers. Connie was a little older than the rest of us and an important figure in the field's history. He was a printer who lived in Queens, New York, and was with us from the beginning, along with Julie Schwartz and Mort Weisinger. He hand-set the type for *The Fantasy Fan, Science Fiction Digest, The Time Traveller,* all the very first fanzines.

Anyway, we went out in the second year of the Chicago World's Fair and got together with a lot of Chicago fans, including Ray Palmer.[14] We once piled into a car to drive up to Milwaukee to drop in on Ralph Milne Farley. Ray was a very small hunchback, but he was very lively. The only thing I remember about the drive up to Milwaukee was that Ray took the cigarette tray out of its slot and threw it out the window!

We also visited Farnsworth Wright in the Chicago offices of *Weird Tales.* You know, a lot of SF people in the early days seemed to have some kind of physical problems, like Palmer. With Wright it was a kind of nervous disorder that made it impossible for him to sit still—in the old days they might have called it St. Vitus's Dance. It was a great affliction for him.

Nevertheless, these were pleasant years. Your questions bring back a lot of memories for me, things I thought I'd forgotten. I hope you keep on asking questions of all us old dodos before we're all gone!

NOTES

1. Damon Knight, *The Futurians: The Story of the Science Fiction "Family" of the 30s That Produced Today's Top SF Writers and Editors* (New York: John Day, 1977), p. 65.

2. *Astounding Stories* had become *Astounding Science Fiction* a year before, in March 1938. The first publication of any kind to use the words "Science Fiction" in its title is believed to have been *Science Fiction Digest,* a fanzine begun by Julius Schwartz and Mort Weisinger in September 1932. A month later, October 1932, Cleveland fans Jerome Siegel and Joseph Shuster, the creators of "Superman," produced their own mimeographed fanzine entitled simply *Science Fiction,* which ran for five issues.

3. Robert A. W. Lowndes said that Hornig had chosen all the material for the final issue of *Science Fiction.* "When the proofs came back, Silberkleit turned them over to me to 'close' the issue. It so happened that Hornig's just didn't fit, in that a couple of stories had to be left out—which left a gap of some pages in the issue. I selected material already set for *Future Fiction* (but crowded out) to fill the gap. And I also took advantage of the situation to replace Taurasi's *Fantasy Times* with *Futurian Times.* [Taurasi was allied with Sam Moskowitz, both then in battle with the Futurians, the fan group to which Lowndes belonged.] You might call that issue something of a collaboration, but that's all; had it been possible to put the issue together using *only* Hornig-selected material, I certainly would have done so. And I think now it would have been better to have just made a few corrections in Taurasi's somewhat sloppy writing and run the sheet he prepared. Partisanship overcame me at that time." Letter to the Editor, *Fantasy Commentator* 6, no. 4 (Winter 1989–90): 297.

4. Frank Paul did not monopolize the covers of *Future Fiction,* as he had those of *Science Fiction.* Indeed, the first issue, illustrating the story "World Reborn," was painted by H. W. Scott, an artist little-remembered today. Scott also painted the first cover of John W. Campbell's *Unknown,* which began in March 1939, simultaneously with Silberkleit's *Science Fiction.* The story illustrated in this case was Eric Frank Russell's classic, "Sinister Barrier."

5. Knight, *The Futurians,* p. 65. Lowndes said that, as far as he

was concerned, he didn't refer to Silberkleit as "Louis the Lug" for very long. "I grew to like and respect him without being blind to his shortcomings. On the whole my relationship with him was a good one, and I remember him with affection.

"While, as correctly noted, there had been interference with my selections for the first issue of *Future Fiction,* I had fleshed out the spring 1941 *Science Fiction Quarterly* with material I had on hand for *Future;* Silberkleit found no fault with those selections, and later, when I turned over my proposed line-up for the August 1941, issue, he gave the manuscript right back to me and said he was satisfied that I knew what I was doing, and he didn't need to oversee any story I had accepted." Letter to the Editor, *Fantasy Commentator* 6, no. 4 (Winter 1989–90): 297.

6. Gardner Fox is an exception, a science fiction comic book writer who later jumped ship to the science fiction magazines. Besides writing for *Superman,* Fox created the space adventures of "Cotton Carver" for DC Comics' *Adventure Comics* (February 1939). He also created the long-lived character The Flash and the superhero team The Justice League of America. In all, he wrote more than four thousand comic book scripts. He made his magazine debut with "The Weirds of the Woodcarver," *Weird Tales* (1944). After 1945 he became a prolific contributor to *Planet Stories.* In 1964 he graduated to books with his first SF novel, *Escape Across the Cosmos.* He continued to produce heroic fantasy novels into the 1970s. He died in 1986.

7. Moore, age seventy-six, actually died in April 1987, but it took some time for the science fiction community to become aware of it. She suffered from Alzheimer's disease and had lain in a coma for many months toward the end. Sam Moskowitz termed Moore "the most important member of her sex to contribute to science fiction since Mary Wollstonecraft Shelley wrote *Frankenstein.*" (Quoted by Don D'Ammassa in his obituary of Moore for *Science Fiction Chronicle* [March 1988], p. 10.) As of August 1997, Moore's *Jirel of Joiry* was still an offering of the Science Fiction Book Club.

8. Leigh Brackett met Edmond Hamilton in 1940 and married him in 1946. She began publishing science fiction in 1940 with "Martian Quest," *Astounding Science Fiction.* Most of her stories appeared in *Thrilling Wonder Stories* and *Planet Stories.* She specialized in

blending SF with sword and sorcery. This was the style of "Lorelei of the Red Mist," *Planet Stories* (Summer 1946), a collaboration with Ray Bradbury. My personal favorite, read as a kid, is *The Sword of Rhiannon* (Ace Books, 1953), previously published as "Sea-Kings of Mars" in *Thrilling Wonder Stories* (June 1949). However, her best novel is usually considered to be *The Long Tomorrow* (New York: Ballantine Books, 1955, reissued in 1974). This is about the secret struggle of survivors in a postnuclear holocaust America to reestablish science and technology.

From 1955 on, Brackett concentrated on film scripts. She wrote many of the films of Howard Hawks, including his adaptation of Raymond Chandler's *The Big Sleep* (1946), starring Humphrey Bogart and Lauren Bacall, and *Rio Bravo* (1958), starring John Wayne. Other Howard Hawks–John Wayne films she wrote include *Hatari!* (1962), *El Dorado* (1967), and Hawks's last film, *Rio Lobo* (1970). Because the producer liked her script for *The Big Sleep,* she was also hired to adapt a second Raymond Chandler novel for Robert Altman's *The Long Goodbye* (1973). The last film she wrote was *The Empire Strikes Back* (1979), the second installment in George Lucas's *Star Wars* trilogy. For this she posthumously won a 1980 Hugo. She died in 1978; Ed Hamilton died the year before.

9. There is some hard evidence to support Hornig. For example, it was Hornig, as managing editor of *Wonder Stories,* not Gernsback, the publisher, who wrote a long letter to agents Julius Schwartz and Mort Weisinger evaluating and rejecting their client Stanley G. Weinbaum's "The Circle of Zero" on August 15, 1934. "We are now in the market for short stories and novelettes propounding new, logical scientific theories, in particular, with original plots, minus any high-toned words," Hornig wrote. "Our chief objection to Mr. Weinbaum's story is that we now have one on hand by Edmond Hamilton propounding practically the same theory (which is new—that is, it hasn't appeared in science-fiction since 1928, to our knowledge), and we couldn't use two so much alike. Furthermore, the science in this story is unconvincing. That is, the scientists admit that they have hit upon one chance in trillions of trillions. Another objection is that it all turns out to be a hoax (apparently) which takes all the fantasy from the story. Re-incarnation is unscientific also, and out of our line." This new story policy

was the one Hornig instituted when he took over as editor from Lasser. Obviously, Hornig was the one passing judgment on the submitted story. See Stanley G. Weinbaum Papers, Special Collections, Temple University, Philadelphia.

10. Robert A. W. Lowndes provided the following information: "The Kraus story Charlie didn't remember is . . . 'Phantom Monsters.' It copped the cover of the April 1935 issue. There's an interesting bit of history behind both the story and the illustration:

> In "The Reader Speaks" section of the December 1935 *Wonder Stories* (p. 766), we find a letter from Henry Lewis Jr., SFL member 682, praising Paul's cover for "Phantom Monsters" and lauding the story itself. To this the editor (Gernsback) replied: "We have proven the theory that 'necessity is the mother of invention' with the April cover, which you like so much. The Editor being at a loss for a cover subject that particular month was offered a suggestion by Mr. Kraus—and it met with his approval, as you can see. After suggesting the scene for the cover, Mr. Kraus went ahead and wrote the story."
>
> That was clearly the first time in science fiction magazines that a cover story was written *ex post facto,* and remains unique in that with later examples, a selected author was presented with a cover about whose subject he or she knew nothing in advance, and invited to write a story around it.

Letter to the Editor, *Fantasy Commentator* 6, no. 4 (Winter 1989-90): 297–98.

11. This was Abner J. Sundell (personal communication, Robert A. W. Lowndes).

12. Evidently, even the better authors who were selling their stories to Hornig agreed with this assessment and many published their lesser work with him under pseudonyms. Typical of these writers was Henry Kuttner; Kuttner's agent was Julius Schwartz, who sold a number of his stories to Hornig that appeared under the name of "Paul Edmonds."

13. Indeed, Lowndes *did* believe Hornig was fired. His version can be found in Knight, *The Futurians,* p. 64. Although Hornig says he

was in New York at this time, Knight believes he was in California, and says that "Silberkleit was dissatisfied with Hornig because it was hard to deal with him at a distance of three thousand miles. . . ."

Knight says that Lowndes was maneuvered into Hornig's job by Donald Wollheim. Lowndes is quoted as recalling,

A batch of pulp magazines appeared on the newsstands, Western, detective, sports, under a new imprint. Donald told me he'd found out these were actually published by Silberkleit. I think the imprint was "All American." So he suggested, "Write a letter to All American, suggesting they bring out a science fiction magazine. And go over all the science fiction magazines and find fault with them, but particularly find fault with *Science Fiction* and *Future Fiction.* And then offer your services to bring out a science fiction magazine." He had found out what Hornig was getting, and the thing was that I would offer my services at five bucks less. Hornig was getting forty. I offered my services at thirty-five an issue. He said, "I'll bet you'll get a letter from Silberkleit." I did. And so early in November 1940, I went down and had an interview with Silberkleit, and when I left, I was the editor of *Future Fiction.*

It wasn't until many years later that I found out that Silberkleit had tried to get Sam Moskowitz to take the job, earlier, and he declined it because he didn't want to throw Charlie Hornig out of a job. Sam told me, "I will never strike at a man's job." Charlie Hornig was not a friend of mine, and so I had no such scruples. [Charlie Hornig was not a friend of Moskowitz's, either, but Moskowitz had scruples.]

Actually, these versions are not incompatible. It's very possible Hornig wanted to return to California and Silberkleit was unhappy with that at the same time that Lowndes was angling for Hornig's job. Silberkleit perhaps didn't try to continue a long-distance relationship with Hornig because Lowndes was presenting himself as an alternative.

Since the original publication of this conversation with Charles Hornig, Lowndes has changed his mind about this episode. "I cheerfully stand corrected and accept Charlie's account without reservation. There's certainly a difference between 'You're fired!' or 'I quit!', both of which imply animosity, and 'I'm sorry, but under the circumstances I'll have to get someone else,' which allows for an amiable separation without hard feelings. I'm glad to know that such was the way Hornig and Silberkleit separated." Letter to the Editor, *Fantasy Commentator* 6, no. 4 (Winter 1989–90): 297.

14. Palmer was a leading fan who later became editor of *Amazing Stories*.

3.

STANLEY G. WEINBAUM AND BLACK MARGOT

A Conversation with Margaret Weinbaum Kay

Lord! That queer creature! Do you picture it? Blind, deaf, nerve-less, brainless—just a mechanism, and yet—immortal! Bound to go on making bricks, building pyramids, as long as silicon and oxygen exist, and even afterwards it'll just stop. It won't be dead. If the accidents of a million years bring it its food again, there it'll be, ready to run again, while brains and civilizations are part of the past. A queer beast—yet I met a stranger one!

—Stanley G. Weinbaum, "A Martian Odyssey" (1934)

STANLEY G. WEINBAUM'S DEATH ON DECEMBER 14, 1935 —less than a year and a half after he exploded upon the science fiction world—deprived the field of a writer who would have been one of the giants of the field. As it was, the thirty-three-year-old Weinbaum nevertheless revolutionized the young genre, and he did so on the basis of his very first story, "A Martian Odyssey," which appeared in the July 1934 issue of *Wonder Stories*. In that story, Weinbaum (who Ed Naha has called "the alien's best friend"[1]) introduced "Tweel," an extraterrestrial alien who was something entirely new in the science fiction world—a sympathetic alien portrayed in a complex extraterrestrial ecosystem replete with other equally alien entities. Thus, Tweel was science fiction's first truly "alien" alien, incomprehensible in human terms. "Weinbaum's Tweel," recalls Frederik Pohl, "showed us all how alien an alien might really be, not simply in physical appearance but in basic ways of thinking and behaving."[2]

"The unique inventiveness, style and psychological viewpoint of the alien," said Sam Moskowitz, "were instantly recognized," not only by fans but by fellow authors as well, for the innovative accomplishment it was.[3] H. P. Lovecraft declared:

> I rejoiced [because here] was somebody who could think of another planet in terms of something besides anthropomorphic kings and beautiful princesses and battles of space ships and ray-guns and attacks from the hairy sub-men of the "dark side" or "polar cap" region, etc., etc. Somehow he had the imagination to envisage wholly alien situations and psychologies and entities, to devise consistent events from wholly alien motives and to refrain from the cheap dramatics in which almost all adventure-pulpists wallow.[4]

"When Weinbaum rejected the alien monsters or too-human aliens from other planets," said Lester Del Rey, "he made the other writers realize how bad their previous conceptions had been."[5] Isaac Asimov recalled that, up until then, aliens were mere "cardboard, they were shadows, they were mockeries of life." For that reason alone, Weinbaum's debut "had the effect on the field of an exploding grenade. With this single story, Weinbaum was instantly recognized as the world's best living science-fiction writer, and at once almost every writer in the field tried to imitate him."[6]

Robert Bloch, author of *Psycho*, was then a teenage member of the Milwaukee Fictioneers. He recalled fellow member Weinbaum as "dark-haired, personable, with a ready smile and a soft Louisville-acquired drawl," who "seemed much more fond of his extra-terrestrials than he was of his earthlings" in his fiction. Bloch thought this was only appropriate, since none of the humans there elicited as much empathy in the reader as did his aliens. "This, of course, was Stanley Weinbaum's greatest contribution to science fiction. He introduced empathy to the field. ... Once it was made and understood, science fiction would never be the same again. In empathy he had found the weapon to destroy the Bug-Eyed Monster, once and for all."[7]

Given his formative importance to the creation of science fiction, there is an amazing dearth of personal memoirs concerning Weinbaum. In addition to Robert Bloch's personal recollections, one of the few other sources of information on him comes from Weinbaum's own autobiographical notes which appeared in the June 1935 issue of Julius Schwartz's and Mort Weisinger's fanzine, *Fantasy Magazine,* seven months before his death. Weisinger, who—along with Schwartz—was also Weinbaum's literary agent, had requested either an interview or an autobiographical sketch and got the latter. Excerpts from these notes were reprinted in the October 1938 *Amazing Stories* when Raymond A. Palmer, by then managing editor, posthumously published Weinbaum's "Revolution of 1950."[8] In them, Weinbaum confesses that he'd always been interested in science fiction from as far back as he could remember, including:

such juveniles as Robinson Crusoe [?] the Motor Boys series, and Tarzan [?], and eventually to the real classics of Verne and Wells. That doesn't exclude a few others who receive less attention from science fiction readers than they deserve, Bellamy (whose "Looking Backward" is still a social influence in such movements as the erstwhile popular Technocracy), Conan Doyle, Poe, and Mrs. Shelley. Those writers wrote with an attention to realistic detail that has been rather neglected in these days of purple, green, or crimson rays, of ant-men, beetle-men, lizard-men, and what not. Science fiction has slipped a peg or two.

Nevertheless, he had great hopes for it. The genre could be used for more than mere juvenile entertainment. "It is, or at least ought to be, a branch of the art of literature, and can therefore quite properly argue, reject, present a thesis, proselytize, criticize, or perform any other ethical function." This, in any case, was what he tried to do with his own stories.[9]

Beyond these brief comments, we have nothing else from Stanley Weinbaum. For that reason, the following conversation with Weinbaum's widow is a welcome addition to our knowledge. Despite the passage of over half a century, she remembered her life with Stanley in great detail and with much fondness. This conversation was held in two sessions, on August 20 and 27, 1988; both have been merged here. Mrs. Kay was eighty-one years old at the time. She died March 9, 1996, at age eighty-nine.

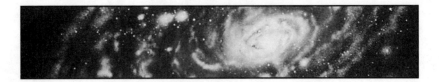

ERIC LEIF DAVIN: *Thank you so much for being able to speak with me about Stanley.*

MARGARET WEINBAUM KAY: Well, this is a particularly high priority to me because I'll always love Stanley. That's no reflection on my husband, because he loved him too.

So, he knew Stanley?

Oh, my lands, did he know Stanley! Eugene came to this country and took out his papers in January of '33. That was the month a man named Hitler came into power and Eugene Kay was a surgeon in a municipal hospital in Hamburg then.

Is your husband Jewish?

Yes, yes. I am too, Stanley was also. But we were all atheists, to tell you the truth. So Eugene resigned from the hospital and he was called before the board an hour later. They said, "Look, if it's because of your religion, we will call Hitler now, we know him personally, and we'll get you immunity for life."

But my husband said, "Thank you, but no thank you." He knew enough about history and politics to know that wouldn't stay true. So he came to this country.[10] Stanley and I met him the first week he was in Milwaukee. We were at a round-table discussion, such as we were always being invited to. We went expecting—at least I expected—to find a little, short, fat, gray-bearded doctor, because they'd said "a doctor from Germany." And then I saw this gorgeous specimen there! We became his best friends, and he was the one who became suspicious about Stanley's health. I wasn't even conscious of it.

Stanley and I used to have Gene Kay come along with us to anything we were going to do. If he could get away, he would. He was new in his practice there, so he worked very hard. We all went down to the beach, a mob of us, on a Sunday afternoon. Eugene wanted to make a call into his answering service, and he asked, "Can you get me to a phone?"

I said, "Yes, my sister lives a block up the hill, let's go." Going up the hill was a very steep set of steps. Later, Gene said to me, "Marge, did you notice how short of breath Stanley got?" I said, "No. I'm not medically trained."

And he said, "Well, I don't like it. Will you bring him up to my office tomorrow afternoon? I want to check him, and I may end up wanting an X-ray." That was the start of the whole thing. It was in June or July of the year Stanley died. He lasted just that long.

A very good friend of Eugene's, Dr. Bloch, was head of the chest department at the University of Chicago Medical School. Eugene called him and asked him to please come and check out his friend. He checked Stanley out and saw the X-rays. It was exactly what Eugene knew it was. That was the first time I knew he had cancer. This Dr. Bloch told me. He had us come down to

Chicago because they had cobalt for radiation treatments there. Back at that time, Milwaukee didn't have any.

I thought Stanley had throat cancer, but shortness of breath sounds like something else.

It was lung cancer. He was a very heavy smoker. I was a very heavy smoker along with him.

Do you still smoke?

No, I don't. Dr. Kay never smoked, either. One cigarette every three months and he didn't inhale it then. The reason I finally stopped smoking was that I fell and broke my hip four years ago. We were in Denver at our oldest grandchild's wedding. He was being married on Sunday, and on Saturday afternoon I fell down two steps at a Hilton Hotel in the only spot in the hotel which wasn't carpeted. I landed on the tile, and that was that! That night, when everyone else was at the wedding rehearsal, I was parked in the hospital.

It was the first time I'd gone to the hospital without leaving something on Eugene's bed for him to find, a cheerful little gift. I couldn't go out and shop, so I thought, he's always wanted me to stop smoking. That's what I'll do. I'll stop and that will be my present. Now, that was the most idiotic thing a person could do the night before surgery, when you need every crutch you have. But I did it and I've never had a cigarette since.

Good for you! It's never too late.

No, it wasn't too late. I was only seventy-eight. I was born on November 25, 1906, Thanksgiving Day, believe it or not. But my birthday falls on Thanksgiving only every few years. Stanley was born April 4, 1902, in Louisville, Kentucky. I have so many birthdays to remember, with the three children and seven grandchildren. . . .

Stanley and I had no children. When . . . my first child [with Gene] was born, a son, my husband wanted to name him Stanley. I said, "Oh, no. It isn't because of any reason except I'm not going to let anybody think 'What a peculiar thing that is.'" So we named him the way I wanted—Eugene, after his father. Our other two children were daughters. One lives here in Santa Monica, the other in West Los Angeles. Our son lives in Denver.

And we always speak of *"The Trunk,"* because everything of Stanley's, all his originals and everything that he published, is in a trunk. We gave it to our son and he's given it to his youngest son, who keeps track of the records and everything.[11]

Are there any unpublished stories there?

You know, I have wondered about that. At one time, right after he died, I went through it and picked out a few things. There's a lot of his poetry—and he wrote beautiful poetry—and *The New Adam* was in there. That was the novel Stanley had planned as his introduction to serious work. It wasn't published until after he died. It's a very odd piece.[12]

You asked about the Milwaukee Fictioneers. It wasn't a large group and the members weren't limited just to science fiction. There was a Western writer. There was a horror-story writer named Bloch, who wrote *Psycho*. He came in toward the end. He was just a youngster at the time; we were much "older."[13] Actually, Stanley had been publishing only a year and a half, two years, before he died at age thirty-three.

So, you don't think there's anything of Stanley's which was left unpublished, except perhaps some poetry?

Nothing that I would say was . . . you know, he started writing in earnest after "The Lady Dances" was published as a newspaper serial in 1933. That was bought by King Features of Hearst. It was his *only* newspaper serial. It was published under the name "Marge Stanley."

See, I did newspaper work after Stanley started writing. I sold a series of articles to one paper on a fluke. Then I sold to another, and finally I was working for four newspapers. It was all freelance—I had only oral contracts. I used "Marge Stanley" for my weekly "society" column in the *Milwaukee Sentinel*. I also used "John Jessel" for another series. I got the magnificent sum of $10 for each of those. Back in the days of the Depression, $10 bought a lot of food.

Then I had a daily article for the *Wisconsin News*, which was a take-off on Ripley's "Believe it or Not." Something about the local area of Milwaukee. That went over big. I also did book reviews for the *Milwaukee Journal*. I just fooled around with it. It was very easy. I made my rounds to turn in all my work on Thursday mornings. Thursday was the deadline at the two big papers. You had to have everything in by noon.

Did you meet Stanley through your newspaper work?

No, no, no. I wasn't doing newspaper work then. I met Stanley the year before I entered college. My sister, who was ten years older than I, was married and lived in Milwaukee. My father and mother wanted to get away from the heat of Texas in the summer—

You're from Texas? And here I thought you were from Wisconsin!

No, no, no. I'm from Waco, Texas.

Ah, West Texas.

No, it's really the heart of Texas, *please!*

Deep in the heart of Texas! Why did your family move to Wisconsin?

My family never moved there. My sister did. She married a Wisconsin man. So we began visiting her in Milwaukee during the summer. I had a bunch of friends there. They convinced my parents to let me go to college in Milwaukee instead of going East. See, I was accepted at Wellesley and was to go there. But this whole gang got on their necks pleading, "Please let Marge stay here in Milwaukee." My parents were hesitant. The other option was Tulane down in New Orleans, because it was warmer. My brother had died two years before of pneumonia. He was in his senior year at the University of Pennsylvania Medical School, and they didn't want to sacrifice another child to the snow.

But in that Milwaukee college, you didn't have to go outside to go between classes; all the dormitories and administration buildings were connected by heated passages with lovely, lovely flower arrangements. So my parents said, "Okay, stay there." They didn't anticipate that I'd be sneaking out at night! But I survived!

This was Milwaukee Downer College. It was a very good girls' school. It was the first one west of the Alleghenies allowed to award a Phi Beta Kappa. About ten or twelve years ago it ceased being a girls' school and joined with Lawrence College, which was a boys' school. Now they're both co-ed.

Who was the school named after?

Well, it was on Downer Avenue. Maybe that had something to do with it.

It must have been difficult to meet boys if all the students were girls.

Oh, no, that's the reason all the girls loved me. I knew so many boys in Milwaukee. I fixed them all up with dates. I tell you, if you have boys to pass out among girls, it's just great! The girls love you, the boys love you!

But, to get back to how I met Stanley. When I was finishing

my junior year in high school the group of girls that I went
around with in Milwaukee decided we had to do something
good. So, we began going down to the Abraham Lincoln House
in the ghetto. Many black children came there during the day,
and twice a week we helped the counselors take care of these
youngsters. Then the counselors asked the four of us who hung
out together if we would consider going out to their summer
camp for a week or two and be counselors ourselves instead of
assistants. Well, of course, that just made all of us feel very
grown up and we said, "Yes, yes, yes!" We had to get our parents' permission, which we did.

The chap I was going with very much wanted to come out to
the camp one evening and see me. I said he had to bring three
other guys along for my girlfriends. I was only fifteen at the time
[which would make this the summer of 1922, and Stanley would
have been twenty], so I wasn't matchmaking. I just wanted to
take care of my girlfriends.

So, he brought three other boys along. He even said to me on
the phone, "You're going to love one of them, 'cause he likes literature as much as you do. In fact, he even writes nice poetry."
So, he made *that* mistake. It was Stanley.

That night we just walked off from everybody else, talking
about literature, poetry and so on, and he turned to me and said,
"I'm going to marry you." How do you like that? Of course, I
just laughed and let it go. But, as time went on I dropped off with
everybody else and it was only Stanley.

What was Stanley doing at this time?

He was a junior at the University of Wisconsin. Let me back-
track a little here. Stanley was always interested in science.
When he was a kid, he blew up the family basement with his
chemical experiments and often managed to stink up the whole
neighborhood. He entered Wisconsin University at Madison
when he was eighteen, majoring in chemistry.

But he'd also begun to write, and by the time he was a junior he was writing a lot.[14] The head of the English Department loved him. One of Stanley's very close friends in college was Eugene Reich, who was also from Milwaukee. He was later a very good friend of mine as well. But he couldn't write. He had trouble even writing his name and address! He had to turn a paper in and so Stanley wrote it for him.

Well, they knew it wasn't Gene's paper, so he was called in. He finally admitted he didn't write it, but of course he refused to tell who had. Well, that's just as much of a sin as having it done. So they went over the records to find out who Gene knew. It turned out that Stanley was one of his friends, and right away they said, "That's who it is!" They called Stanley in and he said, "Yes, I did it and I'm very angry about one thing."

"What's that?"

"You accused Gene Reich of having plagiarized Zane Grey. Now, if I can't write better than Zane Grey, *well!*"

So they suspended Stanley for the rest of the semester. He was allowed to return the next fall, but he said, "No, I'm not returning." He walked out and that was the end of it. He never finished college. This was at the end of his junior year, so you can figure out the date from that [1923, and Weinbaum was age twenty-one].

So he came back to Milwaukee and went into radio. Radio was very new, you know, and it fascinated him. He stayed in it until 1926, when he wanted us to get married. Then he took a job with a large chemical firm in Chicago as their representative in Wisconsin, Minnesota, and the surrounding territory.

Now, here's something you'll be interested in. He had to call on the purchasing agents of all the different manufacturers that needed chemicals. Stanley kept a little notebook in his pocket, and whenever he was waiting he'd write on *The New Adam*. That book actually was all little notebooks.[15]

But soon he didn't have a chance to write very much, because all the agents became so interested in him. They liked him so much they never kept him waiting long. At Christmas purchasing agents always received big presents from the detail men, like Stanley, but he never gave any. Instead, the purchasing agents would ask others for extra gifts for a friend and give them to Stanley! We got the most amazing collection of things.

That lasted until the crash of 1929. His chemical firm cut down and cut down and finally went out of business. So, we'd saved a little money and had a chance to buy a movie house. Not the property, but the lease, on a movie house in Cudahay, Wisconsin, which was a suburb of Milwaukee. This seemed a beautiful idea, because it was already *there*, it was already established, and it was the only movie house in the town. We figured that soon after we got everything organized and going—okay, there'd be enough income to live on, and Stanley would have plenty of time to write. It was just a beautiful set-up. But the stock market crash eventually made the movie crash for us, too.

This was because the biggest employer in Cudahay, which employed several thousand men, was B. F. Goodrich Tires. It was a small community, and a lot of the workers boarded out at houses there. The single men living in these families had nothing to do in the evenings, and they went to movies. It was a very poor community, and the boarders' rent was the pocket money for local people to also go to movies, for their children to go to movies. But when the workers were laid off, they left, and that pocket money disappeared. So, the movie house had to fold with everything else. We couldn't afford to keep losing money on it.

So what did you do?

Well, we counted up our pennies and found we had enough to live a year or so without work and decided Stanley should just write. I had confidence in his writing and it was the thing he loved doing. So he wrote! And he wrote! The very first thing he worked on was *The New Adam,* which he'd started as a sales representative, but he did a serial for the newspaper as "Marge Stanley."

Now at this time we had an older friend who became very

important to us. His name was Edward Schoolman and he was a psychiatrist. He'd been studying medicine and planned on being a brain surgeon, which his uncle was. But his eyesight went bad and they said it would get worse. The only thing he could do to stay in medicine was to be a psychiatrist. That was quite a novel idea at the time. In those days, psychiatrists weren't a penny a dozen, like now.

So, when he finished medical school, his uncle and his father convinced him to go to Europe and study under Freud, which he did. He came back and opened a practice. It was slow going, of course. But he was also a magnificent speaker and he developed a regular lecture circuit. He was from Chicago, but went out to the Chicago area, Milwaukee, and all the different towns around there giving a series of lectures. These were very popular, because people wanted to know what a psychiatrist was.

Stanley and I went to hear one of his lectures. Afterward, Judge Ahrens went over to him and said, "When do you leave for Chicago?"

He said, "I catch a midnight train."

So the judge said, "Come on home with us. We'll have a cup of coffee and I'll have a few of the people here come along."

Well, Stanley was always very popular for anything like that because he was such terrifically good company. I went along, of course, because I was sort of comic relief. This actually started our being in on all of these things.

When it came time to break up, Stanley said to Dr. Schoolman, "We'll drive you down to the train."

The next time, someone else invited him, and we drove him to the train again. After the third time, he began spending the night at our place. His stories about his patients were simply fantastic. One was the foundation—with the psychiatry left out, and a few other changes—of "The Lady Dances."

The next summer we decided we were going to Ontario in the Kickapoo Valley. It was a town of five hundred. We stayed at the supposed hotel, the place which put up the two school teachers who came to take care of the whole area. It cost us only $10 a week to stay there, with food! Ed Schoolman came out and he'd talk. He told one good story after another. Stanley took notes and I typed them up. I was Stanley's amanuensis, because he couldn't type. The mechanics of the machine distracted him. He'd get interested in that, the way he once took a car apart and put it back together. He couldn't type for that reason. He'd want to stop and see what was making the clicking!

Well, we put all these stories about Ed's patients together and got the manuscript of a very fat book. I don't know how Stanley did it, but he found a nursery rhyme which fit in perfectly with each story. So the chapters would be entitled "Little Boy Blue," or "Jack and Jill," or something like that. It was a terrific factual book.

So this book used Dr. Schoolman's patients as a way of explaining psychological problems?

Exactly, to laypeople. We submitted the manuscript to the publisher Alfred Knopf. This was early in the winter of 1934–35. We got a telephone call from Knopf, because they were quite excited about it. They asked some questions, which Stanley wrote them the answers to, because the book was under both names, Edward Schoolman and Stanley Weinbaum. And then they said, "We're going to send some papers that you and Dr. Schoolman will have to sign." Stanley said, "We'll be glad to." Because this would be an expensive volume to put out—a thousand-page book, maybe—they wanted to protect themselves. Unpublished writers had to guarantee them the next book or two they wrote.

Two days later we got a call. Ed Schoolman had dropped dead. Died at the end of a bridge game. Ed wasn't more than in his early forties and the bridge game couldn't have been that exciting. It was very heartbreaking for us. Of course, we went down to Chicago for the funeral, and when we got back, there was the contract from Knopf. Stanley had to return it and tell them that his partner had died.

When did Ed Schoolman die?

It was either the end of May or the first part of June of 1935. And July was when Eugene got suspicious of Stanley's shortness of breath. It looked like Ed Schoolman couldn't get along without his buddy, because in December, Stanley was gone. It was a very odd thing.

"The Lady Dances" had been published by this time, hadn't it?

Oh, it had already been accepted and we were getting money for it. Oh, goody, goody, were we getting money! We were too proud to take help from our parents. We decided we were going to do it on our own. It was fun.

Was the book ever published at all?

No, Ed Schoolman died and Stanley followed him. So the book just sits in The Trunk.

Do you remember its title?

What would it have been? We must've had a title on it, but that I don't recall. You know, Stanley and I always had nicknames for the stories he was working on, and there was one I think we called "Pygmalion." There was the play "Pygmalion" about a girl that had tuberculosis? Well, we called it "Adaptable Anna." That was the title![16]

What was the nickname for "A Martian Odyssey"?

I don't remember. But I can tell you what started the story about the big caterpillars, each of them the size of a boxcar, that went around in a circle.[17] One evening, Stanley and I were driving. We'd had dinner with Dr. Kay. He had a call to make out in

the boonies, so we took him. It was a very, very foggy night. We
were sitting in the car while he went in to take care of his patient,
and we began talking about the fog. We said, "This would be
something for a story." Then the conversation worked around to
the famous French naturalist, Henri Fabre. He wrote about caterpillars, ants, moths—fascinating stuff. He told about the caterpillars that walked in chains, each just following the one ahead.
And we said, "Oh, wouldn't that be great! It's foggy and they
couldn't see where they were going, and they'd just keep following!" That's how one story came about.

*Did a lot of Stanley's stories just sort of evolve when he was
kicking around ideas with you like that?*

I'm trying to remember. I do know that when he was a
youngster he fell in love with anything dealing with nature. That
lasted with him throughout life. We still have a book that was on
his desk when he was writing, *Natural History* by John Woods.
It was published when he was a youngster, in the early part of the
century.[18] He'd sit back and just read it and he'd sit back and read
Fabre. He even had me reading Fabre, because the man wrote so
magnificently.

When Stanley was a youngster, he collected things. He had a
bookcase in his room with glass front doors. That was his
museum. Once he found a wasps' nest, which he dipped in gasoline, or something, to kill the eggs. He had *that* in his museum.
You can probably guess the rest of the story!

Ummm—he didn't kill off all the eggs?

His mother was a fanatic cleaner. She was a terrific dame, but
she had to clean! So, she did a spring cleaning and she opened up
the glass front doors and *wow!* All the wasps flew out! That was
the end of his museum!

Was he a farm boy?

No, no, no, never. He was born in Louisville, Kentucky, and the whole family moved to Milwaukee when Stanley was a young chap. His family was an old family in Louisville. His maternal grandmother was a Jessel, and I mention her name because one of the pseudonyms I used in newspaper columns and that Stanley had a story, "The Adaptive Ultimate," published under was "John Jessel."

You know, at the time "A Martian Odyssey" came out, we got a letter from Mort Weisinger saying he'd like to represent Stanley. Well, this was just great, fine, and Mort became a friend through the mails. After Stanley died he was just as sweet to me as could be. I went to New York that summer, because through him I was offered a very nice job there. But Eugene Kay decided for me that I wasn't taking it. So, I didn't.

You were offered a job at a newspaper?

No, not at a newspaper. It was on a pulp magazine which ran love stories. They'd bought rights to a bunch of short stories from England very cheaply and were reprinting them. They wanted someone who could turn the English into "American." You know, "elevator" instead of "lift," or "hood" instead of "bonnet" of a car, that kind of stuff. That was something my little ol' head would be able to do, so Mort had arranged for me to have an interview.

So, I went to New York City and that's when I met Mort Weisinger. He became a real friend, and later came out to Wisconsin a couple of times to visit us. Every time we went to New York, Eugene and I would see him and his wife and spend evenings together.

You know, I never mind talking about Stanley, and I've done just about everything to keep his stories alive. About two years after he was gone I had a call from Walter Grauman; does that name mean anything to you?

Grauman's Chinese Theater in L.A.?

Well, *that* one was a cousin of Stanley's, but a much older Grauman. Georgie Jessel was also a cousin, *the* Georgie Jessel. When someone in the family, one of the Grauman's, once went down to meet him after a performance, Georgie Jessel said, "They didn't know me when I was poor. Now that I have money, those rich so-and-so's —*No,* I'm not going to meet him!"

Anyway, Walter Grauman was a movie producer, and he wanted to make some movies out of some of Stanley's stories. You see, the whole family adored him and this Grauman was a little bit younger. His stepbrother, who was practically Stanley's age, loved him and was with us an awful lot. He was a doctor, also. All of Stanley's cousins of his age adored him. After Eugene and I were married, the cousins all adopted Eugene and when they met people, they'd introduce us as "Our cousins, Marge and Dr. Eugene Kay." This was their attitude and it always made life very simple for me. There was never any explaining. Eugene was just Eugene, another cousin.

Anyway, Walter Grauman said, "I'd like to do a series of Stan's stories and maybe we'll just specialize in science fiction after that. We'll introduce the direction with Stanley's stories, because they'd make very good movies." I said, "You know, Walter, there's nothing I'd like better than to keep his stories alive."

He said, "I'm willing to pay you . . ." and he mentioned such a silly little amount—I think it was to be part of the profit on the movies—that I said, "Look, let me talk to our agent," who, of course, was Mort Weisinger, "and you get back to me." It just didn't smell good.

So I called Mort Weisinger and told him about it. He said, "Marge, I haven't had anything to do with that kind of thing, but this doesn't sound right at all. I don't like it. Give me time to investigate."

When he called back, he said, "Marge, it is just absolutely crazy. People laughed when I told them the amount." They were offering one-half of one percent. And Mort said, "When Walter Grauman calls you again, you just tell him to contact me. Don't make any arrangement. Don't say anything except 'I'm busy, Walter; call my agent.' " And that's exactly what I did. I think Mort must've given him a good going-over, as that's the last I heard of that.

What about Stanley's sister, Helen. Didn't she finish a story of Stanley's after his death?[19]

No, that is completely untrue. He left some fragments, but she never got her hands on anything. See, she lived in the East, so we hardly ever saw her, and she and Stanley never corresponded. But, all of a sudden, here is a story which appears on the stands as by Stanley and his sister.

All the cousins were in a fury; they were very angry, because Stanley was their idol. He was the one in their age group that was somebody, even before he'd published anything. They thought her taking a ride on his name was very unfair. This was just a story she wrote herself and put his name on it. There was no such fragment by Stanley!

Is Helen still alive?

No, I heard a couple of years ago that she had died. There was never any attempt at any contact with me at the time her and Stanley's mother died. Their mother and father—Stella and Nate—were patients of Eugene's. When Stella fell and had a very miserable broken leg, Eugene had her in the hospital for a couple of months, that's how bad it was. You don't keep people in a hospital for an ordinary broken leg. I went every day to see her.

Stella's younger brother, also a Grauman, of course, often came from Chicago to see her. Afterward I'd drive him to our home and he'd have a drink or two before I'd drive him to the station so he could go back. At those times he told me a lot of stories about the family I hadn't known before. They were great fun for me, as I'd been very close to the family. I was only nine-teen when I married into them and they sort of adopted me.

Anyway, when Stella got out of the hospital, Eugene talked to Helen and said, "You should not leave your mother here alone. She'll have to be in a nursing home. It's up to you, of course, if you want to have her in a nursing home, which is a pretty grim life. If not, take her back East with you." So, Helen did.

I kept in touch with Stella there. I'd call her and we wrote back and forth. When she died, Helen never called me—just for-mally notified Eugene's office and said she'd be buried at such and such a time.

But we went to the funeral. We called the family in Chicago, went down in both of our cars, and met a contingent. We took them to lunch before going to the chapel where the service was.

This was in Chicago?

No, in Milwaukee, where the family cemetery plot was. That's where Stella's husband Nate was buried. After the service Helen walked over and said "Hello" to Eugene and me and said, "We're going back to Ray and Lucia's to have cake and coffee. I don't know if enough is prepared for you as well, but come over if you want to."

Well, if the invitation was put like that, I didn't want to, but I left it up to Eugene. He just nodded his head and we separated. Then Eugene said to me, "You don't want to go, do you?" I replied, "Are you asking me or telling me? You know I don't want to go." And we didn't. That was the last I saw of Helen.

The only other contact we had was when Eugene's office received a copy of Stella's will, with a letter from the attorney about Eugene's signed statement that she was competent when the will was made. No personal note saying, "You've been very good to my mother and I want to thank you" or anything like that, no! It was simply a formal letter from the attorney asking, "Would you please verify this as your signature?"

When did Stella die?

Well, we moved away eighteen years ago and it must have been six, seven years before that, so she's been gone quite a while.

So, we're talking maybe twenty-four or twenty-five years ago? In the early sixties? Stella must have been a very old woman at that time.

Oh, it was a very long-lived family. There's a very strange thing about them. Either they lived very long or they died very young. One of the cousins talked about that when another one died. It was just sort of spooky. But most lived well into their eighties. Stella was very upset that she didn't get any gray hair. She often talked to me about having her hair bleached and said, "Everyone thinks I dye it."

Now, Stanley's father, Nathan—how old was he when he died?

Oh, he was well into his eighties. Eugene had done surgery on him. He had a colostomy. It was always a very close relationship. Can you imagine, after he and Stanley were gone, Stella took Gene, my firstborn, in her arms when she came to see him, looked down at him and said, "You could have been mine, you know." That was very heartbreaking for me. . . .

Nobody could have been more understanding and more . . . more going-right-along-with-everything-Stanley-wanted than I was, and they all knew that. Anything Stanley wanted, I managed to make happen. He was a dreamer! He was a true poet, a true dreamer!

This is the kind of thing Marge had to manufacture: Ed Schoolman once said to us, "Look, one of my patients gave me a due bill on a hotel in New York and I'd love to go, but I can't afford to take a trip now." Remember, this was the depths of the Great Depression, and he had his wife to support, two boys in school and so on. So he said, "If you all could find some way to make the trip and take me along, then I will stay with relatives and you could use the due bill. You'd simply register as Dr. and Mrs. Schoolman."

So Stanley said, "I'd love to go," and he turned to Marge and asked, "Can we afford it?" I said, "You know darn well we *can't* afford it, but give me until tomorrow and I'll have an answer for you."

Now, my mother used to come up to Milwaukee for the summer every year—my father'd died way back—and so I went to her and said, "Mom, how'd you like to visit the family in Philadelphia?"

"Oh, I'd love that."

So, I said, "Okay, here's a proposition. We'll drive you down if you take care of the gas and oil and the motel bills on the way."

"Oh, fine, of course!" Momma was well-heeled, and this was just a joy for her. So, we went. We left her in Philadelphia with Poppa's family, with whom we were very close, and the three of us went on to New York. That's the sort of deal I had to manufacture!

How long were you in New York on that trip?

Oh, maybe five, six days.

Did Stanley use the trip to meet any New York editors or writers?

No, it must have been before "A Martian Odyssey" was accepted in '34. But I went over to King Features and met the editor there, so it was after "The Lady Dances," which was '33.

Did you do any further traveling with Stanley?

We couldn't afford to. We would go down to Texas off and on and my parents would treat us to that trip.

How long were you and Stanley married, altogether?

Nine and a half years.

What attracted you to Stanley, besides his love of literature?

Oh, God! He was handsome enough to be a movie star. I think there's a picture of him on the jacket of *The New Adam*. Now *that* is a story, my friend!

There was a guy in the Milwaukee Fictioneers named Raymond Palmer who went to Chicago to work at Ziff-Davis Publishers. He wrote me and said they were willing to publish *The New Adam*. Well, anything to keep Stanley's stories alive and have 'em in print, so I said, "Yes."

He said, "Well, they have to have $500, but when they settle with you for the stories, they will also pay the $500 back."

Well, I never saw that $500 again, I never saw a penny! What happened, I don't know. But it was published, that's the main thing.[20]

You never received any royalties at all from The New Adam*?*

No, and we were never paid for "A Martian Odyssey," either![21]

That's amazing!

No, it was just *Amazing Stories!*

Well, actually, since it was published in Wonder Stories, *it's a wonder of a story!*

Well, okay. But some things of Stanley's were published in *Amazing Stories*, right? Now I'll tell you about "A Martian Odyssey." I was amanuensis for Stanley. He'd sit and write ten thousand words a day, all in longhand on pulp paper that I'd bring back from the newspaper office for my own work and for Stanley. I'd be in the other room, he'd bring in what he wrote, and I'd type the ten thousand words. When we took a break we'd split a cigarette. So, I typed up "A Martian Odyssey."

Did you comment on the stories as you typed them?

Well, I read them; you know, we always discussed these things. I mean, we had fun with them! We'd joke about them. We commented on ugly ridiculous things to do to the stories, you know—it made life fun.

Anyway, I mailed in "A Martian Odyssey." When they sent back the acceptance Stanley came in simply in a dramatic fury, just in a fury, out of his mind! "You sent it in under my name!" he cried. "Now my name is ruined for good! Nobody will ever read anything I write! I want to do *serious* writing!" And he went on and on and on.

Was he joking?

No, he was *serious!* He hadn't known that I mailed the story in under his name! This just had him bugged but good! But, I calmed him down.

What name did he want to use? "Marge Stanley" or something?

Well, I don't know—it might've been "John Jessel" or something else.

That sounds as if Stanley didn't have a very high regard for science fiction.

He had regard for the *possibilities* of science fiction, but not ... now, this isn't very *nice,* but he said it was pretty sad that none of the authors knew how to write. Jules Verne, yes, and H. G. Wells, yes. But, actually, if you stop and think about most of the SF writing at that time, it was kid's stuff, right? Even the plots weren't very good.

I take it you didn't like much of the stuff being published, either.

May I tell you something? I didn't read much of it. I'm sorry to say that. But there were a few of Campbell's I liked. And a little later Heinlein came along. I liked him. You remember his blind astronaut? He used his poetry in there. This is the kind of thing that meant something to me. But the other stuff? You know enough about this, you have to admit, my friend, it was pretty poor.

So, the only science fiction you really read was Stanley's?

Oh, yes. I loved Stanley's.

So, Stanley was upset that "A Martian Odyssey" was published under his name, but the story was instantly popular and successful. It was also his financial breakthrough.[22]

Isn't that amazing? It really went over big. And that was just the beginning. Within a year, when we were in Chicago for the second series of cobalt treatments, his parents brought down a letter from Mort Weisinger saying he'd made arrangements for one of his novelettes every month in one of the science fiction magazines. They even said they'd also publish his short stories in the same issues under his "John Jessel" pseudonym. In fact, we'd already sent something in under that name.[23]

So, things were just opening up. . . .

Right. But here we were in Chicago and I knew it was over, though Stanley *never* knew it was taps. So I called Mort Weisinger. Now, in those Depression days, when money was tight, making a long-distance call during the day was really something. But I had to tell him we couldn't sign anything—and that if Stanley *did* sign anything, and had me mail it, I wanted Mort to know it just couldn't be done.

Stanley wasn't aware of how serious his illness was?

He *never,* unh-uh. But he was miserable. I told him, "You have a mass on your lung and that's why you're having these treatments, to dissolve it. You'll have to be patient. It's going to take time. When you're feeling better you can go on writing."

I'm trying to remember Larry, the one from the Fictioneers who wrote Western stories—F.D.R. said he read them and always kept some about. I can't remember Larry's last name off hand. I hadn't thought of him until now. But Larry used to come over practically every day to sit and chat with Stanley.[24] Then Stanley got to be very hoarse, and talking was not easy for him, though he didn't know it was taps.

When did Stanley realize that it was "taps," as you say?

He never did. Unh-uh. I told Dr. Kay what I'd told Stanley, so that if Stanley asked him he'd go along with what I said. I remember so well Eugene looking at me as if I was out of my cottonpicking mind. He came in every day to check on him, but Stanley didn't say anything to him that day. I knew how sick he was. His cousin, Dr. Sam Grauman, knew the whole thing. I told him about telling Stanley this garbage, and that he seemed to have swallowed it, and Sam said, "I want to tell you something, Marge. It's the brightest people who can be fooled the easiest."

Did you think if Stanley knew the truth it would have depressed him too much?

I just couldn't visualize Stanley knowing he was dying. I just couldn't allow that. He was much too live a person. He loved everybody, everybody loved him, and the world was always a bunch of roses.

He didn't suspect, even when he went into the hospital for the last time?

No, because we came back home then, and he had visitors. Three young chaps from Chicago had written, saying they'd like to meet him and they came up to Milwaukee to do so. I can't remember, was there someone named "Otto" from Chicago?

There was Otto Binder.

If he was ten or so years younger than Stanley, that could've been him. Stanley was so pleased when these three chaps came up. Later, when we went down to Chicago for his treatments, he said, "How about calling those chaps? Tell 'em to come over and say hello." He was very friendly, very warm, thinking that one of those days, everything was going to be perfect.[25]

So, Stanley liked having fans?

Oh, yeah!

Did he get a lot of fan mail?

No, unh-uh. If any fan mail went to his publishers, they never bothered to send it to him. We met some people who exclaimed, "Oh, you wrote 'A Martian Odyssey'! I couldn't help writing you when that came out!" But we never got anything. This happened in Texas and a couple of other times, but we never received anything. But his attitude was, so what?[26]

When Stanley died did you receive any letters from fans?

Not a word from a publisher, nothing. Mort Weisinger, yes. But our friends outside the writing game were very attentive.[27]

Did he keep writing during this time?

I'll tell you what he used to do, mainly. I would do my book reviews and give them to him to look over and give me his opinions. He'd clean 'em up. I purposely wanted him to keep busy because laying in bed I don't think he was capable of doing real writing. At first he was able to write, but he was too weak toward the end. . . . It seems like a thousand years ago, and yet it seems like yesterday.

. . . .

By the way! Didn't one of Stanley's stories . . . ? Yes, I'm sure! One of Stanley's stories mentioned a cancerouslike growth.

"The Lotus Eaters," "Proteus Island," others. He seemed to be familiar with the disease. You know, that's one of the things I meant to ask you. A number of his stories near the end deal with cancer treatments, using radium to treat cancer, things like that.

Yes! Stanley used to talk with other people about the ideas in his stories. He discussed the brain abnormality of the chap in *The New Adam* with Schoolman. Later he discussed things with Eugene to get background which he'd use.

And he asked Eugene about cancer treatments?

Yeah, right! About different kinds of treatments.

Yet there was really no connection between his own cancer and dealing with that subject matter in the stories he was writing at that time?

No, because he never knew he had cancer. He just never knew it. I want to tell you something. My job was to keep Stanley going, keep him blind to the fact of what was really happening to him, and to do things which would be gay and happy for him.

I remember the night of the funeral, my mother'd come up from Texas. She and I were sitting there when Eugene—Dr. Kay—walked in. He looked at me and said, "Marge, you don't have to keep that smile on your face any longer. It's over." I didn't realize my face had got frozen into a smile until he said, "You don't have to do that now."

But I was under deep pressure. As I said, Stanley's cousin, Dr. Sam Grauman, was aware of the situation. Now, he's another one who died young. They moved to Arizona, I've forgotten where, and he was in practice there when he died very young. The other cousin, Tony Myer, also died very young. It's just amazing. They either live to be very old or they die fairly young.[28]

Let me change the subject and ask your maiden name.

Hawtof. The rabbis have told me that it's a Hebrew word which means an accent mark, like an umlaut, or such. That I found very interesting. Anyway, Papa was born in Russia, but it isn't a Russian name.

How did your family get a strange name like that?

I don't know. It goes way back.

Was the fact that you and Stanley were both Jewish a consideration for your family? Did they say you had to marry a Jewish boy, not a goy?

No, and Eugene and I never said that to our children. Their attitude was, you marry whom you want to. Just know what you're doing. On my own, I didn't consider marrying out of the race, though not because I was religious. As I told you, we were really atheists, but when you have Jewish blood in you, you're Jewish, period! Actually, it's very fine, and I'm proud of my cultural background. I've never been ashamed of it. But I just can't believe that there's somebody upstairs, you know, guiding things.

The reason I would never have married anyone who wasn't Jewish was because I'm the kind of person who likes to have children, and the children would've been neither fish nor fowl. Even though a lot of people can marry outside their culture and be very happy, I was always a little worried that if you had an argument it'd come up—"Okay, that's your background, you're Jewish!" I never had that with any friends, thank goodness. And it just happened that each of the two guys I fell in love with enough to marry were Jewish!

Was Stanley very conscious of his Jewishness?

No. We were very alike that way.

. . . .

Let me ask you about Stanley's early life. What started him writing? Did he have any kind of literary influences as a kid? Any uncles or parents who read?

No, no one at all like that. One of his very closest friends was Horace Gregory. He was an excellent poet. He had the chair of poetry at Sarah Lawrence College. The first thing he became well-known for was a translation of Catallus, the Roman poet.[29] You know, to be a good translator of poetry, you have to be a damned good poet! *The Rubaiyat* would never have become known if the translator hadn't been a good poet himself. Anyway, both Horace and Stanley wrote poetry.

Horace was a spastic youngster. He didn't get around well. In fact, the first time Stanley brought him over, when he came to see me, my parents were a little bit worried. "Was he drinking before he came?" they asked. It wasn't a matter of drinking; he just didn't have his balance right.[30]

When Stanley was of high-school age he wrote. Then he'd go over to Horace Gregory's house. There he met the uncle Gregory, who wrote *The Encyclopedia of Wisconsin.* Of people who might have influenced him, Horace is the only one who could fit that description.

Do you think he had much influence on Stanley?

No, they were simply very good friends. Later we used to see him and his wife—Mary Ann, or something like that—when they came out. She was also a poet. I've forgotten her very difficult last name, which she wrote under.[31] She was Jewish; Horace Gregory definitely was not.

Do you remember the name of the place, the artists' colony in upstate New York? Yahoo?

Chautauqua?

No. There was an immensely rich couple who had a large estate sprinkled with little cottages where artists and writers were invited to spend their summers. If they had children, they could take them along. There was someone to take care of the children of these "geniuses."

I know the type of writers' colony you're talking about, but they wouldn't call it "Yahoo," would they?

Isn't that funny? Why did I say "Yahoo"? I don't know. But Horace and his wife were always invited to go there.[32]

Was Stanley ever invited to go to some place like that?

No, unh-uh. It wasn't even two years, was it, between the publication of his first story and his death? But he had the fun of knowing that he was published. . . . And he never again, after that first time, had a canary about his name being on his science fiction stories.

If he wanted to be a serious writer, what turned him to science fiction?

I think he felt that it could be done in good English. Not only that, he loved nature and was drawn to such man-made scientific things as radio and X-rays. He *liked* all of this.

Do you recall how he got the idea for "A Martian Odyssey"? What was unusual about that story was its very sympathetic portrayal of an alien. At that time, most of the aliens in science fiction were very threatening, hostile.

When you stop and think of his stories, I don't think there were any that were really very threatening. But he really came up with some very fantastic things.

Did he ever kick these ideas around with you before he wrote them down? You mentioned the caterpillars, for instance.

Oh, sometimes he'd say, "What do you think of this? What do you think of that?" We'd chew it around and think about it, but Stanley was his own man. He'd go and write the thing the way he felt it.

By the way, "Adaptable Anna," the story with the plain, sick girl who was put under treatment and came out beautiful, but with no conscience—we found out that it was being made into a movie. I guess Mort had told us. He got me and my daughters tickets, and we watched it being made. We had box seats where they were making this on the stage. It was really exciting. It was when I drove down to New York to pick up my son Gene after his junior year of high school in England. Later we saw it at one of the movie houses in Milwaukee.[33]

What was your opinion of the movie?

I'm trying to think what it was. Oh, this was a hell of a long time ago, my friend! I really don't remember the movie in detail, but it wasn't objectionable in any way. I remember clearly only the way my two daughters got such a kick out of being there, and when their brother got off the boat from England they just couldn't wait to tell him.

Was Stanley obsessive about writing once he got an idea for a story, or did he work in bits and pieces?

He took everything very much in his stride. He was a very casual kind of person. But he loved his writing and never had to be encouraged to do it. He wanted to write about ten thousand words a day, and he stuck to it.

Did he get up in the morning and immediately start writing, or did he write at night?

It was all done during the morning. In the afternoon we'd go swimming, we'd do things.

What kind of things did he read?

He read everything. He was an inveterate reader. He started one practice when he was a youngster; if he looked up a word in a dictionary, he'd also read the ten words above and below it. One of his favorite readings as a youngster was the encyclopedia.

He didn't read for any special thing—he'd just go through it, reading for pleasure. And he retained *everything*. He had the most retentive memory going. He read everything that he encountered. Everything!

You said that you didn't read science fiction that much. Did Stanley?

I guess he did. He usually bought the magazines, but buying them wasn't a *must* with him. Nor did he buy other pulp magazines.[34]

But didn't he try his hand at romance stories?

Yes, he wrote some, but he wasn't very proud of them. He thought it'd be quick money. But we didn't send even one of them in.[35] Maybe we just didn't get around to it, but I know. . . . You see, I took care of that.

You handled the business side?

Yeah. As I said, it was up to me to make things happen.

It's very strange that he could be so very unconscious of money, and yet he wrote golf-club romances and things like that, and we never sent any of them in. Now, in retrospect, it's sort of amazing. He wrote 'em, I typed 'em up, and we didn't do anything about 'em. He must not have been proud of them. We let them sit and never sent one in.

Why did you decide to send in "A Martian Odyssey"?

To me, "A Martian Odyssey" was an excellent yarn. It's just such a *smooth* thing. Anybody could enjoy reading that. You don't have to be a fan of science fiction to like it. Stanley's writing was always polished. He never *tried* to polish it, he just wrote polished.

Did he do many drafts or revisions?

Never any! If you looked at his handwritten manuscripts you would see that every word is the same as in published form. One draft! I typed it and I never changed a thing.

That's absolutely amazing!

I know it! I guess that's why he was shocked at what poor writing was being published. I think that was the reason he blew his stack when "A Martian Odyssey" had his name on it, because who would think that anybody who really knew how to write would write *science fiction?*

He didn't want to be associated with that stuff!

Doesn't it sound like it? But he got over that. I don't remember how I worked around him to calm him down that day. Instead of being upset, I was a little bit amused!

Did he go on for some time over his name being used?

Enough so that I would remember it very well! (Chuckles.) Storming up and down! Throwing his arms around! Running his hands through his hair! And I broke out laughing. He looked at me simply scandalized that I could laugh at something like that. Then he came over and knelt down and put his head in my lap and began laughing himself. . . . It was quite a life I had with him.

What were some of his favorite activities? What did he like to do?

God, he liked everything! He liked sports, he liked eating, he liked music, he liked lectures. Anything intellectual he liked— without making a point of it. We went to lectures just because it was what we were interested in. That's why we went to hear Schoolman on psychiatry.

What were some of his dislikes? Were there things he just could not abide?

No, things he didn't like he could just ignore. He didn't bother with 'em. Nothing ever really worried him. He was a very easy-going chap who felt things would always come out okay.

Did noise bother him when he was trying to write?

No, but there was no noise around. One day the downstairs neighbor came up and said, "Wasn't that a terrible thing last night!" We said, "What?" And she said, "Why, the fire engines right under our windows here!" At first we thought she was kidding, but no. We'd slept through the whole thing!

Sounds like Stanley was very placid, very tolerant, very easy-going.

Very tolerant, very easy-going—but never placid. That'd be the *last* word I'd use to describe him. But, quite a guy!

How did the two of you know "A Martian Odyssey" was so popular? Did you read the responses in Wonder Stories *magazine?*

Well, first from Mort Weisinger. Then we bought some of the following issues of the magazines to read the letters from the readers there. We were very gratified that the story was mentioned and that sort of made up for the *terrible* thing of his name being attached to it.

So he decided to write science fiction after that?

Yes, though he still went on writing other things. But, first we had to make a living. We were too proud to. . . .

How did you make a living at this time? You mentioned that the movie theater didn't pan out and that book with Schoolman fell through. How were the two of you making a living?

That's a good question. I mentioned I worked for four different newspapers. At that time, $50 a week was a lot of money. See, you're used to what things cost now-a-days. But back then I could go into the produce store and buy what they called a "soup bunch"—a bunch of vegetables to make soup, two or three tomatoes, a handful (and the grocers had big hands!) of green beans, a couple of onions, celery, and a few potatoes—all that together for 10 cents! Instead of making soup, I'd separate these out for different meals. So, we didn't have to stint.

We'd share cigarettes, as I've said. Stanley'd come in and say, "Let's take a break." He'd light a cigarette, take a couple of puffs, and we'd pass it back and forth. The way they do with marijuana now, we did with tobacco.

We didn't even realize we were being frugal. We just did what we had to do, and that was that. We also received gifts from our parents, and that was a very big help. For the last few years, my parents owned an apartment building in Milwaukee, and we had an apartment there for free. *That* was a big help. But, it was always a little bit of a hurt to me that we accepted that, but there was no choice. So, with free rent and the little ol' money I was making, we were able to get by.

So Stanley could spend most of his time writing . . .

He spent all of his time writing. We wanted to have a baby, so we'd started saving, because we knew it cost about $1,500 between the hospital stay and the doctor, etc. But that money went toward him going to Chicago for treatment, the hospital bills there, and so on. It was a very handy amount to have then. It was really ironic.

Did Stanley ever receive letters from editors asking him to revise stories?

No. Even in "The Lady Dances," the first thing he sold to King Features, they didn't change anything, just cut it up for serialization. By the way, the money from that was very important to us. That was real money in those days.

Did you ever write to any editor who didn't pay for Stanley's stories asking for payment?

Oh, I wrote to Gernsback, but we never got any satisfaction.

Did he reply at all?

I never wrote to him *directly.* I wrote to Mort Weisinger and *he* went after Gernsback. Just a few years ago I read something about Ziff-Davis selling out to somebody. It was after we retired to the desert, which was eighteen years ago. When Eugene retired we travelled at first, but he had a heart attack and now, with my fractured hip, our travelling days seem to be over, so we bought this condominium.

Anyway, after we retired here, I wrote to Ziff-Davis and said, "Now that you're dissolving yourself, I wonder if you'd like to pay a long-standing debt. I think it'd be only fair if we were paid *something* for The New Adam, at least the $500 that Ray Palmer collected."

I never got an answer. Of course, I didn't expect one, but I thought I'd just let 'em know there was a debt outstanding and they'd been unfair.[36]

When you sent "A Martian Odyssey" off, Mort Weisinger wasn't your agent. . . .

No, no. I sent it direct. But after that, everything went through his hands. He had a partner, Julius Schwartz, but Mort was the one I knew and dealt with. Mort was an awfully decent guy, but very naive.

Oh, God! (Chuckles.) I have to laugh. He sent us a letter, or Henry Kay, Eugene's brother, who was a realtor in New York, sent us a letter saying that Mort had published a story about a ten thousand-dollar bank note and how it passed on and on because no one had change for it.[37] In the story, it also passed through the hands of Henry Kay.

So, we were in New York and I called Mort saying I was Miss So-and-So at Fairchild, So-on and So-Forth law office. "I want to tell you," I said, "that we're serving papers on you because you used our client's name, Henry Kay, without permission."

Well, you could just *see* Mort beginning to sweat! I kept on feeding him this line of garbage and got him really hysterical. Well, God! He almost died! He was going through the whole thing with explanations. After about ten minutes I couldn't help but feel sorry for him and I began laughing and I said, "Oh, Lord, Mort! How you can bite on things!" So, I felt he was really naive in a lot of things, but an awfully nice guy.

And, my God, he made *use* of the writing field! He called us up one time to say he was going to be in Chicago for Sara Lee pastries. Sara Lee wanted a short biography of herself to be enclosed with her cakes, so she'd contacted Mort to come and interview her and write it. So, sure, he went out, and he got good money for it.

He'd often have things published in the *Reader's Digest*. They used to say, "Mort, we want such-and-such a story about a town in Italy," or whatever. "We have arrangements with some other magazine to publish it, and afterward they'll condense it

for us." They'd pay Mort a fee plus expenses to have a great trip!
He did a lot of that stuff.

*Sounds like you were very good friends with Mort. Was
Stanley also good friends with him?*

Stanley never met him! After "A Martian Odyssey" was published, we got a letter from Mort saying that he was very
impressed with this story, and if Stanley didn't have an agent,
he'd like to represent him.[38] We thought, "Goody, goody,
goody!" and, of course, answered "Yes." Oh goody, goody,
goody! Mort told me later that he didn't have any clients at the
time—he was just selling magazine subscriptions door-to-door.

Any time a magazine accepted a story—Hearst or King Features, anything—they sent a special air mail letter. Our postman
knew that meant good news, so he used a special ring when he
rang our bell. When King Features accepted, that was the first
time we had a long distant call from a publisher. Our telephone
was in the dining room and there was an operator calling for
"Marge Stanley." I went in there to take the message. They said
they'd accepted "The Lady Dances," and were sending a contract
to sign. When I hung up I screamed, "Stanley, come here quick!"

I told him about it, and we were jumping up and down. Our
dining room was being painted at the time, and the painter was
up on the step ladder doing the ceiling. Well, *he* got excited too
and began jumping up and down crying, "I'm seeing a live
author! I'm seeing a live author!" And he fell off the ladder and
broke his leg! So, we put him in the car and drove him to Dr.
Kay's office to have his leg set.

You know, the basis of "The Lady Dances" was a true story
from Schoolman. Of course, what wasn't told in that was the
reason she needed a psychiatrist, and that is how Stanley got hold
of the story. Stanley placed it in the South Sea Islands, but they
had nothing to do with it. It was simply a complete disguise.

Of all the things Stanley wrote, what is your favorite?

I think "A Martian Odyssey," because that is a very sweet story that will live forever. Not that I like it *because* I feel it's going to live forever; I mean that no matter what the circumstances are in civilization, *that* is a story any person could enjoy.

Did you like everything Stanley wrote?

Of course, especially the poetry, *particularly* the poetry he wrote to me! All the books he gave me would always have a poem he wrote in the front. When he died I had a line of his poetry engraved on his watch and gave it to Dr. Sam Grauman. For another cousin, Tony Myer, I had a short line of Stanley's poetry engraved on a gold pocket knife. I always loved his poetry. He really did magnificent stuff.

Has his poetry ever been collected and published?

No, no, no.[39]

Does it still exist?

It's in The Trunk, and it's in my books, which have been divided between the three children. Originally, you see, Eugene and I had a five-bedroom house. Every bedroom, as well as every room downstairs, was lined with bookshelves from floor to ceiling. When we broke up our big house we had to dispose of many things, and so we gave the books to our children. My personal books, from when Stanley and I were going together, and after we were married, all had his poems on the front pages.

Did Stanley write love poetry when he was courting you?

Of course! Why do you suppose his poetry was my favorite? He was very romantic that way.

You both once ran a movie house. Did you go to many movies yourselves?

Well, after we bought it and things went haywire, we had to run the projectors ourselves. That was for only a very short time. It was a disappointment, but we didn't go to pieces over it.

Did you and Stanley like to watch movies?

I guess so. But we didn't have a favorite movie star.

I'll bet you liked Charlie Chaplin!

Oh, I *adored* Charlie Chaplin! His pantomime was fantastic. Who could *not* have liked him?

Exactly! And did Stanley like Chaplin, also?

I'm sure he did, but don't forget, movies cost money, and we weren't about to spend money on *that.* Instead, we preferred to go without them, and a few other things, and instead go to the legit.

You liked going to the theater, then?

Oh, yes, yes, yes. And to concerts.

Did he like Shakespeare?

Oh, yes. Helen Hayes used to do wonderful Shakespeare. . . .
Oh, hey! This makes me think—I've talked to you about a lot of personal things. You have too much Marge in this.

. . . .

Of course, so in talking about Stanley, there's going to be a little bit of Marge mixed in there!

When you ask Marge about Stanley, she can't let go of him. The great thing is, there's a pride in Stanley which Eugene has which is beautiful. It's just terrific. He was pleased I'd be talking to you about Stanley. This morning when he came to kiss me good-bye, what he whispered to me was very nice. You see, Stanley is part of us. There's never been any resentment. It's just beautiful.

I like to hear that. I wonder, are there any photos of you and Stanley still remaining?

I don't recall bumping into any for years, now. Originally, yes. But by degrees your family grows, you run out of space for things. Then, when we moved from the big house, I turned The Trunk over to my son. He still hears from Ackerman. It's funny, I must be around the corner from Forrest Ackerman, but I've never called him. . . . (Coughs.)

. . . .

Why don't we talk about Ralph Milne Farley?

Frankly, this idea of Stanley having done a lot of work with him is *not* so. It was only a couple of times. Stanley *never* saw him outside the Fictioneer meetings. Larry Keating was the only Fictioneer he was really close friends with. He didn't know any of them when he first went to the meetings, but he and Larry hit it off.[40]

You might be interested in know a bit about Larry. I know he's dead by now, because the last time I saw him he was a shuffling old man, and this was before we left Milwaukee eighteen years ago. He started writing as a young man just to pass some time away. He had TB and was in a sanitarium. He was restless and so he began writing, never expecting to do anything with it. He ended up making his living that way.

Well, if Stanley never really met Farley. . . .

Oh, he met him at the Fictioneers' meetings. Evidently he said, "Let's do this story together." I recall it sort of vaguely, because of having done the typing. . . . Don't forget, I was busy with these four different papers I was working on, and there was a little bit of housekeeping, too. But I think there was the first half of a story, something about the sea. . . .

"Smothered Seas?"[41]

Yes. What Stanley did was write half of it and then send it to Farley. I guess he wrote the other half. I didn't pay much attention to it, really. And there was one other thing done by the two of 'em, but I don't remember what happened with it.

"Yellow Slaves" was another collaboration. . . .[42]

Well, I don't really remember anything about it. I just vaguely remember a sea story, but I have no idea what it was about.

Do you know whose idea it was to collaborate? Was it Stanley's?

No, it wasn't Stanley's. He got a kick out of the fact that this guy, who'd been doing it so long, said, "Let's do something together." But it was water off a duck's back.

So, Stanley didn't put much effort into the collaboration?

Oh, no.

How did Stanley feel in general about collaborations? Did he prefer to do things on his own?

Well, as I told you, he was his own man. But he got quite a kick out of. . . . I don't know how it came up at one of their Fictioneer meetings. Even when these were held at our place, I never joined in; in fact, I usually got out of the house. They'd go to each other's houses, and when they came to our apartment I just took off. I'd have the food prepared and then they were on their own.

Stanley also got a kick out of another of their ideas. They said what fun it'd be to take a plot and have the Fictioneer writers write their own story around it. Completely different stories in their own veins. Wasn't that a cute idea?

Did they ever do it?

I don't remember, because I can't recall anything of Stanley's which was done with a made-up plot. See, Stanley always did his plots before he started. He didn't outline them on paper, just in his head. He knew where he was going.

Did he also have the titles? Or wasn't that important?

I don't think it was particularly important to him, no.

Do you recall how Farley came to finish "The Dictator's Sister" after Stanley died?

I can't remember. You know, I was sort of in a complete haze at that time. It had been, how many months? From June until December. How I did my work, I don't know.

I just wondered how Farley fitted into that, since there were a number of collaborations. . . .

No, there was not a number! That, I assure you. If anything else had both names on it, it was a fake! Those are the only two I recall at all. I don't even remember typing the second one, the "slaves" thing. But, if I did, I did. I know there would be nothing else except those two.

And there was no one else that Stanley collaborated with at all?

No. Never.[43] You know, when you stop to think about it, his career was a very quick chapter. " A Martian Odyssey" was published in 1934 and in '35 he was gone! So, any other questions?

I just wanted to ask why you think Stanley had so many heroines in his stories, which was unusual for that time. In most of the stories of the thirties, especially in the pulp genre, women were clingy and weepy, sort of like Fay Wray in King Kong.

No, that wasn't his idea of a woman! A dame to him was a glamour princess, not a clinging woman. He was a very romantic person. This was a good part of his make-up. In fact, when he handed me the first section of "Black Margot,"[44] he put a fake front page on it which said, "Dedicated to the Original Black Margot." That was me. Romantic things were always going on.

NOTES

1. Ed Naha, *The Science Fictionary: An A-Z Guide to the World of Science Fiction Authors, Films, and TV Shows* (New York: Wideview Books, 1980), p. 355.

2. Frederik Pohl, *Science Fiction Chronicle* (January 1990): 30. Fan Norm Metcalf has taken issue with me—and those I cite—on this point by stating, "Edgar R. Burroughs' Barsoomians, George A. England's aliens from the fourth dimension in 'The Empire In the Air' (as described by Sam Moskowitz on pp. 388–90 of *Under the Moons of Mars* [I haven't read the story]), England's 'The Thing From—Outside,' Abraham Merritt's Snake Mother, and the whatevertheyweres in

Merritt's 'The Metal Monster' are all alien aliens of varying degrees of alienness." See *The Devil's Work* 2, no. 26 (January 1992): 206.

My answer is that these examples do not present us with aliens unique enough in their "basic ways of thinking and behaving," as Pohl said, to be truly alien to human understanding. For example, the Barsoomians of Edgar Rice Burroughs live on Mars which, except for lesser gravity, may as well be Earth and, despite skins of various hues and multiple arms, these "aliens" are not alien at all. They are really sword-wielding humans on Mars—indeed, the Earthman hero, John Carter, marries one and has children by her! So indistinguishable from humans are they, in fact, that Metcalf has himself long argued in his fanzines that John Carter was, in reality, an amnesiac Martian! And, certainly, none of the examples Metcalf cites had the paradigm-shifting impact on the field as did Weinbaum's Tweel.

3. Sam Moskowitz, "The Marketing of Stanley G. Weinbaum," *Fantasy Commentator* 7, no. 2 (Fall 1991): 104.

4. Quoted in Sam Moskowitz, *Explorers of the Infinite: Shapers of Science Fiction* (Cleveland and New York: The World Publishing Co., 1963), p. 298.

5. Lester Del Rey, *The World of Science Fiction: 1926-1976, The History of a Subculture* (New York: Ballantine Books, 1979), p. 84.

6. Isaac Asimov, "The Second Nova," in *The Best of Stanley G. Weinbaum* (New York: Ballantine Books, 1974), pp. x, ix. Not only did every writer try to imitate him, but editors wanted him to *imitate himself*! Charles Hornig has said that Hugo Gernsback left the editorial work of *Wonder Stories* entirely up to him—except for those notorious European reprints of authors like Curt Siodmak! However, he acknowledged that Weinbaum was an exception. Not only did Gernsback write the acceptance letter to Weinbaum for "A Martian Odyssey," he also wrote the *rejection* letter for "Pygmalion's Spectacles." On December 4, 1934, Gernsback wrote to Weinbaum saying, "This, while a nice story, I believe considerably inferior to your previous two stories ["Valley of Dreams" was the "Odyssey" sequel], not that it is not a good story, but because it is not your *type of story*. [Emphasis in original.] Editors, as a tribe, would like their authors . . . to stay within their domain. . . . Your former true stories struck an entirely new note in science fiction. Not only the editors, but the readers too were favorably

impressed with this type. Now then, the reader will expect you forever
to write this type of story because it made a success. Any deviation from
the formula will be disastrous in your future writings, and I would urge
you to keep to the old formula if you possibly can." See Stanley G.
Weinbaum Papers, Special Collections, Temple University, Philadelphia. Also photo-reproduced in *Fantasy Commentator* 7, no. 2 (Fall
1991): 113. How discouraging Gernsback's desire to have Weinbaum
repeat his "formula" "forever" must have been to Weinbaum—indeed,
to any writer! In this case, however, "Pygmalion's Spectacles" *did*
appear in *Wonder Stories* (June 1935), as Hornig had already written to
Weinbaum accepting the story. Evidently, Gernsback acquiesced in the
contractual *fait accompli* once he learned of it.

7. Robert Bloch, "Stanley G. Weinbaum: A Personal Recollection," in *The Best of Stanley G. Weinbaum,* pp. 301-302.

8. This story began life as "The Dictator's Sister," and Weinbaum
had completed a first draft before his death. He turned it over for completion to Ralph Milne Farley, a fellow member of The Milwaukee Fictioneers, the writing group to which he belonged. On December 14,
1935, the day of Weinbaum's death, Laurence Keating (another Fictioneer) phoned Farley with the news of Weinbaum's death. Farley
immediately wrote a letter to Margaret Weinbaum, the widow,
expressing condolences. "I believe that [Weinbaum] was on the way to
excel Jules Verne," he wrote. Then, "With your permission, I shall continue to use Stan's name on 'The Dictator's Sister,' and shall split the fee
(if any) with you." Farley to Margaret Weinbaum, December 14, 1935,
Stanley G. Weinbaum Papers, Special Collections, Temple University,
Philadelphia. When "The Dictator's Sister" was finally published as
"Revolution of 1950" in the October and November 1938 issues of
Amazing Stories, it appeared under Weinbaum's name alone, although
editor Ray Palmer thanked Farley for "adding the finishing touches."

9. *Amazing Stories* (October 1938): 142. For those interested,
biographical information can also be found in the following: *After Ten
Years: A Tribute to Stanley G. Weinbaum,* Gerry de la Ree and Sam
Moskowitz, eds., 1945, which contains a eulogy by his sister, Helen;
"Stanley G. Weinbaum: A Comprehensive Appraisal," by Sam
Moskowitz, *Fantasy Commentator* 5.3, no. 5 (Winter 1951), which
also contains a checklist of his works; "The Wonder of Weinbaum," by

Sam Moskowitz, in his *A Martian Odyssey and Other Classics of Science Fiction* (New York: Lancer Books, 1962); and "Dawn of Fame: The Career of Stanley G. Weinbaum," by Sam Moskowitz, in his *Explorers of The Infinite* (New York: Ballantine Books, 1963).

As for the fiction itself, in addition to the above cited Ballantine Books edition of *The Best of Stanley G. Weinbaum,* which contains half of Weinbaum's short stories, all of his twenty-two science fiction short stories are collected in *A Martian Odyssey and Other Science Fiction Tales,* Sam Moskowitz, ed. (Westport, Conn.: Hyperion Press, 1974). His editorially-cut novelette "Dawn of Flame" is included in *The Mammoth Book of Classic SF: Short Novels of the 1930s,* Isaac Asimov, Charles G. Waugh, and Martin H. Greenberg, eds. (New York: Carroll & Graf, 1988). However, the complete novel, *The Black Flame*, of which "Dawn of Flame" is a part, was not available in its original and uncut form until 1995 when Tachyon Publications of San Francisco published their restored version with an introduction, "The Saga of the Black Flame," by Sam Moskowitz.

The last "new" Weinbaum short story that will ever be published, which I found in manuscript among his papers, is a hard-boiled detective story, "The King's Watch," published as a chapbook by the Posthumous Press (Rochester, Minn., 1994), copyright Eric Leif Davin; I am also now the literary executor of the Weinbaum Estate. It contains as an introduction a new memoir and evaluation of Weinbaum by Robert Bloch, who also signed each copy. This was perhaps the last thing Bloch wrote, as he died September 23, 1994, at age seventy-six. He was dying as he wrote the memoir and he completed it and the signings as a last labor of love for Stanley Weinbaum.

10. Bringing with him at least his father and his brother, Henry, as we discover later, and possibly more of his family.

11. I later arranged for the contents of this trunk to be turned over to Thomas Whitehead, Head of Special Collections at Temple University, where the Stanley G. Weinbaum Papers can now be found. Included in the trunk was Weinbaum's business correspondence, which was the basis of Sam Moskowitz's article, "The Marketing of Stanley G. Weinbaum," *Fantasy Commentator* 7, no. 2 (Fall 1991). Also in the trunk was the original and complete draft of *The Black Flame,* which was published for the first time in its entirety by Tachyon Publications

in 1995. *The King's Watch*, published by Posthumous Press, 1994, was actually not in the trunk, but in a bureau drawer in Marge's bedroom. Also in the drawer was the manuscript of a romance short story, "Don't Tell Tony," which Marge wanted never to be published, as she felt it not up to Stanley's high standards.

12. Chicago fan and Weinbaum champion Raymond A. Palmer became managing editor of *Amazing Stories,* published by Ziff-Davis, in 1938. Ziff-Davis also published hardcover books and Palmer convinced them to publish *The New Adam* in 1939. According to John Clute and Peter Nicholls, it "is a painstaking account of the career of a potential superman who grows up as a kind of 'feral child' in human society; it stands at the head of a tradition of stories which drastically altered the role allotted to superhumans in pulp SF." *The Encyclopedia of Science Fiction* (New York: St. Martin's Griffin, 1995), p. 1308.

13. There were ten men in the Milwaukee Fictioneers. Laurence Keating was the Western writer, quite popular in the thirties. Besides Weinbaum, those interested in science fiction and fantasy included Raymond A. Palmer; Arthur R. Tofte, who was an occasional contributor to the SF magazines; Roger Sherman Hoar, a Harvard-educated mathematics and engineering teacher and former Wisconsin State Senator who published several SF novels in *Argosy* under the pen name of "Ralph Milne Farley"; and eighteen-year-old Robert Bloch. The other writers wrote detective, romance, and other genre-generated stories.

According to Bloch, "It was the purpose of the Fictioneers to act as a sort of primitive writers' workshop for local professionals. Meeting every two weeks on a rotation basis from one member's home to another's, they discussed story-problems, pitched plots and asked for help on hang-ups." Robert Bloch, "Stanley Weinbaum: A Memoir," in Stanley G. Weinbaum, *The King's Watch* (Rochester, Minn.: Posthumous Press, 1994), p. viii, copyright Eric Leif Davin.

14. Indeed, he was, some of it science fiction. In 1917, as the Great War continued to rage in Europe, Weinbaum had published a story, "The Lost Battle," in *The Mercury,* a high school magazine. In it, he described the end of the war in the year 1921.

15. This notebook was in the Denver trunk and I have examined it. It is indeed, unchanged word for unchanged word, the beginning of *The New Adam*, which is also the title it bears. It is also one of Wein-

baum's college notebooks, containing notes for some of his courses. Sam Moskowitz disputed this dating of *The New Adam*. Based upon the sophistication of the novel and references to it in some of Weinbaum's 1934 correspondence, he felt it must have been written in 1934, when Weinbaum was a more mature writer. See his "The Marketing of Stanley G. Weinbaum," *Fantasy Commentator* 7, no. 2 (Fall 1991). In this, Moskowitz appeared to be mistaken.

16. Here she seems to be conflating two separate Weinbaum stories, "Pygmalion's Spectacles" and "The Adaptive Ultimate," the last of which featured a woman dying of tuberculosis and who became very "adaptable" after treatment.

17. "The Planet of Doubt," *Astounding Stories* (October 1935).

18. *Natural History,* by John George W. Woods (1827–1889), was first published in Britain in 1853. It appeared in numerous editions, including several adapted for young people, and remained in print until 1937.

19. "Tidal Moon," *Thrilling Wonder Stories* (December 1938), was published by Stanley and Helen Weinbaum. Supposedly, Helen Kasson, Stanley's sister, had taken a three-hundred-word beginning written by Stanley and finished it, although there was no outline for the rest of the story. It is considered a trivial story.

A more substantial story is Helen Weinbaum's "Double Destiny," which Charles D. Hornig published in *Science Fiction Quarterly* in 1940. As we know, Hornig was mostly getting rejects from other magazines thru Julius Schwartz, erstwhile partner to Mort Weisinger. Thus, the stories weren't all that good. However, says Mike Ashley, "If any story stands out above this mediocrity it is "Double Destiny" by Helen Weinbaum, sister of the late Stanley G. Weinbaum. Although dreadfully overwritten, it has a curious power all its own, telling of a villainous super scientist and his double from an advanced civilization in the past. A topical story, it is preoccupied with the ominous health hazards of nuclear radiation and with the plans of Fascists to dominate the world." See Mike Ashley and Marshall B. Tymn, eds., *Science Fiction, Fantasy, and Weird Fiction Magazines* (Westport, Conn.: Greenwood Press, 1985), p. 546.

20. Sam Moskowitz obtained photocopies of the complete financial records of the Schwartz-Weisinger Literary Agency, which represented Weinbaum in most of his SF sales after "A Martian Odyssey."

After examining them, he informed me that they show a payment of $400 in 1939, the year Ziff-Davis published *The New Adam*, by Ray Palmer to the Weinbaum Estate for all book and magazine rights to the novel. (For this reason, no additional payment was due when the novel was serialized in Ziff-Davis's *Amazing Stories* during 1943.)

21. This, also, does not seem to be the case. Weinbaum's business correspondence in the Denver Trunk, now at Temple University, tells a different story. True, there was initial tardiness on Hugo Gernsback's part to remit payment for "A Martian Odyssey" and four subsequent Weinbaum stories he acquired, "Valley of Dreams," "Pygmalion's Spectacles," "The Worlds of If," and "The Ideal." According to Weinbaum's calculations, he was owed $215 for the five stories at the official payment rate of a half cent per word. After Mort Weisinger became Weinbaum's agent, he harassed Gernsback for payment and seems to have been successful—to a degree. In a July 10, 1935 letter to Samuel Scheff, treasurer of Gernsback Publications, Weinbaum agreed to a payment schedule for all five stories of four monthly payments, beginning in July, of $25, $50, $50, and $45, for a total of $170, to be paid to Weisinger, as his agent. Further, it seems that Gernsback agreed to pay on acceptance for all future stories by Weinbaum.

Gernsback seems to have kept to the schedule—and perhaps speeded it up. In an August 16, 1935 letter, Weisinger wrote Weinbaum saying, "I am assured by *Wonder* that you'll get the balance due you in about a month. Minus our commission, that makes $58 due you on your *Wonder* account." On August 18, 1935, Julius Schwartz wrote Weinbaum saying, "Since Gernsback came across with the checks, I have let him have, 'The Point of View.' If it's accepted, they'll have to pay $25 on acceptance, as per agreement."

On August 19, 1935, Charles Hornig wrote Weinbaum informing him that he had accepted "The Point of View." On August 20, 1935, Scheff mailed Weinbaum a check for $25 for the story, indicating that Gernsback was honoring the agreement to pay on acceptance.

This is an example of how Gernsback's reputation for nonpayment became well-established in the public mind—even though, at least in Weinbaum's case, he wasn't guilty!

22. Weinbaum, however, never did understand why it was so popular. On November 21, 1934, he wrote to Mort Weisinger saying, "As

for 'A Martian Odyssey,' I'm a little puzzled as to just why that damn thing did take so well; I thought it was lousy." See Stanley G. Weinbaum Papers, Special Collections, Temple University, Philadelphia.

Indeed, Weinbaum thought so little of his masterpiece that he seems to have given away the manuscript to a fan. His correspondence contains a letter from a Texas fan asking for a signed original manuscript. There is also a further letter from this fan thanking Weinbaum for sending such a manuscript. The manuscript in question is not named, but "A Martian Odyssey" was not among the original manuscripts found in the Denver Trunk.

23. "The Adaptive Ultimate," *Astounding Stories* (November 1935).

24. This was Laurence A. Keating, President of the Milwaukee Fictioneers, who wrote the Introduction to the memorial volume of Weinbaum's fiction published by the Fictioneers after his death. Later, for many years, Keating wrote the lead "novel" for *Complete Wild West,* a companion magazine to *Amazing Stories.*

25. These were indeed Chicagoan Otto Binder (who was about ten years younger than Weinbaum, being born August 26, 1911) and Chicago fans William Dellenback and Jack Darrow, as confirmed by Weinbaum's correspondence in the Denver Trunk. All three drove up from Chicago to visit Weinbaum in July of 1935, the same month Dr. Kay diagnosed Weinbaum's lung cancer and six months before he died. Weinbaum, still puzzled as to why people liked his stories, asked the three for elucidation. In a July 25, 1935, letter to Weinbaum, Otto Binder said, "Our visit to Milwaukee will always be a pleasant memory to us. . . . You wanted to know what in your stories makes them so universally liked by the science fiction reading public, and the answer is—realism and humor." See Stanley G. Weinbaum Papers, Special Collections, Temple University, Philadelphia.

26. Although their editorial offices usually forwarded mail at the request of the writer, it was not the policy of most pulp magazines to send authors specific comments received on their stories. They assumed authors read such letters as they were published in the readers' columns—and there were many such letters in praise of Weinbaum.

27. Weinbaum died on Saturday, December 14, 1935. While in his New York synagogue that day, Julius Schwartz received a telegram

from Ray Palmer in Milwaukee saying, "Weinbaum died this morning." Schwartz wept and said kaddish for Weinbaum. See Sam Moskowitz, *Explorers of the Infinite: Shapers of Science Fiction* (Cleveland and New York: World Publishing Co., 1963), p. 308. Charles Hornig wrote an obituary of Weinbaum which appeared in the April 1936 *Wonder Stories,* the last he edited. F. Orlin Tremaine, editor of *Astounding Stories,* also noted his passing.

Weinbaum's friends and colleagues in the Fictioneers sought to preserve his memory by issuing a memorial collection of his fiction soon after his death. New York fan printer Conrad H. Ruppert typeset and printed 250 copies of this 315-page volume, entitled *Dawn of Flame and Other Stories.* He mailed the sheets to Ray Palmer in Milwaukee, who had them bound in black leather with gold lettering. This was the first publication of Weinbaum's "Dawn of Flame." See Moskowitz, *Explorers of the Infinite,* p. 309.

28. Dr. Eugene Kay died in 1992 following a long illness, four years after this conversation.

29. Horace Victor Gregory was born April 10, 1898, the son of Henry Bottom and Anna Catherine (Henkel) Gregory. He began studies at the University of Wisconsin in the summer of 1919, and was graduated in the class of 1923 (Weinbaum was in the class of 1924). On August 25, 1925, he married another Wisconsin graduate, Marya Zaturenska, by whom he had two children. He received a number of awards for his verse, including *Poetry* magazine's Lyric Prize (1928) and the Bollinger Prize for Poetry (1965). He died on March 11, 1982. His autobiography (*A Cycle of Memories,* 1961) does not mention Weinbaum. I thank A. Langley Searles for the information on Gregory and Zaturenska.

30. During infancy Gregory contracted tuberculosis of the bone. This affected the upper vertebrae of his spine, which caused paralysis of the left hand and foot, and a tremor in the right hand.

31. Marya Zaturenska was born in Russia September 12, 1902. She emigrated here in 1910, and in 1914 became a naturalized U.S. citizen. She was graduated from the University of Wisconsin Library School in 1925, and received the Pulitzer Prize for poetry in 1938. She died on January 19, 1982.

32. Chuck Rothman and Fred Lerner suggested to me that this was

undoubtedly Yaddo, in Saratoga Springs, NY. The description and location are both close fits.

33. This was "The Adaptive Ultimate." There is more on the movie career of this story in my chapter on Kurt Neumann, who directed the Hollywood version. Marge and her daughters probably saw the live TV version, which she conflated with the later feature film.

34. In Weinbaum's novel, "The Mad Brain," published as *The Dark Other*, he mentions H. P. Lovecraft's *The Necronomicon* indicating that he was familiar with Lovecraft's fiction, which then appeared in the fantasy pulp, *Weird Tales*. "The Mad Brain" may have been written as early as 1927-28.

35. On June 1, 1933, King Features Syndicate, Inc., bought for syndication Weinbaum's "The Lady Dances," a love story about a Russian girl in the South Seas. On December 27, 1933, King Features rejected Weinbaum's romance, "Without Love," as too, "dryad-satyr for general newspaper syndication." On February 17, 1934, King Features rejected his romance novel, "Mistress Money." It was also rejected by several book publishers. When Desmond Hall became the editor at *Mademoiselle,* Weinbaum sent him two love stories, "Girl in Love" and "Don't Tell Tony," both of which Hall rejected because they focussed on "the old plot of secret love." Weinbaum's agent, Julius Schwartz, also submitted them unsuccessfully to *Serenade,* a slick published by the Woolworth store chain. Schwartz and Weisinger were also attempting to sell Weinbaum's other two love stories, "The Love Mode" and "She Tried to be Bad." These were turned over to agent Lurton Blassingame, who specialized in selling to the slick magazines. He wanted revisions. On September 10, 1935—well into his SF career, ill, and only three months before his death—Weinbaum wrote Blassingame promising to make the requested revisions. On September 16, 1935, King Features rejected the synopsis of "Sensation Girl," which Weinbaum was going to write with Laurence Keating. On November 8, 1935, Blassingame wrote that he liked Weinbaum's new love story, "For Love or Money," and thought it "marketable." It is evident that Weinbaum continued writing and submitting love stories for the entire duration of his science fiction career. See Stanley G. Weinbaum Papers, Special Collections, Temple University, Philadelphia.

This and the following footnote highlight the fallibility of memory and why oral history always has to be checked against the record.

36. See notes 20 and 21. As we now know from both Weinbaum's business correspondence at Temple University and the financial records of the Julius Schwartz-Mort Weisinger Literary Agency, not only did Gernsback pay for "A Martian Odyssey" and all other Weinbaum stories he published, but Ziff-Davis paid the Weinbaum Estate $400 in 1939 for all book and magazine rights to *The New Adam*.

37. This sounds suspiciously like Mark Twain's short story "The One-Million Pound Bank Note," *Century Magazine* (January 1893). It made its first appearance in book form in a collection of Twain's stories called *The One-Million Pound Bank Note and Other New Stories* (New York: C. L. Webster, 1893).

If Weisinger passed off a variant of Twain's story as his own, it's possible he may well have seen it as a great joke and boasted of it in a letter to Marge. It would not have been the first time he'd boasted of literary "jokes" he'd carried off successfully. In an October 15, 1934 letter Weisinger wrote to Stanley, he said, "The January issue of *Super Detective Stories* will carry a short-short of mine, 'Tell Tale Ticket,' under the *nom-de-plume* of Tom Erwin Geris. The reason I used a pen-name was because they have a department there offering twenty dollars for the best short-short by a *new* writer. I won, though illegitimately. But, what the hell, twenty bucks is twenty bucks." See Stanley G. Weinbaum Papers, Special Collections, Temple University, Philadelphia.

38. Actually, this letter, of June 18, 1934, was from Mort's partner, Julius Schwartz. See Stanley G. Weinbaum Papers, Special Collections, Temple University, Philadelphia.

39. Actually, all of Weinbaum's poetry published in the student literary magazine at the University of Wisconsin *has* been collected and published, although without Marge's knowledge or authorization. This was done by Randal Kirsch, aka Randy Everts, aka R. Alain Everts, a Madison fan, as a publication of his small specialty press, The Strange Co. These poems are in the public domain and so this was technically legal—but Everts never told Marge about the publication or showed it to her, even when he later visited her at her home in California. After the Everts visit, I gave Marge a copy of this volume.

40. In October 1934, at Mort Weisinger's urging, Weinbaum joined the American Fiction Guild, an organization for professional pulp magazine writers, to which many science fiction authors belonged. It was organized into regional chapters, with the Milwaukee chapter, which Weinbaum was then affiliated with, being known as "The Milwaukee Fictioneers." Raymond A. Palmer, another Milwaukee science fiction writer, became a member of the Fictioneers at about the same time and soon paid Weinbaum a visit. See note 13 for more information on the Fictioneers and Ralph Milne Farley.

41. *Astounding Stories* (January 1936), which, according to Weinbaum's business correspondence, Weinbaum wrote with Farley in June–July 1935.

42. A detective story, it was published in *True Gang Life* (February 1936). Weinbaum worked on it at about the same time he collaborated with Farley on "Smothered Seas." Then there was the collaboration "The Dictator's Sister." On October 14, 1935, Weinbaum wrote to Julius Schwartz saying, "Farley and I are talking over another collaboration, and I expect to turn out the first draft of it while I am having the next series of X-Ray treatments. I figure that since X-Ray treatments shoot the devil out of you, I might as well spend the time on a first draft for Farley, since it will all be gone over anyway." This story was finished by Farley after Weinbaum's death and published as "The Revolution of 1950" under Weinbaum's name alone in *Amazing Stories* (October & November 1938). See Stanley G. Weinbaum Papers, Special Collections, Temple University, Philadelphia.

43. On July 14, 1935, Schwartz asked Weinbaum to contribute a short installment of about eight hundred words to a round-robin story, "The Challenge From Beyond," for the third anniversary issue of *Fantasy Magazine*. Other authors included C. L. Moore and E. E. Smith. Weinbaum did and the story appeared in the September 1935 issue. See Stanley G. Weinbaum Papers, Special Collections, Temple University, Philadelphia.

44. Published as "Dawn of Flame," part of *The Black Flame*, in which "Black Margot" was renamed the "Black Flame." In January 1946, female fan Jim-E. Daugherty published a feminist SF fanzine entitled *Black Flames*. In her editorial she wrote, "Once upon a time, the story goes, there lived an outstanding, wise and beautiful, Amazon-

type woman. A woman named 'Margaret of Urbs.' Black Flame was the title given her, which stood for authority and power, and also for the raven black hair that crowned her exquisite features and head. She excelled in every field, over man and woman.

"Margaret of Urbs lived in the first stages of science fiction and has become a legend among fans. This supreme character was created by Stanley G. Weinbaum in *Startling Stories,* 1939. The editor dedicates this mag to Mr. Weinbaum's memory and to *The Black Flame*, being the first SF story that, when she was first introduced to the field, left such an individual and vivid impression among the stories she had read.

"All stories and articles will be by Wo-fans only, therefore an S will be added—Black Flames—which will stand for many women, whereas, if it were not added, the name would represent only one."

4.

FROM WISCONSIN TO MARS

A Conversation with
Raymond Z. Gallun

Astronomers, probing toward the outer reaches of the solar system with their telescopes, had just seen some tremendous and unexplained phenomena in the vicinity of the planet Saturn. The orbits of all of its many moons had become elongated in one direction, and its rings, pulled out of shape by the same unknown forces, were disintegrating to form a nebulous haze to one side of the planet. Gaseous Saturn, itself, was bulging ominously; and there was evidence of gigantic explosions taking place beneath the veil of its tremendous atmosphere.

It was as though some terrific gravitational force were being applied to the planet's entire system. But of any invading heavenly body that might cause such colossal distortion, or, in fact, any distortion at all, there was not the slightest evidence. No faint speck of unknown identity had intruded into the pattern of the stars. And the utter, senseless ruthlessness of what was happening denied the theory that it was the work of an intelligent agent. Though there was no discoverable cause, it seemed rather a manifestation of the mad caprice of nature.

Finally something had come which was even more spectac-

183

ular than preceding events. Titan, heaviest of all Saturn's satel-
lites, had exploded, dying space with the red flame of its still
fiery heart.
        —Raymond Z. Gallun, "Godson of Almarlu" (1936)

WHEN STANLEY G. WEINBAUM INTRODUCED THE charming and sympathetic alien Tweel with his short story "A Martian Odyssey" in the July 1934 issue of *Wonder Stories*, he revolutionized science fiction. Although there were a few exceptions, the dominant mode for depicting aliens was as antagonistic and hostile. But Weinbaum presented a sympathetic and appealing alien. As if a new world had been revealed, other writers soon began portraying aliens in this light as a flood of imitators followed where Weinbaum led.

Fellow Wisconsin author Raymond Z. Gallun, whose story "Old Faithful" appeared in the December 1934 *Astounding Stories,* seemed to be one of them. His story portrayed a friendly and sympathetic Martian and was instantly popular—fans liked it so much Gallun had to write two sequels in order to satisfy reader demand.

But Gallun is instead illustrative of the fact that the sympathetic alien was an idea whose time had come, for he was not imitating Weinbaum. Indeed, but for the vagaries of the publishing world, Gallun's story might have appeared first, and Weinbaum would be seen today as an imitator of another's pathbreaking renunciation of a science fiction cliché. Gallun had written "Old Faithful" in early 1932, almost three years before. Upon completion, he sent it to T. O'Conor Sloane, then editor of *Amazing Stories* and perhaps the most conservative and unimaginative editor in the field. Sloane held the manuscript for over a year before returning it without comment. Thinking his idea was too much against the grain of the genre to receive a sympathetic reading from editors, Gallun reluctantly filed his story away and forgot about it. Later, after the sale of several stories to *Astounding* had bolstered his confidence, he decided to give "Old Faithful" another try and sent it to *Astounding's* editor, F. Orlin Tremaine. A little more than a month later a check for the story arrived in the mail and Gallun was established as a writer to reckon with.

Raymond Zinke Gallun (rhymes with "balloon") was born of German parents in the small town of Beaver Dam, Wisconsin. His childhood witnessed the Great War, his adolescence the Roaring Twenties, and his young adulthood the Great Depression. Gallun does not have a "first published story"—his was a double-barrelled debut, for Hugo Gernsback published two of his tales simultaneously in the fall of 1929, while he was still a teenager.[1] Although active mainly in the 1930s, Gallun was in and out of the field and continued to publish into the 1980s, with "A First Glimpse," *Analog* (February 1980), being his best "first contact" story and *Bioblast* (1985), his last novel. But he began as yet another of Gernsback's teenage authors and his relationship with Gernsback helps, in passing, shed some light on the publisher's reputation as a penny-pinching miser. From his early career we also learn a little more about the division of editorial responsibility at Gernsback's magazines during the tenure there of David Lasser.[2] For instance, like Jack Williamson (whose correspondence with Lasser I discussed earlier), Gallun vividly remembered many letters from Lasser discussing stories, but he had no recollection of receiving any from Gernsback dealing with editorial matters.

Finances, however, were different. Although there was no problem with payment for Gallun's first two stories, trouble developed soon thereafter. Indeed, he was eventually forced, like many other authors, to seek legal aid in obtaining the money Gernsback owed him. When Gernsback was the publisher of *Amazing Stories* he was "Uncle Hugo" to the fans and was reasonably prompt in paying writers. Nor did he have financial problems with his writers in 1953 when publishing *Science Fiction Plus*. Both periods indicate that he was willing to pay when financially able to do so.

But at *Wonder Stories* in the 1930s Gernsback was not able to do so. It was, after all, the Great Depression, and he simply didn't have the money. Like many other publishers he was constantly balancing on the knife-edge of insolvency. After October 1935, *Wonder Stories* ceased monthly publication, going bimonthly until the March-April 1936 issue, the last issue Gernsback published. Outside the field magazines like *Argosy* and *Adventure* were having problems, with the latter cutting both pages and publication schedule. Within the field the other SF magazines were also suffering. *Amazing Stories* was forced to put out a combined August-September 1933 issue. After August 1935, it went bimonthly until April 1938, the last issue edited by Sloane. *Astounding Stories* didn't publish July, August, or October issues in 1932. With its November 1932 issue it declared it was henceforth a bimonthly, which it was until March 1933. Then it ceased publication. It was resurrected as a monthly in October 1933, after Street & Smith purchased it from Clayton. Pulps were dying all around Gernsback. That he kept *Wonder Stories* alive at all was, under the circumstances, an accomplishment.

Nevertheless, Gernsback acquired a lasting and undeserved reputation as a miser who literally *refused,* perhaps simply out of contrariness, to pay his writers. From a demigod in the eyes of First Fandom, Gernsback was transformed into the original Scrooge of science fiction, and the black stain has persisted to the present.

It seems clear that Gernsback was acutely aware of his reputation, and that it bothered him. He wrote numerous letters to his authors explaining his financial straits and begging for patience. But, the Depression also made his writers desperate for what he owed them. Indeed, they seem to have dismissed his financial explanations out of hand as the to-be-expected pleadings of someone attempting to weasel out of paying a just debt. Gernsback attempted to alleviate the tension a little by sending his writers Frank Paul-designed Christmas cards offering greetings from the "deadbeat" they perceived him to be. Such attempts at soothing humor were misunderstood, and, at least in Gallun's case, backfired. Rather than encouraging his writers to feel more kindly disposed toward him, these seemingly mocking cards acted as salt in their wounds.

A sad and revealing anecdote shows clearly how aware Gernsback was of his reputation. In the 1950s he was honeymooning in Switzerland with his new bride. Coincidentally, Gallun was at the same time visiting his German friend Walter Ernsting. Ernsting was invited to meet Gernsback. While doing so, he mentioned that Gallun was staying with him. The first words out of Gernsback's mouth were, "Do I owe him money?" Twenty years had passed, yet Gernsback still remembered his financial troubles—and, according to Gallun, seemed willing to lay out some cash then and there to make things right had the answer been "yes."

Gernsback's inability to pay is not a separate issue from the question of editorial responsibility. According to Charles Hornig, the editor who succeeded Lasser at *Wonder Stories,* Gernsback was often also unable to pay his editors and office staff. At the same time, both Lasser and Hornig—who never met or communicated with each other—tell the same story half a century later: Gernsback gave them a free editorial hand.

Yet Sam Moskowitz, who was Gernsback's editor at *Science Fiction Plus* in 1953, said that he had very little editorial control. He also cited correspondence between Gernsback and his writers when Gernsback was publishing *Amazing Stories* which go into explicit detail about requested manuscript revisions. Why should there have been an interregnum of editorial freedom between these periods?

True, Gernsback was in his late forties when publishing *Wonder Stories* and nearly seventy when publishing *Science Fiction Plus.* People do sometimes get crankier and harder to please as they get older. But, he was a young man when he published *Amazing Stories,* where he wielded a heavy editorial pencil.

It is also true that Gernsback did not have as many magazines and other projects to occupy his time and energy in 1953, so details of his science fiction magazine might therefore have commanded proportionately more of his attention. But when he published *Amazing Stories* he was not only bringing out many other periodicals, but running a radio station and a primitive TV station, as well. Yet he still took a close interest in editing the stories appearing in *Amazing*.

As I mentioned before, the only explanation that seems to describe the circumstances adequately is that Gernsback reached a tacit understanding with his writers and staff: If he couldn't pay all his writers, at least they didn't receive detailed letters from him requesting alterations in their manuscripts; and if his office workers didn't always get paid on time, they would get a free editorial hand instead. It was the best deal he had to offer.

Whatever the policy, it was one which worked. In the early 1930s, especially under Lasser's editorship, *Wonder Stories* was the dominant science fiction magazine. Not only did it regularly publish the leading authors of the day, it published the first stories of many who went on to become prominent, including Raymond A. Palmer, Nathan Schachner, Clifford Simak, and John Beynon Harris, the author later known as "John Wyndham."[3]

While it is true that under both Lasser and Hornig, *Wonder Stories* published a large number of translated European stories personally chosen by Gernsback, these turgid efforts had little impact on readers and today are totally forgotten. The tales which excited the readers, and which are now remembered, were those selected and molded into shape by Lasser and Hornig. The first fan-voted science fiction writing award, for example, was not given to a translated writer. The Jules Verne Prize went to Edmond Hamilton for "The Island of Unreason," which appeared in the May 1933 *Wonder Stories* under Lasser's editorship. Stories like this set the tone of the magazine and they owed little to Gernsback's input.

That Lasser was the main editorial force during his tenure is also suggested by letters readers wrote to the magazine. In the

October 1933 issue, for instance (ironically, the last issue of Lasser's tenure), reader John Pratzki wrote to chastise a previous letter-writer who had objected to numerous stories "with socialism as their theme." Lasser, at that time a member of the Socialist Party, used Pratzki's letter as an opportunity to state:

> Although this magazine does not indulge in politics, we must, however, look upon the scientific organization of human society in the same light as the scientific organization of material. A society in which the means of production—farms, factories, mines, shipping, etc., are used for the benefit of the whole people and controlled by them under a scientific plan, seems to us to be only common sense, or good science. No doubt the people are coming to realize this, and some day any person who does not believe in such a society will be looked upon as queer.

That same issue carried as its cover story Frank K. Kelly's "The Moon Tragedy," which Ray Gallun points to in the following conversation as the very type of story that excited him, and which he tried to imitate. And Kelly, again, was not one of Gernsback's translated Europeans, but a Kansas City teenager handled by Lasser.

Lasser was also no doubt responsible for the fact that socialist and feminist utopian literature was still being published in the magazines he edited at this time—and no where else! In 1929, after Lasser took the editorial helm at Gernsback's Stellar Publications, the company published "Lilith Lorraine's" feminist-socialist utopian tale, *The Brain of the Planet,* as "novel" number five in Stellar's Science Fiction Series. The next year, Lasser wrote an enthusiastic blurb introducing Lorraine's new feminist-socialist utopian story, "Into the 28th Century," for the Winter 1930 *Science Wonder Quarterly.*

Nor was "Lilith Lorraine" the only female author whose vision of a feminist utopia Lasser published. In *Wonder Stories Quarterly* (Spring 1930), Lasser ran "Via the Hewitt Ray," by M.

F. Rupert (a woman hiding behind initials), in which women rule, not in the future (as in Lorraine's story), but in a parallel universe. Lasser, it seems, had a certain receptivity for stories of this nature. There was, for instance, "The Woman from Space," by Richard Vaughn, *Wonder Stories Quarterly* (Spring 1932), concerning a female-run society, as well as the male-dominated *dystopia* of "The Last Woman," by Dr. Thomas S. Gardner, *Wonder Stories* (April 1932). The much-despised pulp genre magazines, at least those edited by David Lasser, were thus an oasis of provocative feminist and socialist literature during a time such topics had disappeared from hardcover book publication.[4] Ironically, then, what made Hugo Gernsback's *Wonder Stories* such an exceptionally fine science fiction magazine was the fact that he, himself, had little to do with selecting its most exciting stories. Gallun's experiences help bring this issue into sharper focus.

The following conversation took place on November 15, 1986. Gallun was seventy-six years old at the time. During the following years, I got to know Ray much better. He visited me in Pittsburgh a few times, once for a memorable Thanksgiving dinner at my home. We exchanged many letters, and talked frequently on the phone. I remember one phone call I made to him on January 9, 1993. Ray's conversation was a bit scattered and he had trouble remembering names. He said he'd tried to call me and had gotten someone else. It turned out he'd transposed the digits of my number. He told me that the previous October he'd had surgery to replace an aortic aneurysm. As of January, however, he was up and about and felt fine. On April 2, 1994, his step-daughter was visiting him and heard him answer the phone in his bedroom. There was a short conversation and then silence. When she went into the room, Ray was stretched out on his bed, the phone by his side. He'd finished his conversation, hung up, and then suddenly died, either of a massive stroke or heart attack. Although the obituaries in the SF community said he died at age eighty-three, Ray Gallun was dead at the age of eighty-four.

ERIC LEIF DAVIN: *Ray, let's begin with your birth, about which there seems to be some confusion. I've come across two different dates, 1910 and 1911. Which is it?*

RAYMOND Z. GALLUN: Well, my passport says I was born on March 22, 1911. My birth certificate says 1910. Sometimes I like to be unusual, so I say 1911, as long as I only have to prove it with my passport. But, actually, it was March 22, 1910.

Could you tell me a little about Beaver Dam, Wisconsin, where you grew up?

It was a town of about 7,500, a nice little place. It's about twice that size now. It was the typical small town of Middle America. Very dead.

Was your father a farmer?

Not really. Basically, I think of Pa as a salesman—he was a fairly good agent for the Mutual Life Insurance Company for a couple of years. But he didn't stick to anything very well. He did odd jobs, clerked in stores, did farming, helped neighborhood farmers. Once he had a chicken farm, but he ran that up the crick and it didn't pay out. Still, he stayed on that farm anyway.

That was "Ormund House." Actually, the name of the guy who built it was Osman, but I changed it to Ormund. I always figured that this Osman/Ormund was my spiritual godfather, though I never met him—he committed suicide about a year before I was born. But his guiding presence was there in this place he built and in what he left behind in it. His books were stowed away in the attic. He'd been a science teacher and a half-assed inventor who was interested in lots of out-of-the-ordinary stuff. According to neighbors who remembered him, he was real odd.

Did you have any brothers and sisters?

I had one brother, Arnold, who died before I was born. My sister Charlotte died a couple of years ago. She was eight years older than I. Of course, the Old Folks are long gone. I also had an uncle, Julius Zinke, a younger brother of my mother. Uncle Julius was a pharmacist's mate in the Navy. He was a veteran of the Spanish-American War. He'd spent a lot of time in the Philippines. He went around the world with Admiral Dewey in the Great White Fleet on the *U.S.S. Virginia.* Originally there were fourteen kids in Ma's family, and Pa's was almost as big.

Anyway, Uncle Julius left a sea-chest with us holding a lot of things: Snake skins, Navy pennants, coins and curios from distant parts of the world, a Filipino bolo knife, and what-not. My mother told me he'd been everywhere. Once in a while he'd come to visit us. I guess I idolized him, although he didn't care for small fry.

Once I asked my mother what the stars were. She told me they were places where other people lived, that they were other worlds. So I asked, "Gee, has Uncle Julie been there, too?" I suppose I was almost five-years-old then and already I was not only imagining, but *believing* in interstellar fleets, and that Uncle Julius had been there with the Navy. He was the inspiration for—and appears in—my story "Prodigal's Aura."[5]

How far did you go in school?

I went to the University of Wisconsin for one year in 1929-30. It was mostly a drag. Then bits and pieces here and there through the years, including the Alliance Francaise in Paris, 1938-39. In the summer of 1960, almost inadvertently, I took a

Two views of David Lasser (c. 1935 and 1985), influential editor of Hugo Gernsback's *Wonder Stories* and author of *The Conquest of Space*, the first work in English to explore the possibilities of space flight (see ch. 1). (Photo courtesy of David Lasser)

Charles Hornig (c. 1935 and c. 1985), originally a science fiction fan who launched the fanzine *The Fantasy Fan* and was then hired at the age of seventeen by Hugo Gernsback to replace David Lasser as the managing editor of *Wonder Stories* (see ch. 1 & 2). (Photos courtesy of Charles D. Hornig)

Stanley G. Weinbaum (c. 1934), whose story "A Martian Odyssey" (1934) revolutionized the genre by depicting an alien sympathetically (see ch. 3). (Photo courtesy of Stanley G. Weinbaum Estate)

A young Margaret Weinbaum (c. 1930) around the time of her marriage to Stanley G. Weinbaum (see ch. 3). (Photo courtesy of Stanley G. Weinbaum Estate)

Margaret Weinbaum Kay at her home in Palm Desert, California, 1993. (Photo by Eric Leif Davin)

A middle-aged Raymond Z. Gallun (c. 1952), who had been one of Gernsback's teenage sensations. A story he wrote for a high school English class, "The Crystal Ray," was published in *Wonder Stories* (see ch. 4). (Photo courtesy of Raymond Z. Gallun)

Frank K. Kelly (c. 1935), a much published and highly successful teen science fiction writer, who abruptly gave up writing science fiction when he went to college (see ch. 5). (Photo courtesy of Frank K. Kelly)

An older Frank Kelly (c. 1988), after a distinguished career as a speech writer for President Harry Truman and a director of the Center for the Study of Democratic Institutions, Santa Barbara, California (see ch. 5). (Photo courtesy of Frank K. Kelly)

R.F. Starzl (c. 1934), writer of some twenty science fiction stories from 1928 to 1934, the most important of which was "Out of the Sub-Universe," which depicted civilizations living on electrons in subatomic space (see ch. 6). (Photo courtesy of Dr. Thomas E. Starzl)

Pioneer science fiction author and book publisher Lloyd Arthur Eshbach (c. 1991), founder of Fantasy Press (see ch. 7). (Photo courtesy of Lloyd Arthur Eshbach)

Wolf Man creator and prolific screen writer Curt Siodmak (c. 1991). He was instrumental in transferring science fiction from print to screen (see ch. 8). (Photo courtesy of Curt Siodmak)

Science fiction historian and editor Sam Moskowitz (1993), author of *The Immortal Storm* (1954), a history of the science fiction fan movement from its beginnings up to World War II (see ch. 11). (Photo by Eric Leif Davin)

course at San Marcos University in Lima, Peru, to study Hispanic literature.

I know Spanish pretty well. I'm good at languages. German was actually my first language as a child, English my second, French my third, and Spanish my fourth. I can't speak German very well any more, but I spoke *only* German up until I was four or five. Then my mother told me I had to learn English because I had to go to school the next year. She stopped speaking German to me and from then on it was English.

I've always had a knack for languages, both spoken and written. I loved ancient history and when I was twelve years old I taught myself Egyptian hieroglyphics and could read them pretty well. I also studied written Chinese and Japanese, which are pretty similar. Now I'm into computer languages. The only reason I haven't bought a computer is I don't know where to put it.

How did you become interested in science fiction?

I was always interested in natural phenomena. All of nature was around me, and the stars and the clear skies. In the country you're more aware of the seasons and other things which cities divert you from. When I was a little kid I used to ask my mother, "Why is the sky blue?" "What kind of fire is the sun?" "What keeps it burning?" She didn't know; she supposed it was coal. I had an older cousin, Kathleen, who just then had a great interest in collecting butterflies. She got a long pole and made a butterfly net. So, I said to my mother, "The next time Kathleen comes, I'm gonna borrow her butterfly net and haul down the sun and see what it is."

Then, when I was in the fifth grade, I had a teacher who had a half-hour session after lunch during which she read to us. One of the books she picked was *Tarzan of the Apes.* Of course, that's sort of science fiction, and I was fascinated with Edgar Rice Burroughs from then on. Pretty soon I had all his John Carter books. From there I went to Jules Verne, and then to H. G. Wells and his

War of the Worlds, which is a remarkable piece of writing, even today.

Do you remember the first science fiction magazine you ever saw?

Yes, I do. It was a copy of *Amazing Stories* with an enormous fly pictured on the cover. The fly was attacking a Navy warship of some kind. The background was yellow. That's all I remember about it.[6] That was the first all science fictional magazine I'd ever seen, though, of course, I was already acquainted with other magazines that used science fiction, such as *Argosy, Blue Book,* and *Weird Tales.* I snapped that *Amazing* up right away. School was over for the summer and I was headed for work at the Badger Canning factory where I'd gotten a job at 35 cents an hour. The pea-packing hadn't started yet, but we had to clean up the machinery to be ready. I was in town that afternoon and I spied this magazine on display in the window of Butterbrodt's Stationery Store. I lapped it up. Everything fantastic, futuristic, or spatial was a wonder to me then! It was my main interest.

How did you move from reading science fiction to writing it?

One followed pretty close on the heels of the other. I said to myself, "There's something wrong with this story. They ought to know better than to make such dumb mistakes. Maybe I can do as good—or even better!" So *trying* to write came easily enough. Getting a story plotted and satisfactorily written was a lot tougher!

Actually, science fiction, per se, maybe wasn't my main objective. It was sort of an interim substitute for a reality we didn't yet have. Do you follow me?

Perhaps you could elaborate a bit?

You see, I was fascinated with the still-hidden mysteries about other worlds. I needed some reasonable answers to questions, even if they were only imaginary answers. If you couldn't penetrate such mysteries right away and learn the truth about them, still you had to have some fantasies to fill in the blanks. That remains pretty much my view.

But, I prefer that such imaginings conform closely to whatever facts we have about other worlds. That way, imagining becomes an aid and a possible guide for actual, *factual,* exploring expeditions as soon as the necessary technology is developed. Much of such technology already exists. So, why aren't there more moon landings? Why isn't a manned Mars landing already in the works? To me, science fiction is primarily a forerunner of potentially *near-future* reality. Sure, yarns about trips to the stars are okay. But the local planets are much nearer and within our present reach. They should come first![7] That's part of my annoyance with a lot of science fiction today. There's just so much of it I can't read. Sometimes I think current writers just aren't doing as well as we did in the old days.

Let's talk about your first two published stories, "The Crystal Ray" and "The Space Dwellers," both of which appeared in November 1929, while you were still a teenager.

I wrote "The Crystal Ray" first, for English class in my junior year of high school. I think I got a "B" on it. The teacher was a little miffed because the story was supposed to be ten pages long and it came to over twenty.

I wrote "The Space Dwellers" a year later with more attention; it had more substance. After its original 1929 publication, it was later republished by *Startling Stories* as one of those "classic" science fiction tales of yesteryear. It was a real first shot at something which wasn't even defined at the time, namely exobiology—in this case, radioactive, non-water-based life. The notion here was that all life doesn't have to be water-based and dependent on the oxidation of chemical foods for its energy. It could be energized radioactively. The radioactive element could be one remaining liquid at low temperature, just as mercury does, and also serve the same fluid-flow functions that water does in our biology. I thought of this element as being above uranium in atomic number—say, No. 110. I felt this made a pretty darned good speculative idea.

But, the story isn't too well-written, despite being a "classic." Actually, I did a much better job with this concept in another story which Tremaine published called, "A Beast of the Void." That was a real exploration of the theory.[8]

How old were you when you wrote "The Crystal Ray"?

Oh, sixteen or seventeen. I wrote "The Space Dwellers" for my senior year of high school English. It wasn't a class assignment; I worked it in as extra credit. I had the same teacher as in my junior year, and she agreed to it reluctantly. Again, she was miffed because it was over-long. There used to be a high school magazine published by *The Atlantic Monthly* called *Magazine World.* She got a poem of mine published in it in 1928. She was a good sort, but she's long gone now.

Anyway, I sent these two stories to "Uncle Hugo"—that's what we called Hugo Gernsback then—at *Amazing Stories,* which he still owned. A long, long time passed. I was scared even to write him to ask what happened. Finally, I received two identical letters from him differing only in the names of the stories they referred to and the amount of money mentioned. He offered $25 for "The Crystal Ray" and $30 for "The Space Dwellers."

But, there was a little hitch to it. He asked, "Did you send these stories to me as editor of *Amazing Stories* or did you send them to me personally at my home address on Riverside Drive? This is important, because of certain legal problems." Well, I was an honest kid, so I wrote back saying I'd sent them to him as editor of *Amazing.* His question was a bit phony, because he knew I had no way of knowing where he actually lived; I had only the magazine's address. I think he tried to suggest the legal choice he wanted here, but I was too dumb to catch on. So, he sent them back and wrote me that he couldn't accept them as he was no longer connected with *Amazing Stories,* and I could send them wherever I wanted. All this took a couple of months. I sent them back to him at his home address, he accepted them, and they were published in his new magazines.

Did you ever correspond with David Lasser when he was Gernsback's editor?

Oh, yes, I used to get a lot of letters from Lasser. He wrote on yellow, company-headed, note-sized stationery, and he always signed his name in green ink. Some of those letters were specific favorable comments about my stories; several were responses—and excuses, no doubt relayed from Hugo himself—about why I hadn't been paid for my yarns.

You know, in your interview with Charlie Hornig, he says he never met me. That's not true. I did meet him once. I went to his office in New York to drop off a story, or just to meet him, when he was still editor of *Wonder Stories.* He didn't publish anything of mine, but I did see him for a few moments.[9]

What did the office look like?

I don't have any particular memory of it. There was a large space and then there was a corridor down the side. It was a reasonably good place. I can't recall Charlie too well, except that he seemed very young and very polite.

You spoke of correspondence from Gernsback concerning legal matters. Do you remember ever receiving letters from him dealing with editorial matters—say, requesting revisions?

I don't remember ever receiving any letters of that nature from him, or even doing any revisions at all. Whatever changes made on my manuscripts were done at the office, usually without any notice to me. I don't know who was responsible for editing stories at the office, but I assumed it was Gernsback because he was so rigid about scientific things.[10]

But I *do* remember receiving a letter from Gernsback about a story of mine he published in *Science Fiction Plus* demanding that I present a formula justifying life on an asteroid far out from the sun. At least I'm pretty sure it was from Gernsback. Sam [Moskowitz] wasn't that fussy.[11]

One of the stories I sent to *Wonder* was changed in a way that annoyed me very much. It was damned irritating. I should have sent it to Harry Bates! It was my novella, "Revolt of the Star Men."[12] In it the living mounts of the Star Men—disc-like beasts of the same radioactive life-form as the Star Men themselves—were changed to *machines!* With control levers yet! This, while the Star Men were cast as a primitive nomadic people of interstellar space, living in an entirely *nontechnological* fashion! After the yarn was on the stands someone from the office sent me an unprompted explanation with words to the effect that, if I thought about it, self-propelling creatures in space were impossible—so changes had to be made! At this late date I can't swear who the letter was from, but I assumed Gernsback was responsible.

Poor old Hugo! He was so hung up on the inventive capacities of *Man*—as opposed to those of *Nature*—when there had been fish before there were submarines, birds long before there were airplanes! He couldn't accept the completely valid notion that a living creature of another order of life might emit streams of, say, propelling ions. So he missed a major point of my story. But then, in the 1930s, rigid attitudes of this kind were still common in science fiction. You've seen the Frank Paul drawings of Martians with huge ears, lungs, elephant noses? That weird image came from Gernsback, who was convinced that they had to look like that to exist in the thin Martian atmosphere.

In refutation of his objections to "Revolt of the Star Men," I got no complaints about the concept from *Astounding's* readers, and considerable interest, when I tried to describe this type of life in "A Beast of the Void." Later, in 1954, this was reprinted by Hachette in France as "La Bete du Vide." The editor, Georges Gallet, said it created a minor stir as being a story about a living flying saucer!

Other changes were made at the *Wonder* office on other stories. For instance, "Waves of Compulsion" was originally "The Compulsion Ray," but that title change was surely an improvement.

How was Gernsback on payment?

The money for my first two stories—$25 and $30—came promptly. I was very pleased, as that was equivalent to more than $500 in today's purchasing power. After that—Hugo being *who* he was, *what* he was and the *way* he was—and economic circumstances being what they were, everything got tied up. He wouldn't pay me.

I think I finally scared him. He sent $50 "on account," because I'd written him that if I didn't get paid soon, I was going to put the matter in the hands of an attorney.

There was an agent in New York named August Lenneger. I hadn't done any business with him, but I thought maybe he would help make Gernsback pay up, so I wrote him. It turned out that Lenneger had contact with a lady attorney from Wisconsin who was practicing in New York. Her name was Ione Weber. She took me on and got an arrangement whereby Gernsback would pay the couple of hundred dollars he owed me at the rate of $15 a week. He stuck to that schedule pretty well. Weber took a 15 percent cut, so she was getting a few dollars too, and a few dollars were worth something in those days, even in New York.

Then, since I knew Hugo was holding out on other writers, I wrote to *Writer's Digest,* explaining that I had found a good attorney. They published my letter, omitting Gernsback's name. Then some of my colleagues recognized my name as being one of the "Brotherhood," and they contacted Weber. I understand she managed to collect quite a bit for those other writers, too.

So, the matter was cleared up. I never wrote for Hugo again until many years later, when Sam Moskowitz was his editor at *Science Fiction Plus*. Sam assured me I'd get paid, so I wrote for Hugo again. And I was quite well paid for the novelette I submitted, although the magazine folded rather quickly.

Do you remember exactly when your financial trouble with Gernsback began?

It began early in 1932 with "Revolt of the Star Men." Then there were the novelettes "Waves of Compulsion" and "The Moon Mistress."[13] There was also a story-idea contest Hugo sponsored. Johnny Michel won the contest and they gave me the job of writing the story, which I did with quite a few changes.[14] I wasn't paid for any of this work until Ione Weber took my case. After that, Hugo was out as far as I was concerned.

How did these financial difficulties make you feel toward Gernsback?

I never met him, but he was quite a god to me to start with. However, when you don't get paid, you get kind of pissed off. He had some weird customs. He was great on sending greeting cards and Christmas cards. They were especially made up. I don't know whether Frank Paul designed them or not. There was one in which Hugo declared himself to be a "philanthropic deadbeat." This may have been his card for Christmas of 1933 or 1934. He was very good at poking fun at himself, but he was never very generous when it came down to the cash.[15]

Let me tell you a story about Hugo. I guess this was in 1952. I was visiting Germany, and [the German SF writer] Walter Ernsting heard I was around and looked me up. I'd never met him, but after that we became good friends. Walter wrote all those Perry Rhodan stories under the name of Clark Darlton. He'd fought in the Wehrmacht on the Russian Front during World War II and had been taken prisoner. He always had a loud mouth and this got him treated pretty badly as a POW. They transferred him to a camp for political prisoners and eventually knocked out all his front teeth. When he came home from the war, he was a six-foot man who weighed only 90 lbs. The last time I saw him was years ago in England. He lives in Ireland now because of the tax breaks.

Anyway, this was the time Gernsback had just remarried, and he was honeymooning in Switzerland.[16] I was with Walter in Irschenberg, Upper Bavaria, where he lived. It was a tiny town of thirteen and a half houses, a *Weltkriegsdenkmal* [a World War I monument], a cemetery, and a couple of restaurants. It had a beautiful setting with mountains and a lot of woods around it.

Well, Walter got a letter inviting him to come down and meet Gernsback. Walter wanted me to go along, but I didn't care to butt in. When he came back a few days later I asked, "Did you mention me?" "Yes, I did," said Walter, "and the first thing Hugo said to me was, 'Do I owe him any money?'"

And did he owe you any money?

No, but Gernsback was doing pretty well at that time and Walter made it clear that I could have probably gotten fifty bucks out of him.[17]

Were you ever active in fan circles?

No, I didn't know anybody there. I started out entirely on my own. I wrote to R. F. Starzl once.[18] He'd written some pretty good stories. He lived in Le Mars, Iowa! With a name and an address like that, he *had* to write science fiction! I wrote him saying I wanted to contact another science fiction writer. He wrote back saying, "Your attempt to write to a science fiction author has misfired, as I've just quit!"

Did he say why he was quitting SF?

Yes, he did. He was writing for Harry Bates at *Astounding* when that magazine was published by the W. M. Clayton Company. They were paying two cents a word on acceptance and reporting within one week, which was great. They went bankrupt and we didn't see anything like that again for years. When that market was gone, Starzl stopped writing science fiction.[19]

Then I wrote to an author named Frank K. Kelly. He was a brilliant youngster. He was only seventeen years old and writing beautiful stuff. But, I guess he fell in love, or something, and thought it was more important to make money, so he quit. Kelly lived in Missouri, and I heard he later became a speech writer for Harry Truman. He probably made more money in that line. I once read an article by him entitled, "My Interplanetary Teens." I guess he's passed from the memory of most people in SF circles, but I remember![20]

These were the only two authors I ever tried to make contact with, and neither went anywhere.

Speaking of Harry Bates, did you ever meet him?

No, and I regret that, because he died under very bad circumstances. He was broke and he had a terrible case of arthritis. After he lost *Astounding* when Clayton went broke, Bates never quite seemed to find himself again, though he worked at various small things. He just went down the drain. Finally, in poor health, he couldn't take care of himself and he died alone in that horrible little apartment he had in New York City. I regret never having contacted him because he wrote me some very nice letters near the end of his editorship at *Astounding* telling me he couldn't pay anything because the company was going under.[21]

What other authors did you like in the old days?

Jack Williamson, Laurence Manning, Stanley Weinbaum. I was pretty isolated up there in Wisconsin. I didn't actually meet any science fiction writers until one time I went to Milwaukee and met the Milwaukee Fictioneers. This was in the winter of 1936-37, just after my story "Godson of Almaru" came out. There I met Raymond A. Palmer, Robert Bloch, and Ralph Milne Farley. I didn't meet Weinbaum because he'd died about a year before this time.

What do you remember about Ray Palmer?

He was a very small guy with a humped spine, but a very quick mind and a hard, bright sense of humor. I saw him only that one time in Milwaukee. Later, during 1940–41, I was living in Mexico and I wrote some stories for him when he was editor of *Amazing Stories.*

What about Ralph Milne Farley?

Again, I saw him only that one time at the Fictioneers meeting. He was a sort of lanky chap and I think he had a mustache. A nice man.[22] Robert Bloch was there, too. He was young, tall, and a good talker.[23]

Every once in a while I saw Julius Schwartz around. When I lived in Europe in the late 1930s, Schwartz was my agent. And from early 1940 to June of that year, before I left for a couple of months in upstate New York and then for Mexico, he and I used to be in a group of New York writers that gathered to talk shop and socialize. We met every other Thursday at von Steuben's Restaurant on 47th Street. That's long gone now.

Was Julie Schwartz a good agent for you?

Yes, he was very good. Of course, I knew of Forrest J. Ackerman around this time, too, though I didn't actually meet him till years later. I don't remember our first meeting, though we kept running into each other at various times, at conventions in New York, Philadelphia, Dublin, in Brighton, England, and so on. From time to time Forry gets a story of mine reprinted in some anthology. He never asks permission, or even tells me he's going to do it. He just sends me a copy of the anthology with a check in the leaves.

Let's go back a moment—who was in this writers' group that met at von Steuben's?

Schwartz, myself, Henry Kuttner, Manly Wade Wellman, Otto Binder, and a scattering of others who sometimes dropped in. I'd just returned from Europe about the middle of December 1939. Julie introduced me to the group.

Kuttner was very competent. He could write a ten-thousand-word novelette overnight. He was young, dapper, slender, and looked to be in his middle twenties. Very pleasant.[24]

Otto was doing the Adam Link robot stories, which I'm sure you're familiar with. Otto came to a bad end. His daughter was killed in a very tragic automobile accident. That threw him for a loss, and I guess he took to drinking quite a bit. But at this time he was okay and doing all right.[25]

Wellman was a big fellow. He was supposed to have been a boxer of some sort once. He had one slightly deformed hand, slightly smaller than the other. His favorite drink was Dubonnet and soda, so if you ever get together to remember Manly Wade Wellman, that's what you should order.[26]

Malcolm Jameson also sometimes dropped in. He was a little ex-Navy guy and a very competent writer.[27]

They were all a good bunch.

What did you do at these gatherings?

One of the favorite activities for many of the guys, particularly Wellman, was roasting Campbell.[28] They regarded him as capricious. He'd reject a story for no reason they could see. Another thing Wellman complained about a lot was that Campbell was always busting in on him when he wanted to work.

I thought Campbell wrote long letters explaining exactly why he rejected a story.

Oh, yeah, he did. But, they were hard to understand. He was quite the opposite of Orlin Tremaine, who wrote brief letters which were clear.[29] As far as I'm concerned, Tremaine was a lot easier to work with, because Campbell would write a long letter with plenty of discussion—but he still wouldn't buy the story.

Were Kuttner and Binder having trouble with Campbell also?

I don't think so. But, at that time I believe they were aiming mainly at the Thrilling group,* as I was also. We were more concerned with Leo Margulies.[30] I'd pretty much left Campbell because I found Margulies easier to work with. He emphasized human values more, rather than all these scientific concepts Campbell was stuck on.

Did any of you bring stories you were working on to get the opinions of the others?

No, none of us did that.

If you didn't discuss stories, what, besides Campbell, did you discuss?

---

*The stable of pulps published by Standard Publications, which included such magazines as *Thrilling Wonder Stories*, *Thrilling Mystery*, *Thrilling Love*, *Thrilling Adventures*, *Thrilling Detectives*, et al.

Well, market conditions; who was buying what. A number of times we just picked up as a group and went over to see Malcolm Reiss at *Planet Stories*. Reiss was a very nice chap. One of us remarked that it was nicer to get a rejection letter from Malcolm Reiss than an acceptance letter from anyone else. Later on he was a very competent literary agent, although he used another name. He was an OSS man in Chungking during World War II. The last time I saw him he looked healthy—and, suddenly, within a few months, he was dead.[31]

Would you say you were good friends with this group of writers?

Oh, pretty good, but I didn't seek them out between gatherings. It was just a regular luncheon get-together to have a few drinks, chew the fat, and that was it. It was good to fraternize with other guys in the same deal as you in order to escape being completely lonely. A writer is mostly isolated in his work. It helps to get together with others for an hour or two.

And it must have helped to have Schwartz, an agent, in the group.

Yeah, but all of us spent a lot of time with the editors, anyway. I used to go over to their offices to see what they wanted, so I had a pretty good idea of what was up. The science fiction field then was a narrow circle of people and you could see an editor yourself and ask, "Well, what do you need?" Or, "I've got something here. Can you buy it?"

Once I was in Sam Merwin's office. He worked for Leo Margulies at the Thrilling group. This was later, when Sam was editor of both *Thrilling Wonder* and *Startling Stories*.[32] I had a story I'd just finished and I was short of money so I went over to see him. I said, "Look, Sam, I have this story here I'd like to make a quick sale on. Can you take fifteen minutes off and read it?" So, he took it and went off. A little bit later he came back and said, "Yeah, I'm sure it'll go. I'll have a check for you at the end of the week."

So, it was all very friendly and easy. We all knew each other. Once Leo Margulies asked me, "Do you need any money? I'll lend you $50." Well, fifty bucks was quite a bit then. I never took the money, but it was there if I needed it.

It sounds as if you had friendly relations with your editors.

We *all* did. It was part of the spirit of the thing. They knew you were around, you were always right on top of them, they knew they could depend on you. You were almost a member of the staff. This was true of *all* the writers. Of course, von Steuben's has long since disappeared, and all those guys are gone. The only relic I have of that time is Julie Schwartz.

When your first two stories were published in 1929, did you see yourself as making a career out of writing science fiction?

I saw science fiction as *part* of a writing career. I liked the idea of writing in general.

Did you try to write any other type of story?

Yes, and I had some luck. But this was after World War II. In 1946 I was courting my first wife, Frieda, then Frieda Talmey. She died in 1974. She was a school teacher. We were at her place and we were going out to dinner, but first she had to grade some papers. I had to do something in the meantime, so she brought out a typewriter, put it down on the table along with some paper, and told me to write a story. "Why don't you write something for *Collier's*?" she said. So, okay, I went to work and wrote a little exercise in foolishness. I cooked up a plot on the spot and started something called "A Bright Message."

It was about a girl who was disgusted with her husband, whom she had divorced as a no-goodnik. She had a pretty good job and everyone was living off her, especially an old uncle who kept sending little gifts for her small daughter. The latest gift was a wooden fire engine with a little man in the driver's seat. And she thinks, again, "So, here's another dime-store toy sent to my kid, not for my kid's sake, but just to keep buttering me up to send him another check."

So, then she's down in Acapulco on vacation with her daughter and she's really disgusted with having received the toy, because the kid's already broken it. But then she meets a man on the beach who looks at it and says, "No, this isn't a dime-store toy. This is hand-carved. It took at least a couple of days just to carve that little man on the truck."

So, she realizes her uncle is a pretty good guy, after all, and her faith in humanity is restored. The three of them walk off down the beach and, of course, wedding bells. The story took only about four hours to write.

Frieda had envelopes, so we sent it off and I forgot about it. A few days later I got a letter from John Schaffner, then managing editor at *Collier's*. He'd tried to call me, he said, but I didn't have a phone. Anyway, he offered me $500 for that little yarn! I was so flabbergasted I went to the bathroom and vomited!

So I immediately wrote another story for them called "Final Rite." That one took ten days to finish, and I got $600 for it. The two stories were published in *Collier's* on May 18 and July 6, 1946. But, after that I sort of dried up. I didn't lose interest in writing for the magazine; I just lost the capacity to write in their style. Somehow, I lost the knack. A couple of my rejects from *Collier's* wound up in the *New York Daily News*. I had trouble with word-length. The slicks wanted 3,000 words and my stories always came out either longer or shorter. I did succeed in writing one called "Blurred Barrier" that finally sold to *Family Circle*. It was a nice little story, but I couldn't follow that one up with anything, either. But I was still writing a lot of material. In fact, I picked up Fred Pohl as an agent. He thought he could sell my stuff. Then he passed me on to another agent named Roger Terrill, who sold my novel, *People Minus X*, to Simon and Schuster.[33] Terrill's been dead a long time, now. He'd been an editor with the Popular group.* But I just couldn't consistently produce the kind of yarns the big slicks wanted.

I met a couple of slick writers† and they were physical wrecks. In fact, I bought dinner for one, once. He'd sold quite a lot to the *Saturday Evening Post*. But, his hands couldn't stop shaking. Too much pressure to keep turning it out, and too much uncertainty. I didn't think that was a very good way to make a living, so, ultimately, I wound up as a technical writer where I was paid regularly. Doing that I made a good deal more money for a lot less work.

Getting back to particular stories, you once said that "The Restless Tide" was one of your favorites.[34] Why is that?

I like it because it seems to me to represent human nature. Humans follow something until it wears out. Then they have to change. They're not steadfast about any idea; they have to change. But, that's a process which also assures progress, because change itself is necessary. You can't hold onto a concept for too long or it gets tired, worn out. Then the time will come when you have to change back, too. It's a constant switching back and forth.

I also liked "Prodigal's Aura." I'd been having some trouble

---

*Popular Publications was a major magazine chain which published such SF magazines as *Famous Fantastic Mysteries* and *A. Merritt's Fantasy Magazine*.

†The "slicks" were high-quality magazines such as the *Saturday Evening Post* or *Cosmopolitan*, which paid more money and were so called because they were published on slick paper. The low-quality and poorly paid "pulps" were similarly so called because they were published on cheap pulp paper. *Family Circle, Collier's*, etc., are all "big slicks."

with John Campbell before I wrote that one. I did it in one draft with a very light, worn-out typewriter ribbon. It wasn't right for the Thrilling group of magazines, so I thought, just for the hell of it, why not send it "as is" to Campbell? He surprised me by buying it right away. We'd had our differences in the past, but that didn't stop him from buying this story.

I met him once when I'd just come back from Europe at the beginning of 1940, at the time I was hanging out with the von Steuben gang. The Street and Smith offices were a rambling old place like a barn, and Campbell had this little dinky office off in the corner behind all kinds of stuff. He was a big fellow and very fair-skinned. He was friendly, but only to a degree. But, we had quite a discussion. I was thinking then about the story which later became *People Minus X*. Now, I'd previously written about miniaturization,[35] but not as fully as in *People Minus X*. I was thinking about ordinary folks who'd been changed into androids that could be made in any size, down to the dimensions of dust motes. At that level of miniaturization, the same physical laws would apply, but with different effects. For instance, an android as small as that could actually float in the air. It would also have the advantage of being almost invisible—a useful condition when avoiding or attacking enemies.

So the question came up in our discussion, "Could beings that small hammer metals into shape?" To them, metals would be relatively hard. John thought they would not be able to hammer, but could shape things by compression. Thus, small androids could build smaller ones, and the necessary tools, in decreasing steps downward, until mote-size was reached.

What was the nature of your problems with Campbell?

Not real problems, just annoyances. I'd enjoyed a very good writer-editor relationship with F. Orlin Tremaine, his predecessor at *Astounding*. Then Tremaine was kicked upstairs and Campbell came on the scene. He was superconscientious, writing long letters of criticism. This was all to the good; he was developing new writers, developing the field. But the size of the magazine didn't increase, and space had to be found for his new scribes. So, sometimes the old crowd was left out in the cold. Perhaps this was justice of a sort, but it was unsettling. No matter, the Thrilling group had opened up. They paid just as well and their emphasis was on more human values and somewhat less on science—more my thing.

Once Campbell wrote me asking why I sent him no more scripts. Being a bit peeved at him, and knowing his right-wing political leanings, I sent a flip response stating that I was a card-carrying Communist—which, of course, I was not. Politically, I've always been a middle-of-the-roader. It was just to annoy him.

How did you come to write your most famous story, "Old Faithful"?

In the winter of 1931–32, in the depths of the Depression, I was working ten-hour days in a hemp mill in Beaver Dam. It was a rotten job, but not because of the seventeen-and-a-half cents an hour pay—a dollar bought quite a lot of groceries back then. But the mill was a sheet-iron structure, freezing cold on one side and torridly hot from the dry-kiln on the other. The air was full of black hemp dust and the din of the machinery that tore up the hemp stalks. It was a wonder we all didn't strangle from the dust or die of pneumonia because of the heat and cold. I hated it, but somebody in the family had to earn some money.

I needed some escape, something to take the taste of the job out of my mouth, so evenings after I came home from work I painfully wrote out in longhand and then typed "Old Faithful" on the dining room table by kerosene lamplight. Maybe working in the hemp mill even helped me write the yarn. You see, hemp grown for its fiber is also cannabis—marijuana! Hemp straw was used to fuel the engine boiler, and the smoke from it filled the air we breathed. So, maybe I was actually high on pot!

I was fascinated by Mars at the time. Of course, I was influenced by Edgar Rice Burroughs' John Carter stories, but I knew that was all just entertaining baloney. I wanted to write something as close as possible to what *might* be, if there *were* Martians out there. So I imagined this nonhumanoid Martian whose dream was to learn more about *Earth* and its inhabitants, just as I eagerly wanted to probe the mysteries of Mars. This Martian, Old Faithful, wasn't malevolent, as so many fictional aliens were back then—nor was he totally benevolent, either. He just had this tremendous curiosity, this will, to find out.

"Davy Jones' Ambassador"[36] was a similar story. It was about an alien in a completely alien environment, native to the bottom of the Atlantic Ocean. But, he had enough spiritual similarity to achieve contact with humans.

Those two stories I think a lot of, but my most anthologized story is actually "Seeds of the Dusk,"[37] about sentient plants using life, not fire, as their working tool during the final era of an aging Earth. My most recent novel, *Bioblast,* has much the same concept as "Seeds of the Dusk," but with a far different slant and in a modern setting of a few years from now.

Back in the 1930s, you wrote under several pseudonyms—William Callahan, Arthur Allport, and some others. Why?

It started when I had three stories in the same issue of *Astounding* and they couldn't put them all in under my own name. It was the same issue which carried "Davy Jones' Ambassador." The other stories were "Nova Solis," supposedly by Dow Elstar, and "Avalanche," as by E. V. Raymond. At the time I was turning out yarns like griddle cakes, and I just told the editors to dream up some names for me if they wanted to put some other stories of mine in the same issue.

"Nova Solis" was about the sun becoming a nova. It would destroy everything on the surface of the Earth, but the Earth itself would survive. If you do the mathematics of the thing, you find that if the sun went nova—that is, exploded and expanded to fill the vast volume within the Earth's orbit—its substance would then necessarily be extremely tenuous, really a high vacuum. It would be very hot, of course, but unable in a reasonable time to vaporize or even melt the surface of the planet to any great depth.

Your farewell to science fiction—at least for a while—was your novel The Planet Strappers. . . .

Yes, that was published by Pyramid Books as a paperback in 1961. It was my last story for thirteen years. In 1959 they paid me a $1,000 advance, which was pretty standard at the time, and I wrote the story while I was in Europe with Walter Ernsting. The paperback sold eighty thousand copies at thirty-five cents a copy. I made a couple of hundred extra bucks on it in royalties.

Why did you stop writing SF after that?

I said to myself, "Why the *hell* should I do more of this stuff?" It's fun to do, but you break your back, the pay is poor, and all the glamour of being a writer has worn off." So, I went into technical writing. It was far easier, more secure, and a more lucrative way of making a living—and it was kind of fun, too.

I had a medical checkup about this time and the doctor said to me, "I don't know what you're doing to yourself, but you're headed for trouble. Your blood pressure's up over two hundred." Something had to give, so I gave up science fiction.

I couldn't give up story-writing entirely, but with the financial pressure off, I began a novel, *Ormund House.* Let me tell you about it. I didn't overwhelm myself with the idea of actually selling it, but I do think it turned out to be my best writing. Roger Terrill showed the first draft to an editor at Harcourt-Brace, and they wanted to see more of it.

But, maybe I got carried away. Over a span of twelve years I rewrote it four times, having fun all the way. But, each draft got longer, until it was a 1,450-page monster. It got some good comments—certainly has pace and color, good incidents and characters, and so on. But, the bottom line was, "Too long to be commercially viable." It's sat in a box for years, now. I suppose I murdered it by overwriting. But, I still think it makes a pretty good read.

It's about me and the real, though eccentric, house at the edge of Beaver Dam in which I was raised. It was built by this strange fellow I told you about, a science teacher in a private prep school and a part-time inventor and livestock experimenter. He must have been looking for something special in life, but I don't think he found it because, as I said, he finally shot himself.

We moved into the place when I was just a few months old. Pa wanted the place, which included five acres of land, as a chicken farm. Ma disliked just about everything there—the small, curiously arranged rooms, the fact that the house and barn were joined by a passageway (common enough in Maine, where "Ormund" seems to have originated, but odd in Wisconsin), the gasoline engine–powered water system which "Ormund" devised and which inevitably froze every winter.

Then there were the various gadgets of uncertain purpose which Ma threw out. And there were boxes and boxes of books stacked in the attic: engineering texts, science books, even an E. A. Wallace Budge grammar of Egyptian hieroglyphics! Nobody ever came to claim them, so they became my personal library.

I developed a love-hate for Ormund House. It was my refuge, but also my prison. And, in my mind, "Ormund," though dead before my birth, became my spiritual godfather—a close relative not of blood, but of chafing environment. Part of his effect on me was to lead me to write science fiction. This is what the novel is all about.

While you were writing Ormund House, *the science fiction field made a real resurgence, and established SF writers are now doing very well. Looking back, do you regret that you didn't stay in the field?*

No, because I'd be dead. I understand it might've been better for my reputation and I might have made out a lot better than I eventually did as a technical writer—but I probably saved my life by getting out! It was destroying my health. I had to ease off. Within three weeks as a salaried technical writer, my blood pressure was down to normal. Besides, I'd been at it, with breaks, for thirty years or so—since 1929. That seemed long enough. Payment rates weren't up and I was fairly tired of SF.

Now, quite a few guys did hang in there! Fred Pohl stuck to it and made out very nicely. Isaac Asimov stuck with it. And, of course, Arthur Clarke. I went to an Arthur Clarke book-signing once many years ago where there were only a handful of people to see him. I was embarrassed for him, and didn't want to go up and talk with him. Yet, he stuck it out, and deservedly made good. Fine! He's a good guy and an excellent writer. But I'd had enough.

I saw Arthur Clarke again at the World Con of 1979 in Brighton, England. I'd gone to see him the year before in Sri Lanka, both at his home in Colombo and his underwater safari place in Trincomolee on the other side of the island. In Brighton he was wearing a T-shirt promoting his diving activities. I asked him where I could get one of those shirts. He slid out of his jacket, peeled off the shirt, and gave it to me! This was the only actual, classical demonstration I have ever seen of the generous man who'd give you the shirt off his back!

Another who stuck it out was Lester Del Rey.[38] *Can you tell me about the first time you met him?*

By a curious coincidence Lester del Rey and I had met and talked together many times before either knew who the other was. This was in the last year of World War II. I'd been out in Hawaii for two years. I couldn't get into the service, so I got in the Corps of Engineers; then I worked for a year in the Pearl Harbor Navy Yard as a marine blacksmith.

When I returned to New York I got a job in New Jersey as an inspector for Otis Elevator, which was making crankcases for airplanes. I used to buy snacks at the White Tower hamburger place at the corner of West 56th Street and Eighth Avenue, which was just down the block from where I lived in New York City. I got to know the smooth-shaven, charming young griddle man in the white cap very well. Later I discovered this short-order cook was Lester Del Rey! I don't know why he wanted to do that kind of work—he could have gotten a much better job.[39]

But I really got to know Lester during one of my down periods later on. I figured I ought to have a literary job of some kind, so I worked for one week at a famous literary agency reading short stories that aspiring authors sent in. At that time the agency was charging fees for submissions, and the readers were supposed to comment constructively on the scripts. It had what was called a "plot skeleton" that everything was supposed to fit into. I didn't agree with that format and the boss didn't like my work, so I was sacked.[40]

Anyway, Lester was one of the other people working in this agency. He was really good at it. We used to talk at lunch, and that's when I really met him. He's had a lot of jobs in his time— worked on a farm, was a sheet metal worker during World War II, been up and down. Yes, those were hard but happy years!

*You've had two novels published fairly recently—*Skyclimber *in 1981 and* Bioblast *in 1985. Why did you start writing SF again?*

I starting writing SF again in 1973. Freida, my first wife, had cancer and sometimes I had to stay home from work to look after her during periods when she was in bad shape—which, fortunately, was not always.

While I was home with her, to pass the time, I started writing *The Eden Cycle*, which was published in 1974, partly at the urging of Lester and especially at the urging of Judy-Lynn del

Rey.[41] This was about a dream-culture centered around a device called SES—Sensory Experience Simulator—by which sensory impressions were fed directly into the brains or minds of people so that perfect representations of any sort could be experienced—without any of it being solidly real. Once started, the SES was self-sustaining. It seemed to be the perfect answer for everything. It used very little energy and few materials. Complicated, luxurious things, beautiful houses, yachts, whatever, cost nothing and consumed no resources, since they were only induced mental images.[42]

But Joe and Jennie, the protagonists, reach the opinion that it is all too false and unreal for them. They return to the dangerous and mortal real world, which has been allowed to revert to natural forest and wilderness. For a time they are happy; but illness and mortality catch up with them. Jennie, very sick, wants to die. But Joe persuades her to go back to the SES for another sequence of forgetfulness in the Eden Cycle. Ballantine-Del Rey published it with considerable editorial enthusiasm, but sales weren't too good. Much of this was because, after thirteen years of absence from the field, my original audience had dwindled and the younger readership hardly knew me. I was like a first-novelist.

Do you find there are certain problems you have in writing for the SF market today? It's almost like a different genre.

Yeah, and much of it isn't for me. I've always liked reality more than fantasy, and fantasy dominates the market today. Werewolves, magicians, and unicorns are okay, but on and on? It gets bloody tiresome.

My novel *Skyclimber* represents what I would *really* like to see happen: Let there be an SF movement toward stuff that can *truly* take place with a little expansion of existing technology, things that *should* happen soon, and therefore ought to be pushed in SF. Didn't I say that science fiction, to me, was an interim substitute for coming, though not-yet, reality? And don't let any fatheads say that writing about the first people trying to set up a viable life on "trite old Mars" is old hat! It can be new and alive and about regular, ordinary, rugged people—quite a useful and refreshing contrast to the flood of baloney about unicorns, witchcraft, and magic stuck out in some unknown or fake star system in phoney medieval simulations!

I received an uncorrected proof of an anthology from Arbor House called *Mirrorshades: The Cyberpunk Anthology*, edited by Bruce Sterling. Some of these short yarns were fairly good in their own way—perhaps trying to follow the mood of Chip Delany's *Dahlgren*. Delany's yarns are usually great, but *Dahlgren* is nothing like his best work. It's probably his worst! But what I didn't like most about these cyberpunk yarns was the constant, subcutaneous groan of misery and complaint, often infused with drug imagery and aimlessness. Shoot!

I keep coming back to *Skyclimber* as the kind of SF that should be emphasized today: things possible with present knowledge, things which could be accomplished *in the near future.* Manned Mars landings! A new frontier opened up for human use! Let the distant star system rest for a while!

I worked hard on *Skyclimber* and I'm glad it was a lot of fun because all I got for it from Tower was the small, by 1980s' standards, advance of $1,000. Distribution wasn't very good. Then Tower went broke and *Skyclimber,* along with yarns by other writers, is tied up in the legal tangles that follow a bankruptcy.

I have a number of completed novels in manuscript, but haven't found publishers for them just yet because of their offbeat nature. One, called *Legend Seed,* goes back to the Ice Age and is about the origins of civilization. But I just can't sell it. I get nice words from editors, but no takers. "Not quite what we're looking for right now."

Another script is a novel called *Gemi the Finder,* about ancient Egypt with fantasy elements. Egyptology has been a major hobby of mine ever since I was a kid, when I discovered "Ormund's" book on hieroglyphics in the attic. My novel seems to puzzle some SF editors. One told me over the phone, "It doesn't read or sound like science fiction!" But, trends keep changing, so who knows?[43]

How do you spend your time these days?

Well, I read a lot. I go to the library religiously every Saturday afternoon. I keep writing. I chug along, philosophize with friends in the neighborhood—pretty much do what I want. I'm solvent and, barring utter calamity, in no danger of want or starvation. All things considered, I have pretty good health. I can sit back and relax. My wife and I usually go south every year in early January and come back north in April.[44] I've had as good a life as I deserve.

As far as my writing career goes, I don't really have any regrets. I left the field when I wanted to, and came back when I felt I had something to say. At this point I don't have a very good track record in the book stores. My latest novel, *Bioblast,* was declared out of print after official sales of only 12,000 copies. Why this failure? I can only speculate. My long absence from the field was certainly partially responsible. Success in this business is a matter of building up a following. Most of my following from the early period just got older and drifted away. But, even the old fans forget you when you're away for over a dozen years. In the meantime, a lot of kids were coming up who didn't know me from Adam—and still don't!

There was also the problem of distribution. If you don't get good distribution, you're up the crick. Tower went broke after *Skyclimber*—though I don't believe there's any connection!— and I didn't see it around in many bookstores. *Bioblast* got a little better distribution, but not much.

People who order books for bookstores are like everyone else: They order books by authors they know best, because that's what is selling. Unless a publisher believes in a new book by a less well-known author enough to put a lot of money into a big publicity campaign, that author is at a serious disadvantage, no matter how well he writes. So, all writers, new and old, be warned: It's important to be known! Work on that! And do your best to stay that way after you've achieved it! Otherwise—you'll be forgotten . . . like me!

NOTES

1. "The Space Dwellers" in *Science Wonder Stories* and "The Crystal Ray" in *Air Wonder Stories,* each in the November issue. Truman Capote shared a similar experience. One day the seventeen-year-old Capote received his first, second, and third acceptance all in the same morning's mail. Auspicious beginnings for writers in any field.

2. All but one of Gallun's stories in the Gernsback magazines were published during Lasser's tenure, which ended in October 1933. "The Moon Plague" was published in the January 1934 *Wonder Stories,* under Charles D. Hornig's editorship, but it is unclear if this story had already been accepted by Lasser before his departure.

3. *Wonder Stories* also published the first stories of Laurence Manning and Leslie F. Stone (Mrs. William Silberburg), who went on to become prominent mainly for their numerous appearances in *Wonder Stories.* Stone's first appearance was actually a "novel" Lasser selected for the Stellar Science Fiction Series, books that Gernsback's Stellar Publications was producing. This novel was *When the Sun Went Out* (1929).

4. For more on this point, see Jane Donawerth, "Lilith Lorraine: Feminist Socialist Writer in the Pulps," *Science Fiction Studies* 17 (1990).

5. *Astounding Science Fiction* (April 1951).

6. Gallun got in on almost the ground floor of science fiction. This was only the fourth issue of *Amazing Stories* (July 1926). The cover illustrated "The Eggs from Lake Tanganyika," a story by one of Gernsback's translated Europeans, Curt Siodmak. Gallun would have been sixteen at the time.

7. Ray Gallun left $50,000 in his will to be divided equally between the crew of the first Earth expedition to land on Mars. It was invested so that it will accrue in value until it is awarded.

8. *Astounding Stories* (September 1936).

9. If Hornig forgot ever meeting Gallun, Gallun here forgets that Hornig *did* publish one of his stories, "The Moon Plague," in *Wonder Stories* (January 1934).

10. But so was Lasser. An MIT-trained engineer, he was working hard at this time to produce more scientifically accurate stories. See, for example, his correspondence with Jack Williamson in chapter 1.

11. The story is "Captive Asteroid," *Science Fiction Plus* (April 1953). It was about a giant pleasure palace built on an asteroid that is eventually pulled into Earth's orbit. Sam Moskowitz was the magazine's editor.

12. *Wonder Stories Quarterly* (Winter 1932). Harry Bates was editor of *Astounding*.

13. *Wonder Stories* (March and May 1932).

14. This was "The Menace from Mercury," which appeared under the names of both Michel and Gallun in the summer 1932 *Wonder Stories Quarterly*. Michel, a leader of the Futurians, was fourteen years old at the time. His prize was $2.50, which he apparently collected.

15. Even after the demise of *Science Fiction Plus,* Gernsback published a miniature SF magazine titled *Forecast,* which he sent as a Christmas card to friends.

16. Sam Moskowitz informed me that Gernsback married his third wife, Mary Hancher, in 1951.

17. This seems to contradict Gallun's previous claim that Gernsback "was never very generous when it came down to the cash." Gallun says Gernsback was doing well at this time. Apparently, when Gernsback had the money, he *was* generous with the cash!

18. Roman F. Starzl (1899–1976) wrote about twenty-five SF stories between 1928 and 1934, including a collaboration with Festus Pragnell, plus a detective story for Gernsback's *Scientific Detective Monthly.*

19. William Clayton's *Astounding* ceased publication in March 1933. Perhaps such generous payment rates in the midst of the absolute worst months of the Depression was a contributing factor. Gernsback, on the other hand, kept *his* magazines alive! Starzl did publish SF stories after Clayton went under in such magazines as *Wonder Stories,*

Argosy, Top-Notch, New Mystery Adventure, and the revived Street and Smith *Astounding,* which began publishing in October 1933. None of them paid as well as Clayton, which may very well have discouraged Starzl from continuing, as he ceased writing SF after 1934. He had a full-time job as editor of the only newspaper in Le Mars and wrote all his stories in the wee hours of the night at the end of very long days. The reduced pay rates may not have made it worthwhile. See chapter 6 on Starzl.

20. "My Interplanetary Teens" was reprinted in *Fantasy Commentator* (Summer 1989). Kelly, still a teenager, stopped writing SF in 1935 because a respected mentor disdained SF and told him he was wasting his talents working in the genre. See chapter 5 on Frank K. Kelly.

21. Hiram Gilmore Bates III, aka Harry Bates didn't *entirely* go "down the drain" after he left *Astounding.* He continued to occasionally publish his own SF stories over the next twenty years, his most well-known being "Farewell to the Master" (October 1940), which was made into the 1951 film *The Day the Earth Stood Still,* starring Michael Rennie. Bates claimed he was not an SF fan before being put in charge of the new *Astounding* by Clayton. He came out of a pulp adventure background and he brought these values with him to *Astounding.* His emphasis on strong plots, strong heroes, fast action, and a minimum of Gernsbackian science lectures in the stories brought a welcome injection of story-telling verve to the field, which continued after Clayton's *Astounding* died. Bates himself died in 1981.

22. This was Roger Sherman Hoar (1887–1963), Harvard-educated mathematics and engineering teacher and one-time Wisconsin state senator, who wrote SF under the name of "Ralph Milne Farley."

23. Robert Bloch (1917–1994) was, among many other things, the author of *Psycho.*

24. Henry Kuttner (1914–1958) was a major SF writer who married SF writer C. L. Moore (1911–1987) in 1940.

25. On Otto Binder (1911–1975) and his work in the comic book field see chapter 2.

26. Manly Wade Wellman (1903–1986) first appeared as a fantasy writer with a 1927 story in *Weird Tales.* His first SF story was "When Planets Clashed," *Wonder Stories Quarterly* (1931). His most well-

known series of stories concerned "Silver John," or "John the Balladeer," fantasies set in Appalachia, which began appearing in *The Magazine of Fantasy and Science Fiction* in 1951.

After reading this conversation with Ray Gallun, SF writer David Drake commented, "Julie Schwartz told me that Manly always drank Dubonnet at Steuben's because he'd heard it was a refined drink suitable for a literary man. Manly's brother Paul was a best-seller moving in the same circles as, for example, Harold Lamb; and it was probably from that connection that Manly got the notion.

"When I knew him, from 1970 to his death, he bought modestly priced bourbon (Henry McKenna was one brand, I remember; I'm a teetotaler myself so my recollection is a bit dim for names here) and drank better bourbons, Jack Daniels for choice, if they were available.

"He was never a boxer, but frequently got into fights in New York. His widow Frances tells of walking along the street with Manly, talking, and suddenly looking back to find him halfway down the block behind her battling someone who'd made an insulting remark as they passed. Manly was a good man to have known; I really miss him." See *Fantasy Commentator* (Summer 1989): 223.

Drake also recalled how Wellman won the very first *Ellery Queen Mystery Magazine* short story contest, taking the top prize of $1,000. The second-place runner-up was Nobel Prize–winner William Faulkner, who won $250. Drake says that "according to Faulkner's diary, he was incensed to have been beaten out for the $1,000 first prize by a 'hick from North Carolina.'

". . . The judges in the contest were Christopher Morley, Howard Haycraft, and the *EQMM* editors (for all practical purposes Fred Dannay only). They were absolutely unable to agree on which story was to get the top award. Three submissions were tied: those of Wellman, Faulkner, and T. S. Stribling.

"According to the recollections of Manly's widow, Frances, Dannay broke the deadlock by calling in Rex Stout, a major mystery writer of the day who hadn't entered the contest. He picked Manly's story, which had been Dannay's choice, as well. . . .

"The Wellmans used the prize money to move from New Jersey to North Carolina, where Manly intended to research a book on his namesake, the Civil War general Wade Hampton. Contrary to Faulkner's rantings, he had no connection with North Carolina until after the prizes were awarded.

"This is an interesting story of how a Nobel laureate lost out to a writer who had better connections in the milieu in question; and who, for at least just one story, was a better writer." See David Drake, *Fantasy Commentator* (Fall 1990): 74.

27. Malcolm Jameson (1891–1945) began writing SF in 1938 after cancer put an end to a more active life. He wrote prolifically up until his death and his novels were all published posthumously.

28. John W. Campbell (1910–1971), long-time influential editor of *Astounding-Analog*.

29. F. Orlin Tremaine (1899–1956) succeeded Bates as editor at *Astounding* when it resumed publication in October 1933, as a Street and Smith publication. He relinquished editorship in October 1937, to become editorial director of a number of Street and Smith magazines. He was replaced by his hand-picked successor, John W. Campbell.

30. Leo Margulies (1900–1975) took over as editorial director at *Thrilling Wonder Stories* when Beacon Publishing bought *Wonder Stories* from Gernsback in 1936. He also had overall responsibility for other Beacon magazines, including *Startling Stories, Captain Future,* and *Strange Stories.*

31. Although its sub-editors changed, Reiss was in overall editorial control of *Planet Stories* for the entire life of the magazine, from its winter 1939 issue to its summer 1955 issue. The magazine specialized in "space opera" and was a major venue for Leigh Brackett and Ray Bradbury during the middle and late Forties. Just before it died, it also published the first stories of Philip K. Dick.

Gallun's story, "Return of a Legend," appeared in *Planet Stories.* In reprinting it in her anthology of the best from the magazine, Leigh Brackett declared its Mars setting to be "an astonishingly believable Mars even in light of our latest knowledge. . . . The background is meticulously constructed, interesting in itself and a vital element in the plot." A "psychological story," Gallun's tale "concerns itself powerfully with the effect of an alien environment on Earthmen." See Leigh Brackett, editor, *The Best of Planet Stories*, no. 1 (New York: Ballantine Books, 1975), pp. 5-6.

Difficult to see how Reiss could have been intimately associated with *Planet Stories* throughout World War II while also serving as an OSS man in China during the war.

32. Sam Merwin began editing both magazines with their winter 1945 issues; he edited *Startling* until September 1951 and *Thrilling Wonder Stories* until October 1951.

33. This was Gallun's first hard-cover novel, published in 1957.

34. *Marvel Science Fiction* (November 1951).

35. E. g., "A Menace in Miniature," *Astounding Stories* (October 1937), published by Tremaine.

36. *Astounding Stories* (December 1935), published by Tremaine.

37. *Astounding Stories* (June 1938), published by Campbell.

38. "Lester del Rey" (1915–1993) was a major SF writer and editor who wrote over forty fiction and nonfiction books and was fantasy editor for Del Rey Books, a division of Random House, until he retired in 1991.

39. Sam Moskowitz tells of del Rey working at this White Tower restaurant in *Seekers of Tomorrow* (Cleveland: World Publishing Co., 1966), p. 181. Del Rey was thirty and in a fallow period, doubting his ability to write. He sold two stories that year, both to Campbell at *Astounding*. He was dating Helen Schlaz, a Lithuanian who worked at another White Tower. They married in 1945 and Del Rey quit the White Tower to try full-time writing. Six rejections in a row from Campbell made him doubt his talents even more. He attended the Fifth World Science Fiction Convention in Philadelphia August 30–September 1, 1947, and met Scott Meredith, a fan who'd just launched his literary agency. He first took Del Rey on as a client and then offered him a job in the agency, where Del Rey became a supervisor. See Moskowitz, *Seekers of Tomorrow*, pp. 181–82.

40. The Scott Meredith plot skeleton for successful fiction Gallun is speaking about is the following: "A sympathetic lead character finds himself in trouble of some kind and makes active efforts to get himself out of it. Each effort, however, merely gets him deeper into his trouble, and each new obstacle in his path is larger than the last. Finally, when things look blackest and it seems certain that the lead character is kaput, he manages to get out of his trouble through his own efforts, intelligence, or ingenuity." See Scott Meredith, *Writing to Sell*, 2d rev. ed. (New York: Harper & Row, 1950), p. 58. In the introduction by

Arthur C. Clarke to this same volume, Clarke praised Scott Meredith's literary insights and acumen. Robert Silverberg also claimed that Meredith's book was one of the three books that taught him all he knows about how to write. See Robert Silverberg, "Becoming a Writer," *Amazing Stories* (May 1986).

41. Judy-Lynn Del Rey (1943–1986) began as an SF editor at *Galaxy Science Fiction* in 1965. There she met Lester Del Rey and they were married in 1971. She joined Ballantine Books, a division of Random House, in 1973, and in 1977 convinced Ballantine to establish Del Rey Books, an SF division, with herself as editor-in-chief.

42. Today we would call this "virtual reality."

43. After his death, Gallun's papers, correspondence, and manuscripts were donated to the State University of New York at Stonybrook. SUNY-Stonybrook has also established a Raymond Z. Gallun Award for "Outstanding Contributions to the Science Fiction Genre." Always running from Beaver Dam, Gallun was an incessant traveler to the end who took tens of thousands of slides of his travels. These ended up in Special Collections at Temple University in Philadelphia.

44. Erickson Backman. The two grew up within a few miles of each other in Beaver Dam and met in 1929. They dated, but each married someone else. After the deaths of their first spouses, they met again in 1977 and were married in 1978. Bertha Gallun died of cancer on January 30, 1989, at age seventy-nine.

5.

TEENAGE AUTHOR

A Conversation with Frank K. Kelly

Granton had never been able to understand why gravitation had always been called a "pull"; every phenomenon known concerning the force of gravity would fit as well into the framework of a repulsive theory. He had gone on that principle: that gravity is not a pull, but a pressure pervading all space. The Granton motor was attuned to the matter-radiations of the earth, and it was insulated against the influences of the other worlds of space. It acted as a supertransformer unit, infinitely sensitive in its receiving cells to the pressure of the earth; the result was tremendous propulsive power. In operation tests it proved to be nearly 99 percent efficient—as close to perfect as any man-built mechanism could come; harnessed to a space ship, it would be just about the ideal thing for interplanetary travel.

—Frank K. Kelly, "Into the Meteorite Orbit" (1933)

BETWEEN 1931 AND 1935 ONE OF THE MOST INTERESTING science fiction writers in the magazines was Frank K. Kelly, a seemingly embittered old man who invariably wrote sto-

227

ries which ended on rather somber notes. Readers complained that there surely must be some ray of hope in the future, but Kelly saw only darkness and despair. It seemed evident that something in his life had tinged his outlook with ingrained pessimism. Nevertheless, the editors bought every story he cranked out and among his fellow authors—such as Raymond Z. Gallun—Kelly was considered "brilliant."

Then, in 1935, just as he had begun to sell to the market-leading *Astounding* and it seemed he was destined to evolve into one of the giants of the field—the stories ceased and nothing more was heard of Frank K. Kelly. It seemed the earth had at last swallowed up the disappointed old man.

But the real Frank Kelly fit few of these misanthropic perceptions. Perhaps most surprising was that, despite the tone of his stories, his entire science fiction career blossomed, grew, and faded while he was yet a teenager. *In this, Kelly was representative of a young genre which was both consumed and created by the young.* Ray Gallun, as we have seen, wrote his first two published stories for his high school English class. John Michel shared a professional by-line with Gallun when he was only fourteen. Charlie Hornig became a professional editor when he was seventeen. Frederik Pohl became a professional editor when he was nineteen. Frank Kelly himself was only sixteen when he became a professional SF author. Isaac Asimov, perhaps the best-known SF writer of all time, was another such. Beginning to publish SF only a few years after Frank Kelly and, like Kelly, a teenager at the time, it is tempting to speculate about their careers. Kelly, a teenager with great promise in the field, abandoned it in embarrassment. Asimov, a teenager who never wanted to do anything else but write science fiction, stayed with it all his life. One wonders if Frank K. Kelly might have been a name as well-known as that of Isaac Asimov had he, too, stayed with it.

One reason teenagers were so prominent in the new field was that older and more mature writers avoided the new field as declasse, even more "trashy" than other pulp genres, a reason

Kelly was shamed out of the field by his respected academic mentors. The resulting inexperience of the writers who remained to create the evolving genre was one major reason so much of the writing seemed juvenile. It *was* juvenile because it was *written* by juveniles! It was literally "kid stuff." In such a context, a writer such as Stanley G. Weinbaum, who began publishing in his early thirties, would naturally stand out as a more mature writer if for no other reason than the fact that he had more life experience. Only as the genre itself aged and more mature writers entered or stayed in the field did the phenomenon of the teenage author or editor fade from the scene. But the birth of science fiction belonged to the young, to writers such as Frank Kelly.

While most readers viewed Kelly's stories as overwhelmingly stark and jaundiced, Kelly himself saw his work as deeply religious, hopeful, as attempts to discover the "Love at the heart of the universe." Further, Frank K. Kelly, while disappearing from the science fiction world, was not swallowed up by oblivion. He continued to write and his stories not only appeared in the top mainstream magazines, but also were selected for annual year-end "best of" anthologies. He served as a war correspondent in World War II, attended Harvard as a Nieman Fellow, and wrote Harry Truman's back-of-the-train speeches for his successful 1948 whistle-stop election campaign. After helping to found and lead the noted Center for the Study of Democratic Institutions in Santa Barbara, Kelly went on to write a half-dozen history books before turning full-time to international peace advocacy, which he continues to this day. No doubt if he had continued in the science fiction field, such life experience would also have made him a renowned master of the genre. Even so, Frank King Kelly was typical of many of the early pioneers of the field who helped bring it into existence and shaped it as a separate genre.

Concern with and opposition to nuclear war has been a constant theme of Kelly's life. In his first story, "The Light Bender," written when he was sixteen and published in 1931, he described a nuclear world war between Germany and America in 1990. In his 1932 story, "Red April, 1965," he posited a nuclear war between Russia and America in 1965. His fictional concerns carried over into his real life when he helped found the Nuclear Age Peace Foundation dedicated to the abolition of nuclear weapons.

The following conversation about Kelly's SF career and later life took place on September 24, 1988. He was seventy-four years old at the time. I last spoke with him on October 24, 1997. He was still the senior vice president of the Nuclear Age Peace Foundation and, at age eighty-three, was still working to eliminate nuclear weapons from our world.

ERIC LEIF DAVIN: *In the early thirties, when your science fiction career was in full-bloom, many readers thought you must have been an embittered old man, judging from the pessimistic tone of your stories. But you were still a teenager for most of those years, weren't you?*

FRANK K. KELLY: Yes, actually I was born in Kansas City, Missouri, June 12, 1914 and was only sixteen when I sent my first story off to David Lasser at *Wonder Stories*. By the time I was twenty-one, when I entered the University of Missouri at Kansas City in 1935, it was basically over.

Teenagers are usually pretty optimistic. Why do you think your stories were just the opposite?

I think I was—unconsciously at the time—really conducting a religious search in all my science fiction stories. I felt that I didn't belong anywhere, and I think I thought science fiction might help me find my place in the universe. I know that ever since I was a young boy I had this yearning to explore the night sky. I often felt I didn't belong, that I actually came from somewhere else other than this place called Earth. My parents said I had this feeling from a very early age. When I discovered science fiction, I didn't imagine aliens coming here, so much, as our going out into space—and finding our real selves on other planets. There was a mystical element in my feeling for space very similar, I suppose, to that expressed in the movie *E.T.* I had a really fine family life, with good parents and a loving sister and brother, but I still had a yearning to be connected with other worlds. I thought of myself as a dreamer—a wanderer, a sojourner.

How did you discover science fiction?

Well, I must have been about thirteen years old. I was a student at St. Vincent's parochial school in Kansas City. On my way home from school one day I stopped in a drugstore and found a copy of *Amazing Stories,* with a cover of Martian tripods burning London, illustrating "The War of the Worlds" by H. G. Wells.[1] After that I was hooked. I felt I had a resonance with Wells, with Jules Verne. I began reading everything I could find. Some of my favorite authors of the time were E. E. Smith, Jack Williamson, David Keller; I was really surprised to learn from your conversation with David Lasser[2] that Keller was actually pretty bad at grammar and needed to be cleaned up a lot before he could be published. His ideas impressed me, so I assumed he could write fluently.

How did you go from reading science fiction to writing it?

Despite what I just said about writers I liked, I felt most of it was awful and that I could write stories just as good as those I saw published. So, I tried my hand at a story without telling anyone and slipped it into the mail to *Wonder Stories* on the way home from school one day. This was "The Light Bender," and, to my surprise, it was accepted and published![3] It was about scientists who invented a device for bending light rays, which allowed them to enter alternate universes. It also predicted atomic power and a *third* world war—not a second one!—in 1990, possibly a nuclear holocaust fought with the Germans. My belief that the Germans might launch another terrible war came from my father. My dad fought in World War I as an infantry captain and was wounded at the Battle of St. Mihiel. He told me the Germans weren't really beaten and would try again, so I guess I put that into the story. I think David Lasser's blurb for it said that I was a "brilliant young author," so that just inspired me to do more writing.

The Depression was beginning when I was graduated from high school. My dad, Francis Kelly, lost his job in 1931 or 1932. He had led an adventurous life. When he was sixteen he served in the navy, and sailed on Teddy Roosevelt's Great White Fleet around the world.[4] Then he was a fireman in the days when fire engines were pulled by four huge white horses. The only memory I have of that was of a collision between his engine and a streetcar. After fighting in France he worked for the National Cloak & Suit Company, but that collapsed in the thirties. A man who had been his lieutenant in the army offered him a job in Indianapolis, and we moved there.[5]

I got a job in a box factory working twelve hours a day for 25 cents an hour and was exhausted by the hard manual labor. Despite that, I wrote stories. I wrote for the joy of being published—I was just happy to be published. Shortly afterward, Dad found work and he bought me a typewriter. Also, I was able to stop working, and I enrolled at Butler University in Indianapolis for half a year. Mostly, though, I just wrote. We moved back to Kansas City in 1932, when my father became an executive with the branch office of Sears, Roebuck, and Company.

Where did you send your stories?

Mostly to David Lasser at *Wonder Stories*. He was the one who wrote to me and accepted my first story, so I sent them to him and we developed a close working relationship. I have a vivid remembrance of David Lasser. I had great respect for him. He was really a creative genius. He wrote me long letters scolding me for various things in my stories, but he never drastically changed anything I wrote. I do remember I did a revision for him on "Exiles of Mars," which he still didn't like, but he published it anyway, just as I rewrote it.[6] Much later I wrote a piece for the *Atlantic Monthly* called "My Interplanetary Teens" in which I talked about the problems I had had with editors— plural—but I think I was talking about only one editor in that piece, and he was David Lasser. We seemed to hit if off well, despite his criticism of my stories, and I appreciated his guidance and concern. That *Atlantic Monthly* piece is a tribute to Lasser. If my stories were ever any good, it was partly because of him.

Did you ever receive any communications from Hugo Gernsback concerning any of your stories?

No, all my contact with *Wonder Stories* was from Lasser. Hugo didn't actually write to authors, did he?

Well, it seems he did with some of them. How about payment? Was there any problem getting paid by Gernsback? Did you hear from him about money?

No; Hugo was slow to pay, but I think I was always paid. But, even when I wrote to *Wonder* asking about my money it was always Lasser who answered me. I never had any contact with Gernsback himself. At least I don't recall any.

What kind of criticisms did Lasser make of your work?

Mostly they had to do with plot, believability, technical accuracy; he wanted the stories to be as realistic as possible. I also showed some of my stories to my eighty-year-old Irish grandfather, Mike Kelly. He'd just chew on his mustache as he read them and then tell me, "Too many God-damned super-fluous words!" I think he was right. I loaded on the adjectives. I gradually learned to eliminate "super-fluous" words.

Were there any themes you were trying in particular to explore?

I remember sitting on my porch on the Paseo in Kansas City in 1927 when I was thirteen. I watched Charles Lindbergh ride by in a car and was greatly excited by seeing him. His lonely flight to Paris was a tremendous feat. He was my model for some of my heroes. I was always interested in how people summoned up the courage to be heroes, the boldness to be explorers—and the changes this made in them.

But I also believed that invisible forces for good and evil were at work in the universe, and this tension, I think, was reflected in my stories. I had been very religious and there had been some fantastic nuns at St. Vincent's who encouraged me to write. They didn't try to restrict my mind. So, I was filled with a sense of wonder at the enormity of the universe and our role in it. I tried to explain that feeling in my stories, to show how we are all connected with each other and with the universe. I felt science fiction—like religion—was an attempt to explain the universe. I was engaged in a search for ultimate truth. I was always grappling with the mystery of consciousness. How do the dancing atoms of which we are composed make it possible to converse—as we are doing—or for a writer to create? Many years later I had a long conversation with Linus Pauling about this, and he said it was all an accident of physics. I told him it took tremendous faith to believe that physics and chemistry could explain the development of life and thought.

I guess I was terribly romantic as a teenager. I expected a lot and was often disappointed. I was frustrated at the way things were. I often had a foreboding about technology. I went through a very lonely period of complete skepticism. I guess you could

say I lost my faith in everything for a while. I felt there was no
hope beyond this transitory life, and that this life itself didn't
look so great. Science, I felt, couldn't explain the powers of the
universe after all. My readers at this time must have felt I was
engaged in a pretty pessimistic search. Look at my stories, like
"The Moon Tragedy," or "Star Ship Invincible," just to name two
which ended on a dark note![7]

But experience eventually convinced me there is an amazing
Love at the heart of the universe. There is something greater than
we are—greater than we can imagine—which guides our des-
tinies. I can't explain many of the events in my life otherwise. For
instance, in 1932 I wrote "Red April, 1965," for David Lasser at
Wonder Stories.[8] It was about a rocket war between the USA and
the USSR, a war supposedly occurring in April 1965.

One day, in the actual year of 1965, a strange anxiety came over
me in my office at the Center for the Study of Democratic Institutions in Santa Barbara, where I then worked. My secretary buzzed
me and said a madman was running around in the lobby. I went out
and found a well-dressed man who was pacing about in an agitated
state. He turned to me and said, "I am the Son of God! I want the
Center to publish my New Testament! I've come to tell you there
will be a nuclear war between America and Russia in April 1965!"

It turned out he was a Santa Monica dentist who'd lost all his
money in the stock market, which pushed him over the edge. But
why did he come and confront me? This was one of the eeriest
episodes of my life. But events like this made me think there's a
directing force to our lives. The war that I had predicted for 1965
didn't happen. Perhaps my story was a factor that helped keep it
from happening.

*Did any of these feelings affect the way you went about your
writing?*

I think so, because I never knew where I was going with my
stories. They just came to me and I wrote them down. I believe in

a creative spirit. Otherwise, I just can't account for how I poured out those stories in an endless stream. I'd write sixteen thousand words in two or three days at top speed with no outline or idea of what the plot might be. I'd just start out with a few sentences and go with the flow wherever it took me and then I mailed it directly off. Every story I wrote was accepted and, except for "Exiles of Mars," I was never asked to do any substantial revisions. It was a transcendental experience which convinced me that writing comes out of deep psychic wells and can't be explained.

Your stories may have been first drafts, but they also seem to have been increasingly welcome by 1934, 1935, with the editors, if not the readers.

Yes, I had editors writing me asking for stories. The money was also welcome. I was able to buy things for my family we wouldn't have been able to afford otherwise.

In 1934 you finally broke into Astounding, *which was the top science fiction market at the time. According to Mort Weisinger, Desmond Hall, their associate editor, read your "Into the Meteorite Orbit" in* Amazing *and wrote to you asking for something for* Astounding. *You then retrieved "Crater 17, Near Tycho" from* Amazing, *which had already accepted it, and sent it to Hall at* Astounding.[9] *Can you tell me about that?*

I'm glad to be reminded of how I began my friendship with Desmond Hall. He later became my literary agent and a very close friend when I lived in New York.

I sent the story off to him and heard nothing at all for the longest time. Then I received a check for $150, or something like that. It came to a cent a word, double what I'd have gotten from *Amazing.* But no letter—just the check. Weeks later I did receive a letter from Hall saying he'd been too busy to write before that, but that he loved the story.

When F. Orlin Tremaine, the editor of Astounding, *was asked around that time to comment on various stories, he said that he chose "Crater 17, Near Tycho," for "pure beauty of style."* [10]

I'm delighted to hear that, because I always cared deeply about style—about the shape of sentences, the flow of words, the musical rhythm of good writing. I continued to care about it even after I stopped writing science fiction.

Speaking of which, why did you stop writing science fiction? It seems you were not only successful at it, but that it met a spiritual need, and yet you stopped cold in 1935.

Well, in 1935 I entered the University of Missouri at Kansas City and studied under H. Robertson Shipherd, an Englishman from "Oxbridge." I showed him my published stories and he said I was wasting myself on trash, and I ought to write serious literature. He convinced me that what I was doing wasn't worthwhile. That ruined me as a creative science fiction writer.

So, I turned to mainstream literature instead. I tried to write out of my own experience. Even with this type of writing, however, I tried to do the same thing I'd tried to accomplish with my science fiction. I wanted to make people understand that we're all connected, we're all one.

I showed Shipherd a story I called "With Some Gaiety and Laughter." It was about a wounded World War I vet who was obsessed by a recording of laughter. The sound of laughter kept him from going insane. He liked it and sent it off to *Story Magazine,* which printed it in 1935. It was then picked up and included in Edward J. O'Brien's anthology, *Best American Short Stories: 1936,* after which it was reprinted in Sweden, Norway, and France. Then NBC Radio bought the broadcasting rights for $50 and I got a literary agent out of it, so it seemed to me then that abandoning science fiction was the right decision.

What was the next step along this new career path?

I was graduated from college in 1937 and began looking for a journalism job, which seemed to be the closest salaried work I could get to writing. C. G. ("Pete") Wellington, night editor for the *Kansas City Star,* took me on, though he was reluctant. He said the last "restless writer" he hired had been Ernest Hemingway, and Hemingway had left after a few months. "Just when you get good as a journalist in four or five years," he said, "you'll leave to write novels, just like Hemingway."[11]

And he was right! I worked as a reporter there for four years and then made my break in 1941 for New York City to become a "serious" writer. This was when I finally met Desmond Hall, who'd accepted my stories at *Astounding.* We became good friends and he certainly encouraged me. He told me I could write absolutely anything! He read and edited all my stories and became my literary agent. He sold my stories to *Esquire, Liberty,* and other top markets, but I just couldn't make a living at it. Then another friend, Hal Boyle, helped get me a job as a reporter in the New York bureau of the Associated Press.[12]

Needless to say, this drastically cut down on my fiction, but I wrote a lot of other things. William Rapp, editor of *True Story,* wanted me to write for him, so I did. I gave him a first-person story entitled, "Miss Smith Goes To Washington," about competition between women for men in Washington, D.C., because of the great expansion of the federal bureaucracy taking place at that time. I got the story by interviewing girls in Washington. This piece was later reprinted in *The Best True Stories of 1941.*

Didn't you also marry about this time?

Yes, I married Barbara Allen Mandigo of Kansas City—a beautiful poet and pianist—at the Cathedral of St. John the Divine in New York City on Friday, December 5, 1941. At the reception at Hal Boyle's the next night everybody was talking about the crisis in the Pacific. On Sunday morning we heard on the radio that the Japanese had attacked Pearl Harbor. I immediately called the offices of the Associated Press to see if they wanted me to come in and help out. An editor there, Norman Lodge, told me, "It's only a damn war, go back to your honeymoon!" My wife appreciated that.

When did you get your journalism fellowship at Harvard? The Nieman Fellowship?

In 1942. I happened to read about it and applied at the very last minute at the urging of my wife. I had to hurry up for the interview later, and almost didn't get the fellowship, because I was very nervous and serious. They thought I was stodgy and had no sense of humor and didn't like that, but they accepted me anyway for the 1942–43 academic year. I was amazed. I hadn't believed that I could possibly get such a fellowship. My wife actually drafted the application and mailed it.

And what was the Nieman Fellowship like?

It was wonderful! It was a year off from journalism during which we got to live in Cambridge and sample Harvard. I remember we lived at 21 Chauncy Street, near Harvard Square. But the winter of '42–'43 was very hard and we almost froze because there was very little fuel. The war was on and Nazi submarines sank many oil tankers off the Atlantic coast.

I took whatever courses I wanted with no exams! In addition, Barbara had an opportunity to take some courses at Radcliffe. Harvard paid you whatever salary you'd been making at your previous job. At the end of a year, they expected you to write a report on your experience. It was very enlightening. There were good weekly seminars with world leaders, such as Heinrich Bruning, the former Chancellor of the Weimar Republic, and I gained a real insight into world affairs.

But then, toward the end of 1942, my draft board called me in for a medical exam. I was extremely near-sighted and I thought they'd reject me, but I passed! In January of 1943 I found myself drafted into the army. The Harvard faculty gave me a big farewell party and I was shipped off to Ft. Devens in western Massachusetts.

Were you drafted into the infantry, or something else?

Well, I went through Basic Training at Ft. Devens, but then a battery of tests revealed that I was eligible for the Army Specialized Training Program. So they shipped me back to Harvard for six months of schooling. There I was, marching through Harvard Yard in formation! My friends on the Harvard faculty really got a kick out of that! The other Nieman Fellows were astounded. But then, for some reason, these units were disbanded and I was sent down to Virginia for infantry training.

So, you ended up in the infantry after all! Did they send you to Europe?

Yes, we were shipped off to England. My convoy across the Atlantic was a real nightmare. A Nazi submarine wolf pack attacked us, and the ships in our convoy were mauled pretty badly. The tanker next to the ship I was on was hit by a torpedo and sank in flames. It was all chaos and confusion. Men were screaming and writhing in the burning oil. Two torpedoes narrowly missed our ship. We thought we would be hit, but we weren't.

When we reached England, I was stationed in a supply depot. An officer came through looking for a soldier with experience in journalism, so I jumped on that, which is how I became an army correspondent.

What did that entail?

Mostly interviewing a lot of wounded soldiers. It was a sad business. Many of them had lost their arms or legs. The horror of war was burned into their faces. After D-Day I was sent to France and was eventually promoted to sergeant. I was attached to General George Patton's Third Army and took part in the liberation of Paris in August 1944. The whole city went wild. We were hugged and kissed by screaming Frenchmen and Frenchwomen.

I was back in England in early '45 when the Nazis started hitting London with their V-bombs. These really shocked the British, as they thought the Nazis were licked. It really surprised them, but the V-bombs made me think of my science fiction stories—it was like they were coming true!

Were you still trying to write fiction during these years as a war correspondent?

Oh, yes! In fact, I wrote one of my best stories at this time, "Crossing the Volturno."[13] The Volturno is a river in Italy. Our soldiers fought their way across it under fire. I overheard the story of the crossing in a bar while I was in France. I sat down, scribbled out the story, sent it to the *New Yorker* and they published it. They put it into a special issue distributed overseas and I got fan mail from readers all over the map. It really seemed to touch people. They all said it was a powerful story—but they didn't understand the ending. The reason for that was that the *New Yorker* actually chopped off the last paragraph! The magazine was famous for its cryptic stories, and this seemed to be how its editors operated.

[After the war ended Kelly returned to Harvard to complete his Nieman Fellowship. This was followed by stints at the Associated Press, as a speechwriter for President Truman during the 1948 campaign, and as a journalism teacher at Boston University. In 1959 he joined the Center for the Study of Democratic Institutions in Santa Barbara, California, where he eventually became vice president. He retired from the center in 1975.]

Have you thought of trying your hand at science fiction again?

No, but ten years ago my whole science fiction past was brought back to me in a rather unusual way. In 1978 there was a small earthquake here in Santa Barbara which did very little damage. But it did jar open the door of the closet in my second-floor study and tossed out a bundle of old *Astoundings* which I'd kept only because I had stories in them. Actually, there were only three of them. I never kept track of my career; I always wanted to move ahead, not look back, so I kept few things.

But in a way this earthquake brought the past back to life. I showed my stories to Noel Young, a friend who owns a small local publishing house called Capra Press, and he thought there might actually be a market for them. He published a small anthology of the three under the title *Star Ship Invincible* and sold about three thousand copies!

Right now I'm not writing any science fiction, but maybe I will. That book and this conversation have stirred me up. First, though, I'll have to finish my autobiography, of which I have three chapters completed.

Do you have any regrets about the direction your life and career took?

I hope I've gotten past the stage of regrets. The old, you know, like to be part of everything. I'm reminded of Robert Frost's poem on "The Road Not Taken." You can take only one road, no matter how attractive others might be. I wish I could have kept on writing science fiction and still have done all the rest! I wonder what would've happened if I'd stayed with it? But basically I believe regrets are futile.

Would you say a few words about your family?

I'm still married to the same woman I married more than forty-seven years ago and it gets to be a better marriage all the time. She is a woman with spiritual wisdom. Barbara's volume of poetry, *Uncovering Memories*, was published two years ago, and some of her poems have been translated into Russian. Many are autobiographical. Some of them tell of our long-lasting love.

We have two sons. The oldest, Terence F. Kelly, of Madison, Wisconsin, is a vice president of Dynatech Corporation and is a great reader of science fiction. His wife Mary is a talented artist, and they have three sons—Christopher, Matthew, and Michael. Christopher is a gifted child, already interested in science fiction and exploring the universe. Matthew and Michael are also talented. If I do say so myself, all three of our grandsons are bright and handsome.

Our second son, Stephen D. Kelly, is a brilliant pianist who has given concerts in France and Spain, as well as this country. He has an enormous repertoire. He is also a marvelous dancer, a philosopher, and a teacher of music.

I have so many blessings I can't begin to count them all.

If you had to sum up your life, what would you say?

Well, I've been involved in so many interesting things. My wife wondered if they'd all come together. Admiral Hyman Rickover once asked me how to make sense out of my career. I quoted Hamlet and said, "There's a Divinity that shapes our ends, rough-hew them how we will." He turned to his wife and told her to write that down. Perhaps it helped him to understand his own life.

My concerns grow out of my feeling that every person has a spirit or soul of value. I'm a man of faith, and I feel that every one of us is of importance in the sight of God—and therefore each one should be important to us. Jesus prayed that we all may be one. But all religions talk about the unity of humanity. Now it seems to me there is a pattern, a purpose, to my life, erratic though it may appear. As in the title of my *Saturday Review* article, that purpose seems to be in becoming "A Spokesman for Mankind."

NOTES

1. This was the August 1927 issue, with a cover by Frank Paul, which confirms that Kelly was thirteen years old, instead of the eleven years of age he mentions in his memoir, "My Interplanetary Teens," *The Atlantic Monthly* 180 (July 1947): 102–103, reprinted in *Fantasy Commentator* 6, no. 3 (Summer 1989).

2. *Fantasy Commentator* 5, no. 4 (1987), and reprinted here in chapter 1, "The Age of Wonder."

3. It appeared in the June 1931 *Wonder Stories.*

4. This would have made Francis Kelly a shipmate of author Raymond Z. Gallun's uncle, Julius Zinke, of whom Gallun was greatly impressed.

5. C.L. Moore was also in Indianapolis at this time, but had not yet begun writing.

6. *Wonder Stories Quarterly* (Summer 1932). This is probably the "Exiles of Saturn" mentioned in "My Interplanetary Teens." To a follow-up query, Kelly replied that he, "may have changed the locale to Mars in the course of revising it."

7. "The Moon Tragedy" appeared in *Wonder Stories* (October 1933), the last issue to be edited by David Lasser. Kelly never sent another story to *Wonder Stories* after Lasser's departure. "Star Ship Invincible" appeared in the January 1935 *Astounding Stories* and was his last science fiction story.

8. "Red April, 1965," appeared in the March 1932 *Wonder Stories.*

9. See Mort Weisinger's column, "The Ether Vibrates," *Fantasy Magazine* (May 1934): 27. "Into the Meteorite Orbit" appeared in the December 1933 *Amazing Stories.* "Crater 17, Near Tycho" appeared in the June 1934 *Astounding.*

10. *Fantasy Magazine* (October 1934): 43.

11. Wellington must have had a dearth of "restless writer" applicants, since Hemingway left the *Kansas City Star* twenty years before this to drive an ambulance in World War I.

12. Frank Starzl, brother of fellow Midwestern SF writer R. F. Starzl, was at this time head of the Associated Press in New York City.

13. *The New Yorker* (June 2, 1945).

14. Dr. Isaac Asimov was also a member of the Boston University faculty at this time, but the two never met. Certainly Asimov would have been familiar with Kelly's SF work.

6.

THE SCIENCE AND SCIENCE FICTION OF R. F. STARZL

A Conversation with Thomas E. Starzl

"I blame myself," said Professor Halley sadly, "for overlooking this important point. While it is true that the sub-universe resembles our own; while it is true that the electrons follow their orbits in a manner analogous to the planets around the suns; yet I overlooked the fact that due to the great difference in size there is also an enormous difference in time. It takes the earth a year to go around the sun; an electron circles its positive nucleus millions of times a second. Yet every time it completes its orbit it is like a year to the inhabitants.

"Before I had time to even blink an eye, Shirley and Hale had lived, loved, died, and many generations of their children had gone through their life cycles. It was normal to them—to us it was unthinkably brief."

—R. F. Starzl, "Out of the Sub-Universe" (1928)

LIKE FRANK KELLY, MANY OF THE EARLY PRACTITIONERS OF magazine science fiction were just kids. As Robert Silverberg, who began publishing at a young age himself, points out, "we see Isaac Asimov selling stories at 18, and writing the classic 'Nightfall' at 21; we have Algis Budrys on every magazine's contents page before he was 22, Harlan Ellison doing the same, Bradbury famous for his weird tales at 23, Theodore Sturgeon turning out 'Microcosmic God' at about that age . . . and so on and so on."[1] Youthful writers were a phenomenon of this youthful genre. And, not to disparage these fore-named excellent writers, most of the young writers did not display outstanding literary skills, even by pulp standards. This was because "the editors of the early science-fiction magazines had found it necessary to rely for their material largely on hobbyists with humpty-dumpty narrative skills; the true storytellers were off writing for the other pulp magazines, knocking out westerns or adventure tales with half the effort for twice the pay."[2] Early science fiction was truly a labor of love, for even within the pulp universe science fiction was considered trash and was left to the enthusiastic young. Thus, a writer such as Kelly, who might have brought needed maturity to the field as he matured, was shamed by those he respected to abandon his beloved literature.

But there was another kind of writer and enthusiast who was attracted to science fiction. This type tended to be older and tended to be attracted to the genre because of its early Gernsbackian emphasis upon science and innovative technology. Such a writer was R. F. Starzl.

As mentioned by Raymond Z. Gallun in chapter 4, he grew up and started writing in the backwoods of Wisconsin during the 1930s. He was never a member of any fan circle, nor was he able to associate with other genre writers, as did fellow Wisconsin author Stanley G. Weinbaum. Recall that in 1934 he finally tried to break out of his isolation by contacting R. F. Starzl, a fellow midwesterner whose work he had long admired. But Starzl wrote back saying, "Your attempt to write to a science fiction author has misfired, because I've just quit!"[3]

Before he suddenly did so, however, he had produced a solid body of science fiction totalling some twenty stories in the period 1928-1934. Some of these stories were featured, complete with garish covers, as the main draw of the issues where they appeared. One such was Starzl's November 1930 tale in *Amazing Stories*, "The Globoid Terror," with a delightful cover by well-known genre artist Leo Morey. But perhaps Starzl's best-known story, and certainly his most important contribution to the field, was his very first, "Out of the Sub-Universe," which appeared in the summer 1928 *Amazing Stories Quarterly*.

The idea of "sub-universes"—entire microscopic universes, with planets, suns, and galaxies, contained in the atoms around us—was perhaps originated by Fitz-James O'Brien in "The Diamond Lens," which appeared in the January 1858 issue of the *Atlantic Monthly*. In it, a scientist invents a microscope of great power which enables him to observe people living in a world inside a drop of water. Ray Cummings came up with the first real twist on this concept—and gained immediate literary fame—with his best known story, "The Girl in the Golden Atom," printed in the March 15, 1919 issue of *All-Story Weekly*. Here he became the first writer to shrink a human being to atomic size, and recount his hero's amazing adventures in a microscopic world. Readers clamored for more, and Cummings followed with a novel-length sequel entitled "The People of the Golden Atom," serialized in *All-Story* from January 24 through February 28, 1920. The two stories were combined and published as a book by Methuen in 1922 and by Harpers in the United States in 1923 as *The Girl in the Golden Atom*. Cummings spent much of the rest of his career retelling the same story in such derivative works as *The Princess of the Atom* (1929), *Beyond the Vanishing Point* (1931), and so on. Others also derived stories from Cummings' idea, e.g., Philip M. Fisher Jr. with his "Worlds Within Worlds," *Argosy* (May 13, 1922).

None of these stories, however, contained any significant variation on the theme. It was left to R. F. Starzl to contribute the last significant thematic twist. In "Out of the Sub-Universe" a scientist sends his daughter and assistant into the microscopic world of Elektron via a "Cosmic Ray." In the single hour between shrinking the two to subatomic size and trying to retrieve them, however, millions of years have passed on Elektron. The two adventurers have long been dust, but they have founded a civilization which worships them as gods and patiently awaits the appointed time for the return of the Cosmic Ray. "While it is true that the sub-universe resembles our own," the scientist sadly realizes, and "that the electrons follow their orbits in a manner analogous to the planets around the suns; yet I overlooked the fact that due to the great difference in size there is also an enormous difference in time. It takes the earth a year to go around the sun; an electron circles its positive nucleus millions of times a second. Yet every time it completes its orbit it is like a year to the inhabitants. Before I had time to even blink an eye, Shirley and Hale had lived, loved, died, and many generations of their children had gone through their life cycles. It was normal to them—to us it was unthinkably brief." Starzl had discovered the "enormous difference in time" that seemed logical to suppose existed between the macro- and microscopic worlds. Once formulated, the idea seemed obvious. Time relativity has been a part of the "worlds within worlds" concept ever since.

Starzl's last SF story was "Dimension of the Conquered," which appeared in the October 1934 *Astounding Stories*. After that, he ceased writing, and his name slowly faded from memories of everyone except old-timers like Ray Gallun. Of all his stories, only "Out of the Sub-Universe," through occasional reprintings, seems well-remembered. More than thirty years after it was first published, for instance, Cele Goldsmith found it worthy of republication in the April 1961 *Amazing Stories*. Even more importantly, Mike Ashley chose the story as a representative one of 1928 for his first volume of the *History of the Science Fiction Magazine*, published in the United States in 1976, the very year Starzl died.[4]

Roman ("Rome") Frederick Starzl[5] was born of an Austrian immigrant father on December 10, 1899, in Le Mars, Iowa, and spent his life in that small, heavily Catholic, farming town of five thousand, almost equally divided between Irish and South German immigrants and their descendants. There he ran the family newspaper, the *Globe-Post*, for nearly forty years. The *Globe-Post* had been founded in 1880, and was purchased by his father, John V. Starzl, in 1917. R. F. Starzl began working there in 1923, after serving eight and a half months in the army during World War I, another year at college, and three more in the advertising department of the *Chicago Tribune*. His father died in 1931 of uremia at the age of sixty-five and his mother died of arteriosclerosis at age sixty-seven in 1937. R. F. Starzl became sole owner of the family newspaper in 1934, working in partnership with his younger brother Francis ("Frank") from 1938 until 1940. Thereafter he was the paper's combined editor, publisher, and columnist until 1962; after a fire destroyed the plant on St. Patrick's Day, 1964, it was sold to the publisher of the competing Le Mars *Daily Sentinel*. Meanwhile, on November 14, 1923, R. F. Starzl had married a Sioux City nurse, Anna Laura Fitzgerald, and began raising a family. He married his second wife, Rita Kenaley, on July 27, 1948. After his stroke of 1962 she ran the *Globe-Post* for two years before its sale.

In what spare time he had R. F. Starzl read omnivorously and worked ceaselessly on inventions of various kinds. He reminds one of the character played by Jimmy Stewart in Frank Capra's movie *It's a Wonderful Life*—he seemed to long to travel far and do great things, but that was a life reserved for his younger brother Frank, who moved to New York City and became head of the Associated Press.[6] Meanwhile, R. F. Starzl remained trapped in a small and stifling midwestern farm town, taking care of the family's business. But in his imagination he travelled farther than his brother ever dreamed.

In 1926 a son, Thomas Earl, was born. Thomas Starzl went on to a career in medicine which his father could only imagine, and which even today some see as virtually science fictional.[7] Although he worked on the family newspaper as a youth, he seems to have been more inspired by his mother's profession; eventually he pursued a career in medicine. There, almost single-handedly, he created the new field known as organ transplantation.

Dr. Starzl built the University of Pittsburgh into perhaps the world's foremost center of human organ transplantation and transplantation research. It was there, on Valentine's Day in 1984, that he performed the first successful simultaneous heart and liver transplantation. In 1988 he successfully performed the first "cluster" transplants on seriously ill cancer patients, replacing diseased organs with clusters of healthy organs—the liver, kidney, pancreas, and parts of the small intestine. In 1993 he saved the life of Pennsylvania's then-governor, Democrat Robert P. Casey, by implanting a heart and a liver in a single operation.

Starzl now devotes all his time to research, seeking to develop techniques that will routinely provide animal sources for the thousands of people who currently die for lack of a human organ. As part of this research, he performed the first transplantation of a baboon's kidney into a human with the HIV virus in 1992. (Unlike humans, baboons cannot be infected with the HIV virus, thus making a baboon kidney appropriate in this case.) As with his first liver transplant, the patient eventually died, but an autopsy revealed that death was due to a surgically blocked duct, not to rejection of the kidney. Routine animal-to-human organ transplants may well be the next science fiction idea Thomas Starzl turns into science fact.

Today he serves as the director of the Transplantation Institute at Pittsburgh. As such, he has a modest office in an old wood and brick building above what used to be a Pizza Hut franchise across the street from the University Medical Center. It was there that I visited him on November 16, 1992, for the following conversation. His office was cluttered with books on world affairs and classical music. CDs of such music were littered over piles of correspondence, and there were photos of his family adorning the walls. As usual, he was in the midst of a whirlwind of activity, and we were interrupted several times by visitors. Nevertheless, Dr. Starzl was eager to talk about his father, science fiction author R.F. Starzl, who died April 8, 1976, of a blood clot in the main artery to both lungs after a series of debilitating strokes that began in 1962. He was bedridden from then until his death.[8]

ERIC LEIF DAVIN: *"Roman" is an unusual name. How did your father come by it?*

THOMAS E. STARZL: It used to be common in South German Catholic families. I haven't seen the name in years.

In your autobiography, The Puzzle People, *you mentioned that your father began writing science fiction in order to earn extra money so he could buy the family newspaper.*

That's right. His parents owned the *Le Mars Globe-Post*, for which my father worked. It had originally been known as *Der Herold*, but they changed the name because of tensions during World War I. My grandparents paid my father a miserly salary, but when they died he determined to buy out all the shares owned by the family. He had a sister named Adele who died prematurely, and a brother named Frank. Frank changed his last name to "Starzel" and later became CEO of the Associated Press in New York City. So, my father bought both of them out. As soon as he was able to do that, he stopped writing fiction and just ran the newspaper.

His first professional SF sale was perhaps his most important and well-known, "Out of the Sub-Universe." This was the heyday of the pulps, and he could have written in any genre if it was just for money—boxing stories, ranch romances, air war stories, railroad stories, South Sea stories, all of which paid far more money. Why did he pick science fiction?

I think it was what he was most interested in. He had a scientific inquisitiveness. I think he read science fiction, and he was always inventing little things of one kind or another, like a photo-engraving machine and a blood oxygenator. I remember that he was fascinated by airplanes. His favorite magazine was *Popular Mechanics*, which bored me stiff. He also signed up for correspondence courses in various things, like calculus, or how to build a house, or making boats. He was a great student, and always did well. He spent his whole life doing that. For example, he would never go out and buy a linch for a trailer. He insisted on making his own. He had a machine shop in which he made these things.

Would it be correct to call him an "autodidact"?

I'm not sure I know what that means, but I'm sure you're right.

An "autodidact" is a self-taught person.

Yes, he was. For one year he did go to Northwestern University, the same school I went to, but then dropped out and came back to Le Mars to run the newspaper.

Did he leave because of finances?

I think mainly it was that. His parents were growing old, his sister had married, and Frank had run off and was getting famous, so there really wasn't anyone else in the family to maintain the newspaper.

Did he subscribe to any magazines besides Popular Mechanics?

Well, he always had a big supply of science fiction magazines, but I don't know if he subscribed to them. *Popular Mechanics* stands out in my mind because he went through that with a fine-toothed comb. The *National Geographic* was also a favorite of his. Other regulars were *Collier's* and the *Saturday Evening Post.*[9]

I used to go down to the newsstand where they had an enormous array of pulp magazines of all kinds, and stand there for hours on end speed-reading them. I read *Amazing Stories* and *Astounding Stories* and other science fiction magazines. I'd read all the comic books like a buzz saw, and this would drive the newsstand owners nuts.

Did you ever run across any stories by your father in these magazines?

Oh, yeah. I knew he was writing, but because he was my father I suppose I didn't pay as much attention to his stories. It was no great thrill to see my father's name in print. I bought some and brought them home, but I was interested at least as much in war stories and football stories and things like that. I didn't completely appreciate what he was doing. In fact, I wasn't really aware of the extent of his activities until I was quite a bit older when I went into that mystical trunk in the basement where he kept copies of all these things. That trunk of magazines was really the only complete record of his publications.[10] I found there that he'd even published in magazines like *Collier's*. He also wrote about real-life nursing experiences—usually about some terrifying event—to which he signed my mother's maiden name.[11]

You're now a medical doctor. Were these nursing stories, supposedly written by your mother, inspirational to you at all?

Well, my mother herself was inspirational to me. She was in love with the medical profession and highly respectful of it, and I guess I concluded that anything she was so attached to must be highly worthwhile. She'd worked in Sioux City for a surgeon named Doherty or Donahue—some Irish name—and she thought very highly of him. So, I felt that a profession which could command so much respect from her must be worthwhile.

Your father's first science fiction story appeared when you were about two years old. You must have been about eight when he stopped writing in 1934. In your autobiography you had a passage which stuck in my mind. You wrote that late at night, while lying in your bed in the dark, you could hear your father's typewriter clacking away into the wee hours of the morning.

Yes, he was writing his stories. I think that sometimes he'd stay up all night, then take a bath and go to work on the newspaper. He'd come home the next night and do the same thing. It was hard work, as I later came to learn—I found writing my autobiography wasn't easy! My father had his own technique of typing which didn't use the touch system. He used only two fingers, and was all over the keyboard like an octopus. He was very fast.

But when he'd earned enough money to buy out his siblings, the typing at night stopped?

It stopped—bang!—just like that. Then he started building things. He spent ten years working on his photo-engraving thing.[12]

And yet he really did a lot of work researching the science fiction field. I don't know if you ever saw this, but I have here an article your father wrote for the October 1931 Author and Journalist *magazine. It's an analysis of the fantasy and science fiction market; he goes into extensive detail on what the various magazines were looking for, what the payment rates were, who the edi-*

*tors were, and what kind of stories they wanted. This is just one
of a number of such factual articles he wrote on the field.*

I'm going to read this article with interest. I wasn't aware of
its existence until now. May I make a copy of it?

*Be my guest. Later on, your father was paralyzed by a series
of strokes. I understand these left him with very limited motion,
but nevertheless he carried on an extensive correspondence and
even wrote a book.*

Yes, he typed it out himself. It was a lengthy thing, hundreds
of pages. Because of his paralysis it was very difficult for him.
He had motion only in his eyes and a single finger. He couldn't
talk. He communicated with the world through that one finger
and an electric typewriter.

I read the book. It wasn't befitting him. It contained a thread
of regret and covert anger which really wasn't like him at all. I
never tried to stop his getting it into print, but I hoped that publishers would find no value in it. He sent it to an agent in New
York, and I was hoping very much it would never see the light of
day. And it didn't. That was the end of that.

I don't remember exactly what kind of novel it was. I do
recall it had some racial themes in it. And, although my father
was a very abstemious person in all matters, it contained some
uncharacteristic sexual passages. Perhaps he was trying to
accommodate to a market which by then had become less
Puritan. But, I didn't think it was representative of his true grain,
so I was glad it never found a publisher. I really don't remember
too much about it, but I do think it was very clumsy, compared
to what he'd written in the past.

*You say it contained racial themes. Do you mean it was
racist? I'd find that odd, given that you are married to a black
woman and so that attitude—*

No, I don't mean that it was racist. It just dealt with topics with which he was really unfamiliar, and for that reason it was very clumsy.

Why do you think he didn't return to science fiction, with which he'd previously had much success?

I don't know. He wrote about space travel and rockets when only Goddard was taking them seriously.[13] He had a lot of background material he'd gleaned from all his reading. We lived at 205 Central Avenue, right across the street from the Le Mars public library. It was only fifty feet from our living room, and like an extension of our home. We all used the library extensively. I don't know why he didn't use this research for more science fiction at that point. A lot of the things he was doing were more advanced than what you might find in the technologies industries. He had great insight. But, it's very difficult to keep up with developments, and perhaps his information was outdated by that time. He must have realized that.

He did a very valuable thing for me. When I was in the navy I was stationed in Missouri at Westminster College. I was a biology major there. I had never written a scientific paper, and I had to write a senior thesis. Now, my father had a tremendous interest in rabies, and also in Louis Pasteur's life, so he'd collected a lot of material on the subject. He knew everything about it, down to the last detail. So, he suggested the topic to me. I said, "Fine, send me all the material which you've collected," which he did.

But he not only collected all his material on rabies, he'd also gone ahead and written a thesis for me on it! I then handed the thesis in under my own authorship. That always bothered me, because it was a beautiful piece of work and I got an "A" on it—but I didn't write it. I did read all the source material, but I realized my father had a capacity for expression that was far beyond anything I could command.

This was an important lesson for me. When I later started writing scientific articles, in many ways I mimicked him. His writing style was a curious mixture of journalism and literature. Or perhaps a more accurate description would be that his was a strange blend of scientific and literary styles. This still comes up today. A reviewer of my autobiography drew attention to my style, which is in this mode. I'm sure it's heavily influenced by my father's. Our parents make us what we are.

I think I was also influenced, or at least impressed, by his great honesty. When FDR became president we went off the gold standard, and anyone who had any gold was supposed to surrender it. I remember that he had a small sack of gold coins up in the attic. We got a ladder and climbed up there to search for it. He then turned them in. But you only got their face value. If you had a five-dollar gold piece, you got five dollars in paper. Of course, the gold content made it worth much more than that. At that time, when everything but gold was so devalued, a five-dollar gold coin might've been worth a thousand dollars. And if my father had held onto his coins, they'd have been worth a fortune. But, as I said, he was a very law-abiding guy.

Was he a coin collector?

No, he just realized there was going to be a depression, so he'd converted a good deal of paper money into gold. He was prepared.

You comment in your autobiography on the discontinuity between people who have education, or at least credentials, and how their contributions are accepted, while others, such as your father, may have much to offer but are ignored because they lack such education or credentials.

That's only part of what I was trying to say. I think the principal message is that there is sometimes a loss of primitive knowledge through being too "smart." I can see that in myself, for example. My wife can solve certain types of problems better than I can. Given certain kinds of problems in science, I can sometimes solve those better than experts in an isolated corner of science.

Recently I made a discovery about how organ grafts are accepted by the body. It's a very big discovery about a field that has generated a hundred thousand publications of one kind or another, each looking at some detail. But I saw the whole picture, even though in all the myriad of small pockets of expertise I didn't have enough sophisticated knowledge, sometimes, even to speak the language of particular elites. But I was able to stand back and survey the entire scene, while the specialists could see only pieces of the mosaic. So I discovered something that had escaped everyone's attention for forty years. It's like the dark side of the moon, the bright side being a kind of dogma which grew out of some discoveries made in 1953. In a sense, what I discovered reads like science fiction.

Could you synopsize your discovery for me?

Well, a big problem in organ transplantation is the body's natural immune response to an alien invader, such as the transplanted organ. In order for the organ to be accepted, the body's natural urge to attack it has to be suppressed. My theory is that there is a two-way traffic in white blood cells between the donor organ and the recipient, and it is this traffic which determines the success of any transplant operation. White blood cells within the grafts leave these tissues and migrate all over the recipient, where they learn to live in harmony with the body, provided they are given protection during their nesting. These cells, the soldiers which normally cause graft rejection, become instead the missionaries of graft acceptance and, ultimately, tolerance. That is what happens, but nobody saw it before, or understood fully how grafts are ultimately accepted by the body.

But I felt intuitively the process had to be there. So I wrote up my theory first, and then went looking for the evidence. Usually it's the other way around; you have evidence which you attempt to explain with a theory. My article describing this was published in the *Lancet*, the prestigious English medical journal, in June 1992. It's opened a whole new field in organ transplantation.[14]

If you're too specialized, you miss these things. I said at the time that seeing some of those people work in their very limited, esoteric areas is a little bit like sitting at a microscope in the middle of a snow storm examining the crystallography of single snowflakes and not having the foggiest idea of where you are. So, people like my dad, who have a good primitive intelligence, can sometimes see everything. He did just that with his heart-lung machine.

That's the blood oxygenator he developed. As I recall, when he sent it to you, you were disdainful.

I totally ignored it. I was ashamed of it, contemptuous of it. In 1953 I was at Johns Hopkins and we were trying to develop a heart-lung machine. I wrote letters to my father explaining one of the big problems we were wrestling with, how to oxygenate the blood. A few weeks later he sent me a God-dammed farm cream can which was supposed to do this by direct exposure of the blood to air, a method everyone said was unsound. Because he had a primitive mind he thought, well, here you've got oxygen, there you've got blood, so put them together! This he did via a jet spray. But also realizing that undissolved oxygen could do harm, he devised a means of defoaming the blood of bubbles before returning it to the patient. Well, I never even bothered to test the thing. I just put it in a corner of my office and ignored it while it gathered dust. I didn't even write my father back about it.

A couple of years later the big medical breakthrough finally came when a team at the University of Minnesota developed a machine that could oxygenate blood. We all went breathless to examine this medical marvel. When I saw it I exclaimed, "Shit! That's my dad's cream can!" And it was—the same thing, *exactly*. He was working with the only equipment he had at hand, a cream can, but he had the principle right and had it right before any of the experts did! By ignoring him I had cheated my dad out of his deserved immortality.

You ignored your dad because he didn't have the credentials to invent a working blood oxygenator. Does this mean there really isn't much room for those who lack the proper credentials?

Actually, I think there's more room than we realize. The discovery I made about white cell migration was very difficult to get published, but I *did* get it published. Because it was pointed in just the opposite way the mob was going, I didn't want to send it out for the usual anonymous peer review. Instead, I sent it to twelve scientists in the field. I explained that I wasn't looking for a testimonial, but I wanted their opinions because I didn't want to be humiliated late in life by something so bizarre. The wisest of these people said, "How could we have missed this concept?" The smartest guy I know told me it was like looking out a window overlooking a bay and having docked right outside a battleship so big you couldn't see it.

You are now the most published scientist in America, and the sixth most published scientist in the world. How do you manage to be so prolific and still be an active surgeon? Do you think your father's journalism background had anything to do with this?

Oh, it had a lot to do with it. Starting with that rabies thesis he wrote for me, which I appropriated for my own, I went on to develop the skills which I so much admired in him.

What are those skills?

The power of expressing ideas in a simple way. Sometimes one confuses the creativity involved in doing an experiment with that needed to write it up, but the writing itself is a very creative part of the whole process. I did my own experiments, but with the writing comes the interpretation. That's where you make sense of it all, construct the big picture, explain what everything really means. I don't think it's a matter of form, which would be the sense of your implication, but a matter of the formal construction of ideas in some kind of intellectual architecture.

So, you don't fully understand what you've done until you've written it?

I think that's very close to the truth. You have a scientific jigsaw puzzle sitting there in pieces. Each piece is clear, but the whole picture isn't. You have to sit down and give the problem much thought, and writing about it is a powerful means of thinking about it. I try not to talk in public about any new or important thing I'm working on until I've had a chance to write it. Otherwise, I'd just be talking off the top of my head. But, once it's written down, it's organized, you've made sense out of it, you really understand what it means. From that point on, it can be expressed in a thousand ways.

This attitude didn't come simply from reading that one piece on rabies by your father, did it?

Well, of course, I worked on his newspaper, too. What he wrote there was always very clear. He was quite careful about everything he wrote. He was a perfectionist about spelling, grammar, and all kinds of things. I used to get long letters from him—which I didn't save—that were filled with his ruminations about the meaning of life and all kinds of arcane subjects. He could also do everything on the newspaper, from the lowliest to the most sophisticated jobs. I have never come up to his level of Renaissance expertise. He was learning up to the day he died.

Was he at all religious?

He was toward the end of his life and at the beginning of his life. He was raised in a very strict Teutonic Catholic mold. I think he went through a mid-life phase in which he didn't believe in anything, but before he died he returned to Catholicism. He was probably what some call a "Black Catholic"—one of those people who love and embrace the Church, but don't believe in all its dogmas.

You say you've read your father's science fiction. What's your opinion of it?

I found it very entertaining. If you're fair enough to judge it within the context of the scientific knowledge we had sixty years ago, you'd have to say it was very advanced. I liked the sub-universe theme, worlds within worlds especially.

Several years ago Somerset Maugham wrote a famous short story on the same subject. I think the title was something like "To See the Sparrow Fall." In this, a missionary on the way to Africa, or some other primitive place, talks to someone who tells him about the concept of universes within universes, from the macroscopic to the microscopic. For every one of these universes there was a cosmos. The missionary embraced this concept, and by the time he arrived in Africa, his belief in conventional Christianity had been completely distorted. He walked off into the jungle. Search parties were sent out, following his trail from native village to native village. In each they found strange rituals and symbols. Instead of crosses, they found concentric circles, like diagrams of atoms. Slowly these symbols changed, becoming more recognizably human. Then they came to the last village. There he'd died and been buried. The last thing he had done was to create something the natives could make no sense of, the portrait of a Christ-like figure looking down at a sparrow. The missionary had come full circle—from Christ through all the sub-universes back up to Christ who sees the smallest sparrow fall.

The twist your father put on the concept was emphasizing the relative nature of time among the various universes. Time at the subatomic level passes so much faster than it does in our own that hundreds, thousands of years there might occur in the blink of our eye. That final elaboration pretty much summed up everything there was to say about that theme, and for that alone R. F. Starzl deserves science fiction immortality.

Well, in that case I hope you won't let his memory die.

NOTES

1. Robert Silverberg, *Reflections and Refractions: Thoughts on Science-Fiction, Science, and Other Matters* (Grass Valley, Calif.: Underwood Books: 1997), p. 195.
2. Silverberg, *Reflections and Refractions*, pp. 149–50.
3. See chapter 4 on Gallun.
4. In addition, however, "The Last Planet" was reprinted in *Fantastic Story Quarterly* (Summer 1950); "Madness of the Dust" in *Avon SF Reader* 1 (1951); "Planet of Dread" in *Avon SF Reader* 3 (1952); and "Hornets of Space" in *Startling Stories* (March 1942). Several of his stories also appeared in British, French, and Danish magazines. Plans for reprinting a selection of Starzl's SF in book form in 1948 were never realized because the potential publisher, Oswald Train, was unable to finance it.

In 1988 Don C. Thompson printed an outline of a proposed article (which appears never to have been subsequently written) about R. F. Starzl (*Rim-i-nis-cent* 4 [August 1988]: 14–16). In it he noted that Starzl's stories had elicited generally favorable response in the magazines' readers columns and were "credited with some new twists and with scientific accuracy." He himself felt they were "pretty typical" of the era, "perhaps just a cut above average," although their "women do seem to be a bit more gutsy and active" than typical pulp heroines of the time.

5. According to his second wife, Rita, Starzl's mother recorded his birthname in the family Bible as "Romanus."

6. Francis Joseph Starzl was born February 29, 1904, and died in Denver on June 14, 1994, at age ninety.

7. Indeed, shortly before Dr. Barnard's successful heart transplantation, a medical doctor friend of mine, whom I greatly respected, scoffed at the possibility of such a procedure.

8. Some six years after Rome Starzl was felled by the strokes that left him severely paralyzed, staff writer Robert Gunsolly composed a moving memoir of the man which was published in his paper, "Voice of Brilliant Northwest Stilled, but Mind Remains Active, Undulled," *The Sioux City Sunday Journal*, December 8, 1968, page C2. For those wanting to know more about him, this is the best source extant. It tells of his Le Mars upbringing; his politics (he was an anti-New Deal Democrat who despised FDR and opposed "Roosevelt's War"); and his family (in addition to his brother he had two deceased siblings, Adele and Oswald; besides Thomas Starzl he had another son, John, and three daughters, Nancy, Mamie, and Kathleen; and at the time of his death there were eleven surviving grandchildren). Gunsolly recounts Starzl's vivid reporting of the 1933 Farm Holiday movement in Iowa, when foreclosure of farm mortgages brought about the near-lynching of a local judge and subsequent invoking of martial law. He also quotes from Rome Starzl's memorable and often controversial column for the *Globe-Post*, "Between Deals."

9. He probably did subscribe to several science fiction magazines. Given the extensive knowledge of the field displayed in his October 1931 article, "The Fantastic-Science Market," for *The Author and Journalist*, it is unlikely that Starzl would rely on haphazard purchase of the magazines at newsstands.

In addition, I have a photocopy of a letter Starzl wrote to fellow SF author Lloyd Arthur Eshbach on October 4, 1930, commenting on two of Eshbach's stories. Starzl writes, "this morning the *Air Wonder Stories* came. They must have had trouble finding a copy, as the one they sent me was the worse for the wear." That issue carried Eshbach's story

"The Invisible Destroyer," which Starzl said "held my interest without interruption for an hour this morning when I should have been working."

The letter also suggests that Starzl subscribed to *Astounding*, as he comments on Eshbach's "The Gray Plague" in that magazine. He found it fast moving, believable, and "above the average level of *Astounding* stories," implying he'd read enough to make the comparison.

This same letter indicates that Starzl and Eshbach both belonged to the same organization, the "S.C.C." Eshbach had complained that some members' names had been omitted from a list and Starzl promised to correct the omissions in the next *S.C.C. Bulletin*. This was the Science Correspondence Club, the first organized fan group in science fiction. The mention shows that Starzl had some responsibility for maintaining its membership lists and for producing its bulletin. For more information on the S.C.C., see Moskowitz's *The Immortal Storm* (Atlanta, Ga.: Science Fiction Organization Press, 1954), pp. 8–10.

In addition to holding official positions in SF's first fan organization, Starzl was also a member of David Lasser's Interplanetary Society and seems to have carried on an extensive international correspondence. For instance, perhaps because of his membership in the Interplanetary Society, Starzl sent Willy Ley, the vice president of the German Society for Space Travel, the first issue of Gernsback's *Science Wonder Quarterly*. Reportedly, it instantly converted Ley to science fiction and, after immigrating to this country to escape the Nazis, Ley went on to become a mainstay of the SF magazines in the 1950s with his science fact essays. See Marshall B. Tymn and Mike Ashley, *Science Fiction, Fantasy, and Weird Fiction Magazines* (Westport, Conn.: Greenwood Press, 1985), p. 763.

10. This trunk and its contents were left behind when the Starzl family sold their home. A subsequent tenant discarded both.

11. R. F. Starzl is also the author of the article "Small Camera Easy to Convert for Aerial Use," *Popular Mechanics* 54 (September 1930): 521–22.

12. See the chapter on Gallun and my conversation with him in *Fantasy Commentator* 38, p. 86. Gallun recalls that Starzl stopped writing science fiction after *Astounding*, which was then paying two cents a word, went bankrupt.

Additionally, Thomas F. Starzl, Rome's grandson and Dr. Starzl's son, a science-fiction fan who lives in Colorado, told me that he has letters from Rome's wife, Anna, which, he recalls, say the same thing. (Unfortunately, he has been unable to locate these for verification.)

Both versions are probably true. Starzl was selling to other markets (*Popular Mechanics*, *Argosy*, and *Top Notch*, for example) and it is clear he was familiar with what they wanted and what they paid. Had he truly wished to continue selling, there seems no doubt he could have done so successfully. Probably the collapse of the field's best-paying market just happened to coincide with Starzl's reaching the financial goal he'd set for himself. The incentive to persevere in a shrinking market would naturally not have been as strong.

13. He was, of course, also a member of Lasser's Interplanetary Society.

14. In the autopsy following the 1992 baboon liver transplant into the HIV patient, Starzl discovered that white blood cells had, indeed, migrated into the body of the patient from the liver. He believes this might have implications for AIDS treatment, since baboons are impervious to the HIV virus. The baboon's immune white blood cells, migrating into the patient's body, may help replace the latter's AIDS-depleted supply.

7.

THE BIRTH OF SCIENCE FICTION BOOKS

A Conversation with Lloyd Arthur Eshbach

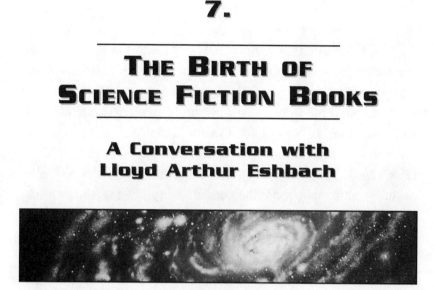

Sarig, seated in a pool of slime, was straining with all his strength at the cords that bound his hands. Suddenly as one of the plants burst above him, he made a supreme effort, and the cords broke.

Slowly the dust settled upon him. As it touched his skin, sending tiny rootlets through the pores, into his flesh, and drawing life from his living body, he gave utterance to one piercing shriek.

Strangely formed plants sprang from all parts of Sarig Om's body then. With mad, frenzied haste, the scientist tore them from him, leaving ugly, bloody wounds where the growths had been. But only for a moment was he able to struggle with his vegetable destroyers; several plants, having reached maturity upon him, burst simultaneously, enveloping him in a thick cloud of dust.

He seemed to grow larger before my eyes. Countless plants grew upon him, swelling him to three times his normal size. Grew—and decayed. The figure remained thus for only a moment, then it collapsed and lost itself in the slime and plants upon the floor.

—Lloyd Arthur Eshbach, "The Voice from the Ether" (1931)

L LOYD ARTHUR ESHBACH WAS PRESENT ALMOST AT THE creation of modern magazine science fiction. As yet another of the teenager authors then so prevalent in the new genre, he sold his first two stories on the same day, October 14, 1929, to *Amazing Stories* and the brand-new *Scientific Detective Monthly*, the latter a short-lived sister publication to Hugo Gernsback's *Science Wonder Stories*. In those halcyon times when the postal service made more than one delivery per day, the morning mail brought an acceptance from T. O'Conor Sloane at *Amazing* for his "The Voice from the Ether," while in the afternoon came another from David Lasser at *Science Wonder* for "The Man with the Silver Disc." Sloane finally got "The Voice from the Ether" into print in 1931, and more than forty years later Mike Ashley published it again as a representative story from that year in the first volume of *The History of the Science Fiction Magazine* (1974).[1] Over the course of that decade Eshbach wrote thirty-nine stories, selling thirty-four. He wrote fewer in the forties, but sold all of them. He went on to publish more than fifty short stories, and sixty years later his *The Land Beyond the Gate* tetralogy gained him an entirely new audience of fantasy fans.

But it is not as a writer that Eshbach made his greatest mark on the history of science fiction. Rather, his importance lies in having pioneered publication of the new genre in book form. Without question, science fiction became a distinct literary category when Hugo Gernsback launched *Amazing Stories,* the first all-science fiction magazine, in 1926. The next two decades, when it was a magazine phenomenon, were formative. The trailblazing authors of that period were breaking new ground, establishing new literary conventions. Nevertheless, as Isaac Asimov confirmed in my conversation with him, they viewed their work as essentially ephemeral, having no life beyond a month on the newsstands in some garishly illustrated magazine. The possibility of a more enduring existence for their efforts—of, say, relative immortality between the covers of a book—was inconceivable.

Nevertheless, this had to be the next stage of the genre's development. It was evolve or die, as the first bloom of magazine science fiction was over. Wartime paper shortages had severely curtailed pulp magazine publishing. In the aftermath of the war, the new challenge of comic books had to be faced. True, comic book heroes such as Superman and Captain America had been born in the Depression years, but only in the late forties were they beginning to supplant the pulp magazines in the loyalties of young readers. Facing this new reality, Street and Smith, one of the major publishers of pulp magazines, decided in 1949 to kill all of its pulp titles—but for one. The sole survivor was *Astounding Science Fiction,* under the brilliant editorship of John W. Campbell. But even *Astounding* and Campbell, though they survived, did not occupy the dominant position they had previously. Science fiction in book form was the obvious next step and, with the end of World War II, some in the science fiction universe began to conceive of this possibility. Eshbach was one of these.

There had been a few early anthologies from the commercial publishers, such as *The Pocket Book of Science Fiction*, edited by Donald A. Wollheim in 1943, and *Adventures in Space and Time*, edited by Raymond J. Healy and J. Francis McComas in 1946. In addition, Holt published such SF authors as Fletcher Pratt and L. Sprague de Camp. But most mainstream houses remained unconvinced of the profitability of science fiction, and were reluctant to chance many experiments in its direction. Into that breach stepped Eshbach and his Fantasy Press, a small specialty publishing house he launched in 1949. He followed by establishing Polaris Press, a short-lived companion, in 1952.

Technically, Fantasy Press was not the genre's first press. August Derleth's Arkham House had published its first book, *The Outsider,* in 1939. But that was a collection of horror stories by H. P. Lovecraft. And while Arkham House would and did issue an occasional purely science fiction volume, its stock in trade remained horror, fantasy, and particularly the work of Lovecraft. There were also others who felt science fiction should move on to the book publication stage—Tom Hadley, Ken Krueger, and Donald Grant of Buffalo Books, and Martin Greenberg and David A. Kyle of Gnome Press—and who launched specialty presses at roughly the same time as Eshbach.[2] But, with the exception of Gnome Press, founded in 1948 and which was first to put Asimov between book covers in the early 1950s, these other efforts were transitory, producing a handful of books, and then fading. Fantasy Press, however, survived and thrived for almost a dozen years, gathering into handsome hard-cover volumes some of the best magazine science fiction of the previous era. The authors thus assured of recognition and longevity in this manner included such early giants as Stanley G. Weinbaum, E. E. ("Doc") Smith, A. E. van Vogt, L. Sprague de Camp, Jack Williamson, and John W. Campbell Jr., who as editor of *Astounding* was also attempting to take science fiction yet a new stage further. In addition, in 1947 Eshbach edited and his Fantasy Press published the very first book *about* the genre, *Of Worlds Beyond: The Science of Science Fiction Writing*. In this were the papers from a symposium of seven science fiction writers—Campbell, de Camp, van Vogt, Williamson, Smith, Robert A. Heinlein, and "John Taine"— which Eshbach himself had organized.

By 1958 commercial publishers had begun to awaken to the fact that science fiction fandom bought books. Their belated entrance into the field as competitors with more money and infrastructure support ended the virtual monopoly of the small specialty houses. According to Eshbach, Fantasy Press therefore sold "a trailer truck-load" of its stock to Donald Grant, while Marty Greenberg of Gnome Press also bought, at most, a couple of hundred books from its inventory. At the time, it was thought by some that Gnome had bought both Fantasy Press and its entire inventory, a story Eshbach contends was bruited about by Greenberg in order to stall Gnome's creditors.[3] If so, the ploy was but partially successful, for the firm struggled on for only a few more years before it, too, folded.

In a larger sense, the end of Fantasy Press didn't matter, since it had served its purpose. It had made possible the evolutionary leap of science fiction to a new stage of existence. It had demonstrated that there was an audience for science fiction between hard covers. It had kept the flame alive until the torch could be passed to a new kind of publisher. The inconceivable had become reality. Primarily for this reason Lloyd Eshbach was made Guest of Honor at the seventh World Science Fiction Convention at Cincinnati in 1949. Forty years later he was given the Milford Award for "Lifetime Achievement in Fantasy and Science Fiction Editing" for his work at Fantasy Press, and for the same reason First Fandom inducted him into its Hall of Fame.

Lloyd Arthur Eshbach was born of Pennsylvania Dutch stock on June 20, 1910, in Palm, Pennsylvania. Brought up in Reading, he attended school there until the tenth grade. In 1931 he married Helen Margaret Richards, with whom he had two sons. Although active in the science fiction field, he supported his family mainly as an advertising copywriter, advertising manager, and sales representative for a series of department stores, paint companies, and publishers.

In 1983 he returned to science fiction in a big way. In that year he edited and introduced *Subspace Encounter*, an unfinished novel by "Doc" Smith, and also edited and introduced *Alicia in Blunderland,* a parody by his friend P. Schuyler Miller, which had originally appeared as a fanzine serial half a century before. He also published his memoirs of the age of specialty presses, *Over My Shoulder: Reflections on a Science Fiction Era.* He followed this in 1984 with his popular *The Land Beyond the Gate,* the first of a tetralogy which concluded with *The Scroll of Lucifer* seven years later. These fantasy novels reestablished him as a writer in the field.

In 1988, at ICON 7, the State University of New York at Stonybrook awarded Lloyd Eshbach the Raymond Z. Gallun Award, which it administers, for "Outstanding contributions to the genre of Science Fiction." After hearing Eshbach's praises sung, Ray Gallun turned to Eshbach and said, "Gosh, I had no idea you'd done so much!" Now in his ninth decade, Lloyd Eshbach remains active and betrays no hint of retiring from the field with which he has been identified all his life.[4] The following conversation took place on February 3, 1991. Mr. Eshbach was eighty years old at the time.

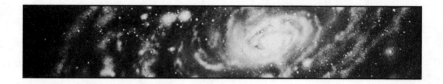

ERIC LEIF DAVIN: *Why don't we start with some personal information? Can you tell me a little about your wife?*

LLOYD ARTHUR ESHBACH: Well, when I made my first sale, in 1929, I called up my intended, Helen Richards, to tell her. I later married her, and we were married for forty-seven years. She died of pancreatic cancer in 1978. Donald, my elder son, died of lung cancer in 1990. My younger son Daniel is forty-six or forty-seven, and lives just a few miles from me. He has two sons. Donald had three children, so I'm a grandfather five times. The Eshbach name will be around for a while.[5]

How did you meet Helen?

We met in church in Reading. She was eighteen and I was sixteen, but I looked older than my age and she didn't know I was two years younger. When she found out, she broke it off. She wouldn't be going with a kid! A couple of years later we picked it up again, and finally married in 1931.

Was she also Pennsylvania Dutch?

Well, "Richards" was originally "Reichert," a German name, so we had the same ethnic background, but her family hadn't spoken Pennsylvania Dutch for generations.

What was your family background?

On my father Oswin's side we came from a long line of farmers who emigrated from the Rhine Valley of Germany in 1734 in the St. Andrew galley. They came over to escape religious persecution, but I don't know their religion. On my mother's side I believe we are half Jewish. Her ancestors came over from Switzerland in the same year. They were all landowners, businessmen, farmers, and what-not.

My mother, whose maiden name was Kathryn Leeser, had a really marvelous mind. But she married at fifteen and had six children, so wasn't able to develop it as much as she might have. I remember once when I was nine or ten and I was home from school because I was sick. To keep me entertained, Mom started reciting poems she'd memorized in school. She recited *one hundred poems!*

I got my creativity from her. My dad used to read my stories and say to me in amazement, "Where do you *get* this?" I'd point over my shoulder and answer, "From Mom." She was absolutely in favor of my writing. In fact, she just about burst with pride when I started making it. She wasn't demonstrative, but boy, she just beamed! Naturally, this pleased me.

What about your schooling?

I left school in the tenth grade. I always hated and loathed math. I learned ordinary arithmetic, because I knew I'd use it. But when it came to algebra and geometry, I didn't know anything about them and I didn't want to. I found a good student who let me copy all his papers so I got good grades, but I didn't understand any of it. When I got into tenth grade he was in another class, so I got zeros for the couple of months I was there. My dad, who encouraged me to study harder, said if I flunked math I'd have to quit school. I said, "Then I may as well quit now, because I'm going to flunk. There's no way I can make up my deficit."

So at age fifteen I quit and went to work as a sign-painter's apprentice. Originally I thought I was going to be an artist. Seven months later I became a show-card painter in a department store. Then I moved into white collar work for the rest of my life. During the Depression I worked in a variety store as a window decorator and show-card writer. Through my writing on the side I got a copy-writing job in advertising—and so it went.

Have you ever regretted dropping out of school?

Nope. No one's ever asked to see a diploma. Everyone just assumed that I was not only a high school grad, but in most cases that I was a college grad. I never claimed to be, but I also never corrected them. However, I did work on a doctoral dissertation once—not my own—because I needed the money. It was on the Agrarian Movement as represented in the work of Theodore Dreiser and two other well-known writers I no longer remember. I finished the first chapter for the guy. It was just a matter of editing; I found I could cut the wordage in half without losing anything. But it was boring as all get-out, and my conscience bothered me. I couldn't go on with it. I told him to find another sucker. He must have, for he eventually got his degree.

Do you feel you may have missed out on some knowledge by dropping out?

No, I've been an omnivorous reader all my life. I don't put much stock in it, but my I.Q. once tested at 145. I started writing science fiction when I was seventeen and selling it when I was nineteen. I once read an entire college freshman chemistry text just to get the science I needed for one story! I've done the same kind of research for other stories. I'm one of those freaks who can speed-read if I want to. I've absorbed so much in so many different fields that I don't feel I've missed a thing in not getting a diploma. Recently I was contacted by the Reading High School

Alumni Association. They wanted to make me the "Alumnus of the Year" at their summer reunion. I told them I'd never graduated. So they're going to give me a "Lifetime Achievement Award" instead, and add me to the list of alumni anyway. That's the equivalent of an honorary high school diploma, I guess.

In my high school science class I used to raise my hand to answer every question. No matter what it was, I knew the answer, so after a while the teacher stopped calling on me. Once I mentioned in passing that the moons of Mars were Deimos and Phobos. The teacher was amazed, and asked me where I'd learned that, as they weren't named in our textbook. I couldn't tell him that I'd got it from *A Princess of Mars* by Edgar Rice Burroughs, so I simply said I'd read it somewhere.

I've also been blessed with a good memory, but in recent years it's begun to fail me in the matter of names. Five minutes after hearing someone's name I've forgotten it.

You mention Burroughs. How did you become interested in science fiction?

From my older brothers' copies of Munsey's magazines, where I read "A Princess of Mars" and the other Burroughs' Mars stories, "The Moon Pool" by A. Merritt, and so on. This was long before *Amazing Stories*. I had four older siblings (as well as a sister three years younger), and each week one older brother bought *Argosy* and the other bought *All-Story*. They cost ten cents a copy, and that was all each could afford in a week. I had access to their magazines, but I had to be very careful about how I handled them. My brothers were very careful about their collections.

My next older brother wanted to write, but he never got beyond the first page of anything. He was into sports and was very rough in his grammar. He had a creative mind, but lacked the technical skills of writing. He became a candy maker. Meanwhile, my eldest brother became a mechanic.

What was it about this type of literature that excited you and your brothers?

It was the sweep, the opening of new worlds, the imagination. But, understand, we read *everything*. I read all of the Frank Merriwell stories, all of Horatio Alger, not just science fiction and fantasy—but that appealed to me most.

You mentioned your mother reciting poetry. Did you get your love of it from her? I know of some poems you published in Wonder Stories.

Not knowingly, but I enjoyed reading poetry. In junior high school, about the seventh grade, I discovered I could make things rhyme. I decided to try writing verse and found I could. I submitted some to a column called "The Poet's Corner" in the school newspaper. In the next issue of the paper, "The Poet's Corner" was entirely my work! I thought, hey, this is fun!

At that time I was going to be an artist. I was in a special arts class and I did illustrations for the school paper. I even sold some paintings at age eleven—some visitor from New York wanted to buy all I had. Well, I sold them, happily. I can still draw anything I can see, though I can't create a picture from just a mental image. Both my brothers had the same ability. But when the school paper started publishing my verse, I decided I liked that better.

My first prose appearance was also in the school newspaper, when I was in eighth grade. It had a page entitled "I Think." I had written an essay in response to a question in civics class and the teacher, Katherine Haage, put it in the school paper under that heading. Then she asked me to write a short story for the next issue. So I did. I still have it, and it isn't bad for a thirteen-year-old kid. It was a sports story, which was popular at the time. Then she asked if I'd write another for the next issue. So I wrote a longer one, which she published as a two-part serial. That's when I decided to become an author instead of an artist.

In the thirties I tried everything. I wrote juvenile stories for Sunday School papers. In the forties I wrote mysteries. My niece is a successful writer, and just after she graduated from high school we collaborated on several love stories. They were published under the name of "Judy Schuyler." From about 1934 to '36 I edited a journal for the Galleon Writers' Guild, an Italian writers' club in Reading, and I wrote some verse for it. Then I started acting as an agent for a lot of the local versifiers. I'd send out their material as well as my own. I wrote quite a bit of verse at that time. But I wouldn't call it "poetry," even though some appeared in a number of poetry journals.

Why?

Because "poetry" is something which is going to *live,* and I don't think we have a right to determine whether anything we write will live. I consider Robert Frost's work "poetry." The same applies to a lot of the old-timers—many, not all of them.

Why did your teacher think you could write fiction when all you'd written for the school newspaper was an opinion piece and some verse?

I have no idea. Up until then I'd never thought of writing any fiction. Katherine Haage was really responsible for my becoming a writer. She was a civics teacher, and didn't even have me for English composition. I don't know why she thought I could write.

When I tried to write my first science fiction story, "Up From the Pit," it was a very bad imitation of A. Merritt. My second story was a ghost story. The third was "The Valley of the Titans." The first draft of that was rejected; I rewrote it and later sold it to *Amazing Stories.* It appeared in March 1931.

What was there about A. Merritt that excited you?

His vivid, wild imagination. That fascinated me. And his purple prose, as they called it, certainly appealed to me. Now, while I read everything by Edgar Rice Burroughs I could get my hands on, I never tried to imitate him. Both P. Schuyler Miller and Jack Williamson also—I won't say imitated—but were deeply influenced by Merritt. But when T. O'Conor Sloane, then editor of *Amazing,* compared my A. Merritt imitation to Merritt's "The Moon Pool" and "The Metal Monster," I thought, hey, this is getting too close for comfort. So I stopped imitating him. But, by that time I'd learned how to write and felt I'd found my own style.

Besides Merritt, who else excited you?

H. P. Lovecraft's "The Colour Out of Space" is one of my favorite stories. "Doc" Smith excited me, but not so that I wanted to write like him. Beginning with *Skylark of Space* I enjoyed all his stuff.

However, when I completed his unfinished sequel to *Subspace Explorers*, published by Canaveral, I purposely imitated his style. He'd been using me as a sounding-board during the original writing. He'd call from Florida or California or Illinois or wherever he happened to be, and we'd discuss it. He also sent me a copy of each portion as he went along. When Doc died Fred Pohl sent out a notice asking if anyone had unfinished Smith manuscripts which might be completed. I had some, and either I sent them to him or—we were both living in Chicago at that time—he may have come to get the manuscripts himself. I can't remember, but it doesn't matter because nothing ever came of it.

Then I was reading and offering suggestions to Dave Kyle, who was writing the "Dragon Lensman" under contract with Pohl. I was the Kyles' house-guest at the time. Fred had sent Dave a lot of Smith material he thought might be of use. In it was a manuscript of this unfinished *Subspace Explorers* sequel. Lo and behold, notations with my initials were in the margins. It was my copy!

So with Dave's permission I took it home, photocopied it, and sent the original back to him to return to Fred. I'd mentioned to Dave that somebody ought to complete the work, but he didn't think it could be done. Evidently, Fred didn't think so either, because he'd never done anything with it. They thought there wasn't enough to go on.

But Doc had discussed it with me, and I knew what he had in mind. No one else did. I looked it over again and decided I could finish it. I contacted his daughter and got her permission. I also asked her to look for the very first draft he wrote. She found it, and with all the material I had I put everything together, writing about twelve thousand words myself to complete it under the title *Subspace Encounter*. (The original title had been *Subspace Safari*, but Doc didn't like the title.) Now I defy anybody, no matter how rabid a Smith fan, to discover where Doc left off and I began. (So far, no one's been able to.) Berkeley issued the novel in 1983. I suppose I'd have been entitled to call it a collaboration, and I debated doing that, but I finally decided no, it's Doc's story and I shouldn't. So, it was published as "Edited and with an Introduction by. . . ."

Just recently a complete holograph manuscript of *Subspace Safari* came to light, and is now in my possession. Apparently it was never retyped and the handwriting is very hard to decipher. This dates from the time Doc decided to make the work part of a trilogy. He planned to write an unrelated novel set in the same universe as *Subspace Explorers*, but with totally new characters. A third novel would connect these two, but would really be the second book of the series. This was what I "completed" as *Subspace Encounter*. Confusing, isn't it?

After starting out as a writer, in 1947 you became a genre publisher. What led you to launch Fantasy Press?

You might say it was Doc Smith. After the war I was working at Glidden Paints in Reading. I got a badly printed postcard from Tom Hadley in Buffalo, New York, advertising publication in book form of Smith's *Skylark of Space*, which, like almost everything else in the genre, only existed in magazine form. I dearly wanted a copy of *Skylark* as a book, so I sent my three dollars off to Hadley and waited. And waited.

Hadley had launched Buffalo Books immediately after the war. His mother was a somewhat wealthy heiress, and gave him $5,000 to publish a book he wanted to put out. Supposedly Ken Krueger and Donald Grant were copartners, but basically the project was Hadley's. Grant shortly went into the military, and I don't know what happened to Krueger. I eventually recommended to Hadley that he change the firm to "Hadley Publishing Company," because "Buffalo Books" said nothing and he was the sole operator, anyway.

Well, *Skylark* never came, so eventually I wrote a letter of complaint to Hadley, asking where it was. In return I got a phone call from him, in which he apologized profusely. This set a pattern for our subsequent relationship. There had been delays, he said. There would always be delays. In the meantime, he'd published Taine's *Time Stream*. He asked if I wanted my three dollars to go toward that, and order *Skylark* when it was actually published. I agreed.

It turned out that Hadley was one of the most disorganized people you can imagine. He dealt with me entirely by telephone. He had no mailing list. He never kept records of any kind, never wrote letters. He just tried to deal with each order as it came in, and then threw the letter into a big box and never looked at it again.

Well, *Skylark* finally came out, but then I learned that he'd never heard of the concept of review copies! I told him to send me ten copies and I'd make sure it got reviewed. I sent them out, including one to *Amazing Stories*. On the basis of the review there the entire press run of about one thousand copies sold out.

Because of all this, I'd printed up some stationery for Hadley and started doing other things for him. I told him to send me the box of all the orders he'd ever received and I'd turn them into a mailing list. He did, and I compiled a mailing list of about a thousand names and addresses. Then, since he never wrote anyone, I started answering his mail for him. One day I got a letter from the Spokane Better Business Bureau on behalf of an irate fan in Washington. A book he'd paid for had never arrived, and the bureau wanted to know what was going on. I decided I'd gotten in too deep, and called Hadley to tell him I didn't want to do this for him anymore. He said that was okay, as he was thinking of getting out himself.

Meanwhile, my coworkers at Glidden Paints knew all about this, because Hadley always called me at work and I had to tell them what was going on. So I just turned to them and said, "How would you guys like to start a book publishing company?" I wasn't really serious—just joking. To my surprise, two of them immediately agreed. "How much would it take?" they wanted to know.

These two were A. J. Donnell, who was the artist on a newsletter I produced for Glidden, and Herbert MacGregor, assistant sales manager for the company. Donnell agreed to do the art work and MacGregor agreed to do the packing and shipping. Then MacGregor pulled in his next door neighbor, Lyman Houck, who was an accountant in an insurance company, to keep our books. I'd do everything else. Each one of us chipped in $20, and the total of $80 launched Fantasy Press. Donnell designed a letterhead for us, and I composed a letter announcing our first publication, Doc Smith's *Spacehounds of the IPC*. We mailed the letter to everyone on the list I'd compiled for Hadley, and got enough prepublication orders to pay for printing that first book. We were immediately profitable, and in our first year had over $25,000 in sales. And it all happened because I wanted to own Doc Smith's stories in book form!

After almost a dozen years, Fantasy Press finally shut down in 1958. You say most of your stock went to Donald Grant, who was then back in the specialty press business, and that no one ever bought the company itself. Yet most of the reference books say that Gnome Press took your stock, and that Greenberg bought you out. How did that happen?

I think it happened because I wasn't on to what was happening at Gnome and probably unwittingly aided this impression. I allowed Greenberg to reprint Smith's *Grey Lensman*, which Fantasy Press had published. What he did was just produce a facsimile edition from my original, even keeping the "first edition" notation on it—though he did add the Gnome Press name. Perhaps this confused the identity of the two presses in people's minds.

Also, I arranged to have the company I was working for print the last two books Gnome published. One was John W. Campbell's *Invaders from the Infinite*, and the other was another Smith title. Greenberg never paid for the last book, by the way. As a side point, David Kyle, supposedly coequal partner with Greenberg, never got a penny out of the operation. Anyway, this may have contributed to the confusion as well.

But the truth is that Gnome Press was *not* a continuation of Fantasy Press in the slightest way. My company just folded and the stock went primarily to Grant.

After not having written anything for quite a while, you're now writing fantasy. What got you started again?

The death of my wife. She died in 1978. I'd actually started writing my reminiscences, *Over My Shoulder*, before she died. It was a very long project because it required extensive correspondence with the agents, writers, and other publishers involved. Then I visited Dave Kyle and read his first draft of *Dragon Lensman*. I offered him some criticisms and suggestions which he followed. That made me think, hey, maybe I can do this again, too. The first thing I tried was a science fiction novel. I figured if I could write a thousand words a day, in sixty days I'd have one.

Which do you find easier to write, short stories or novels?

Novels are much easier. The first two stories I sold were twelve thousand and thirteen thousand words. The third was twenty thousand words. The fourth was thirteen thousand words. I went for length, always. Now, I did write shorter pieces, but I've always been more comfortable with the greater length. These weren't novels, of course. And until I started writing again the length of a novel scared me. All those pages—that was quite a challenge! Oddly enough, now it doesn't bother me at all.

Which novel was this that you began work on?

You haven't seen it because all the editors rejected it. It was a space opera, a world-saver, an ancient idea. I'd actually thought of the plot thirty years before, and I started it with no plan, just wrote off the top of my head. I can do that; years ago I usually did. I showed it to Don Wollheim in his New York office before he died. He said it would have sold right away in the thirties, maybe even the forties, but not now.

So, I rewrote the beginning, outlined a new middle and end, and sent it to my agent. He sent it to Shelley Shapiro at Del Rey, who rejected it because of its hackneyed plot. The new beginning seems okay to me; in fact, I think it's excellent, and I believe she thinks so too. But she said the plot was too ancient—and it *was*. I've come up with a new plot now, and I'll *still* sell the blooming thing! I haven't done anything with it so far, though, except make a few notes.

So, I wrote that in the allotted sixty days. Then I finished Doc's novel, which I told you about. I followed that with *The Land Beyond the Gate*. It now has three sequels,[6] though I wrote it without any sequel in mind. However, I put in the portals, gates to other worlds, in case anyone wanted a sequel. At the time I had no idea at all what was beyond those gates.

When Lester Del Rey accepted *The Land Beyond the Gate* he wanted only two very small changes. They were both science fictional, and he said they should be deleted. Science fiction fans will tolerate fantasy, he said, but fantasy fans don't like science fictional intrusions. So, I cut 'em. Then he said, "If you have a sequel in mind, I'd like to see it."

So I immediately came up with not just one, but three, and sent him outlines for all of them. On the basis of these we signed a contract and he sent me an advance payment for thousands of dollars before I'd written a word! Then he sent me a check again after I completed each novel. The first book is now in its fifth printing, the second in its fourth printing, the third in its second, and the fourth has just come out. The third, *The Sorceress of Scath*, is better than the first two. The fourth, *The Scroll of Lucifer*, really winds things up.[7]

Did the acceptance of these novels surprise you?

By Del Rey? Not really. I thought the first was a good book and that Lester would go for it. But as far as the market is concerned, you never know. That's a sheer gamble. Today, with space in bookstores at a premium, the merit of a book doesn't mean a whole lot.

You must have been in your late sixties when you started writing again. How did you accommodate yourself to current tastes and styles?

I had no trouble at all, really. I just wrote what I wanted to write. I haven't read much of the new generation of writers. Most of the new stuff I don't care for, and I don't want to write like that. I don't want a lot of sex and gore and four-letter words. Fortunately, Lester liked what I did.

Also, fantasy doesn't age as much as science fiction.

That's correct. But I think I can make a saleable manuscript out of that first science fiction novel, and I'm stubborn enough to keep on trying.

Do you think that writing fantasy made it easier for you to get back in the field?

Probably so. There's more fantasy than science fiction being written now, and more *bad* fantasy than good fantasy. So, if you can write good fantasy, you should have no trouble selling it. And personally, I enjoy reading fantasy. Therefore, I'm doing what I want to do.

I also do a tremendous amount of research in the mythology of ancient peoples, such as the Celts who figure in *The Land Beyond the Gate*. In *The Scroll of Lucifer* I introduced the mythology of ancient China and India.

Lester now has the synopses of a new fantasy trilogy that takes place in 2350 B.C. The first locale is Egypt, the second one is in Crete, and the third is in Akkad, which was a successor to Sumer. I've done extensive research on them already, although I still don't have an okay on them. Until I get this I don't want to mention trilogy's overall title.

Do you feel you've slowed down in your writing?

Yes—but I've slowed down intentionally. I've gone back to writing in longhand. I used to do all my composing on a type-writer. I went back to longhand because I write better that way. When things are going well I average about a thousand words a day. That comes to about three legal pad pages.

Right now I'm struggling with a short fantasy story. I have to write one of four thousand words for Pulphouse Publishers. It's for an anthology of my stories which will be titled *In Wonder's Way: Tales from Seven Decades of Science Fantasy*. It'll have a story of mine from each decade, starting in the thirties. I'm writing the one for the Nineties now. Not many writers can match seven decades of publication. Anyway, this story has to be short because there's a space limitation. The book can't be longer than thirty thousand words.[8]

You're eighty now, so if you hang on for just another decade,
you can write a story in 2001 as well!

That's a good idea! Actually, longevity runs in the family. My
older sister is still alive at ninety, and I had two great-grandpar-
ents who lived to be one hundred and one hundred and one.[9] My
father died two months short of eighty-five. My oldest brother
died at eighty-four.

In the meantime, I'm working on seven projected novels,
including the outline of one set in the modern-day Scottish Highlands. That part of the world fascinates me—I own thirty or forty
books on Celtish mythology alone. This is a story I mentioned just
casually to Lester. It would be a single novel, not part of a series.

What's your normal writing routine?

Generally, I try to write in the morning, when I'm fresh, but
sometimes it doesn't happen until late in the afternoon and occasionally not until late at night. As I said, I shoot for a thousand
words a day, but I don't limit it to that. If I happen to write two
thousand, fine; if I can only get five hundred, well, that's okay too.

Do you write seven days a week?

Often, but not religiously. I know Fred Pohl writes every day.
I suppose Asimov does, too. But I usually write five, maybe six
days a week. Sometimes seven. Occasionally none. It all depends
on how well it's going.

Do you do all your research first, or do you research as you
write?

I do an awful lot first, and then some more while I'm writing.
Things often turn up in the writing that require more research. By
the way, I have a personal library of some four thousand books. I

live in what used to be a frat house of Albright College. The rooms have fourteen-foot ceilings, so there's plenty of room for them. It's like a library. I have seventy books on mythology alone, few of them on Greece and Rome because my interest in other areas of the ancient world is greater. I found you can't rely on the public library, for it just doesn't have all the specialized books you need.

How many drafts do you write?

I write a draft of a scene in longhand, which may be four or five pages. I type that up, making changes as I go; that's my second draft. I then edit the typescript. But if in typing I run into things which change the direction of the story, I may have to go back and rewrite portions on my legal pads. When I have a completed typescript I go over the whole thing, noting changes on the copy. Finally, I have a professional typist do the final draft. So, usually three drafts.

Lester does the copy-editing on my books himself. I was told by his associate that this isn't the usual practice, but we've been friends for a lot of years. I just received from Ballantine the copy-edited galley for *The Scroll of Lucifer* and there wasn't much editing done. My final draft stayed pretty much final.

Invariably, Lester has input which can change things substantially. In *The Sorceress of Scath* I had what I thought was a finished novel when he pointed out that there were two major scenes which, while interesting in themselves, didn't really advance the story. And he was right. So I took them out and rewrote the last half of the book. Actually, that led into a much more interesting avenue with new developments. Rewriting is one of the necessary hazards. That's why I'm not going ahead with my Egypt-Crete-Akkad trilogy until I get Lester's okay.[10]

Looking back, what's your favorite story or novel from all you've written?

Oh, brother! Man alive, that's difficult. . . . I suppose *The Land Beyond the Gate*. I enjoyed writing that story, and I enjoy reading it now! That may sound vain, but, nevertheless I really like it.

By the way—here's something I don't think has ever been mentioned: my collaboration with P. Schuyler Miller. We broke into the science fiction magazines around the same time. I recognized the Merritt influence on his work and wrote to him. He admitted the Merritt influence. We became correspondents, and then friends. Eventually we arranged to rendezvous in New York City, where we spent a day together. In the course of that day we decided to collaborate on a novel. We would have two lead characters; he'd write one character's viewpoint and I'd write the other. Well, I wrote my half, but he never finished his. I still have my half and what Sky wrote of his, which come to about forty-five thousand words together. One day I just may complete the thing! It'd have to undergo some major changes, though.

Another thing which isn't generally known is that I have a complete unpublished Doc Smith novel—a murder mystery. I did some revising and polishing of the first chapter, and George Price at Advent will bring it out in a collector's edition. But, that's the end of the Doc Smith material.[11]

Speaking of "lost" novels, didn't you once announce that Fantasy Press would be publishing a novel by Harry Stephen Keeler, the noted mystery writer?

Yes, and after Fantasy Press folded, I sent it, with Keeler's permission, to Marty Greenberg at Gnome. It was a time travel story in which the hero met himself. It was written with a logical plot development, but in the typical Keeler complex writing style. He took an utterly fantastic idea and made it convincing. But Marty didn't like it.

Anyhow, Keeler sent it to a firm in Portugal, which printed it in Portuguese—the only time it was ever published. There's a

Keeler society in New Jersey or Maryland which once wrote me about it. They'd been trying to trace the novel and found out about this Portuguese edition, but were never been able to find a copy. I've kicked myself all over the lot for never photocopying the manuscript while I had it in my hands. So far as I know, it no longer exists.

It sounds like Heinlein's "All You Zombies. . . ."

I never read that.

Or "By Your Bootstraps."

Yeah, that sort of thing, where the hero goes back in time to meet himself. Keeler wrote the most complex, involved stories, and this novel was like that. One thread which leads to another thread which leads to another. In fact, he even drew charts to follow all the ramifications of his plots. I have a copy of an article he wrote for *Author and Journalist* in which he discussed these charts and his almost mathematical plot complications.

Did you ever try anything like that?

I tried it to see if it would work, but it was too mechanical. I like to just let it flow. I have a general idea of where I'm going. The synopsis of that trilogy I sent Del Rey totaled thirty-eight pages. I described the beginning, the ending, and some of the middle of each novel.

When I start on a novel, I outline each chapter as I begin it. I don't outline subsequent chapters before I start on them, because things may change in the current chapter which would change the later ones. Nothing is carved in stone; I plan it as I go along. There are some authors who write totally blind, with no idea where they're going. I can't do that; I always have the ending in mind. I know where I'm going, but the route I follow may change.

Getting back to publishing, I believe in 1955 or so, as a Polaris imprint, you put out two Burroughs novels, Beyond Thirty *and* The Man-Eater. . . .

Oh, I'll have to tell you about those. By the way, they weren't anything like Polaris books, and no Polaris imprint was involved. I got copies of the stories from Ozzie Train, because I wanted one of each for myself. Then I realized that other collectors would want copies, as well. Copyrights on both had lapsed into the public domain, though I didn't check into that at the time. As it happened, there wasn't any need for secrecy, but I didn't know that.

I had a gal who did some typing for me type them up, two book pages on a single sheet. I had them reproduced cheaply, not by a mimeograph, but something comparable. Offset printing, not the good offset printing of today, but on letter-sized sheets. I hand-stapled three hundred copies of each. Then I had a color stock cover printed, and I sold them for three dollars per copy. They weren't copyrighted and no publisher was named because I thought at the time I was violating copyright. Today I don't even have copies of my own! That's the story behind those two.

I've been selling, over the last year or two, some things I've held on to for a long time. At one time I considered publishing *Skylark of Space* in a format to match the other Fantasy Press "Skylark" books. Julius Unger, the New York fantasy dealer, urged me very strongly to do this. He said he'd buy five hundred copies on publication. While I was considering this, I had A. J. Donnell, the artist, make a black and white drawing for the cover. I also had the binder make a binder stamp. They gave me a proof on the blue cloth that I used for the Smith books. Eventually, however, I decided against publishing it.

But Donnell held onto the original drawing, and recently I sold it for him to Barry Levin on the West Coast. I think he got $800 or $1,000 for it. Just last week I came across the cover proof in my files. I mentioned this in a letter to Levin, and he offered me $175 for it! Well, I mailed it to him, believe me! It's a unique item. He'll make a profit on it.

Where did Ozzie get copies of the Burroughs novels?

He had original tear-sheets, or perhaps typed copies. "Beyond Thirty" had been published in a pulp magazine like *All-Story*—I can't remember which—and "The Man-Eater" had been serialized in some newspaper.[12]

Did you get much feedback on those Burroughs novels?

Nothing. Not even from the Burroughs people. They probably never heard of them. Those three hundred copies are big collector's items today. A while back Barry advertised one in his catalog for several hundred dollars.

Since you're interested in history, let me ask you this. If you could travel in time back to any event in history, what would you like to see?

Oh, my word! (Pause.) My goodness, that's an impossible question! My thoughts flow from ancient Sumer to ancient Egypt to the ancient Scottish Celts. But I don't know. I've never given such an idea a thought.

Okay, let me narrow the field a bit. If you could visit any science fiction event of the past, what would that be?

Possibly to watch H. G. Wells or Jules Verne write one of their novels. But then, it wouldn't be interesting to watch someone write. My mind has just never gone in that direction.

What other plans do you have besides writing the trilogy you spoke of?

Well, I'm liquidating Doc Smith's science fiction at the request of his daughter, Verna Smith Trestrail, which is how the sequel to *Subspace Encounter* came to light. I think the most collectible item may be a three-hundred-fifty-page holograph synopsis in a desk diary of the entire Lensman series, from *Galactic Patrol* to *Children of the Lens*, which he wrote before beginning his first Lensman book. That should be very desirable. I'm not getting a penny out of this, by the way. Outside of Verna, the family doesn't have any interest in science fiction, and doesn't know what to do with the stuff. So I've taken it in hand as a way of paying thanks to Doc.[13]

Also, I've edited and written an introduction for the complete stories of an old English author who wrote under the pseudonym of "Fionna McCloud." McCloud was very popular and influential in the old days. In fact, Merritt got the idea for "The Woman of the Wood" from one of his stories. I collected all of them, which are now in the public domain, and sent them to Donald Grant for publication. He agreed on their high quality, but at this moment it's unclear what will happen with this collection. I'm also sketching out ideas for a number of other novels.

I'm also an expert lapidary and a fairly good silversmith. Five of the stones I've cut are in the Smithsonian. I was a rock hound as a kid. I'd read a book from the Reading Public Library called *The Boy Mineral Collector*. I got what I thought was a knapsack and a stone mason's hammer—they turned out to be a gas-mask bag and a shoemaker's hammer—and went around the countryside collecting minerals. Over the years this interest gradually faded.

But when I was in Chicago in the early sixties as an advertising manager for Moody Press, of the Moody Bible Institute, I took a walk along Chicago's Antique Row one day and stopped in a junk shop. There was a box of rocks, somebody's collection. It had some really nice stuff, including one of the best examples of tiger's eye I've ever seen. I bought maybe half a dozen of the rocks for peanuts.

Back in the office afterward I mentioned to somebody that they took me back to my childhood. He said, "You know, they teach lapidary work through the park system here in Chicago." I didn't know anything about that, so I investigated. I found that it cost only $1.25 a month for instruction, and you could go there up to eight hours a day and five days a week if you had the time.

So I signed up. After work I went there a night a week, and I took to it like a duck to water. I'd been going to classes sporadically for about six or eight months when I learned about a competition to be held by the Chicago Lapidary Society. I decided to enter.

Like everything else I do, I went into it whole hog. I do nothing by halves. Some of the other students would go up to the instructor and say, "Mitch, what do you think of this?"

He'd answer, "If you like it, that's all that matters."

But I'd go up to him and say, "Mitch, what's wrong with this?"

And he'd reply, "Well, it doesn't have the shine it should have," or something like that. And he'd teach me stuff the other students never heard of because they weren't sufficiently interested.

I was learning silversmithing as well, and combining the two to make jewelry. So I designed a piece for the competition, which I entered. I'm looking at this very moment at a trophy on top of one of my bookcases which says, "Best of Show." I won it for this first piece I ever entered in competition! The next year I won two second places. The year after that was the last one we were going to be in Chicago, so I said to my wife, "I'm going to go for broke," and I entered nine pieces. I won Best of Show, four firsts, two seconds, and two-thirds!

I have a shop in my basement with about $5,000 worth of equipment. Diamond saws and polishers, grinding wheels, the whole works. A regular lapidary shop. Now and then I spend a couple of hours a day working on stones. When I was on the road I'd stop at any rock shop I saw. If I liked something, I bought it, because I figured I'd never see it again. So now I have a huge accumulation of rough slabs—enough to keep me busy if I live to be one hundred fifty! I love the work.

Also I love the idea that each of these unique stones I turn out will be worn by someone. You can't find any commercial stuff anything like mine. Right now I'm turning out stones for Laurie Edison, a silversmith in San Francisco who operates a shop called "The Sign of the Unicorn." I met her at a World Con where she was exhibiting. She buys all her cut stones from me, several thousand dollars worth so far, and I'm sending her another shipment in a week or two. She says my stones are "utterly marvelous," but I told her that'll be the last shipment for about six months, because I'll be concentrating on writing. I have my new trilogy to write!

NOTES

1. "The Voice from the Ether" was also anthologized in Martin H. Greenberg's *Amazing Stories Science Fiction Anthology: The Wonder Years, 1926-1935,* (Lake Geneva, Wis.: TSR Publications, 1987), the contents of which differed generally from the Ashley anthology.

2. The Buffalo Book Company was the first of these ventures, in 1946. Later, Tom Hadley continued alone with the Hadley Publishing Company, in 1947. The Martin Greenberg of Gnome Press, founded in 1948, should not be confused with the current prolific anthologizer Martin H. Greenberg.

3. This point needs to be emphasized, since it differs from that found in reference books. I have this version from Eshbach himself. Curiously, the older one is repeated even by the official curators of the Eshbach archives and papers. With others in the field, these can be found in the Department of Special Collections at Temple University, with Tom Whitehead, long active in Philadelphia fandom, as head curator. In the listing of Temple's Eshbach-Fantasy Press holdings, *Register* 37 (June 1981): 14, it is stated that he sold both "the company and its stock to Gnome Press." This, Eshbach says, is "a total lie." Donald Grant purchased the great bulk of the stock and the company itself was never sold to *anyone.*

4. Gallun himself died of a possible stroke April 2, 1994, at age

eighty-three. The SUNY-Stonybrook Raymond Z. Gallun Award, established by the Gallun estate, continues to be awarded to those who have contributed significantly to science fiction.

5. In August 1994, Eshbach told me that he also has five *great*-grandchildren, with another on the way.

6. *The Land Beyond the Gate* was published by Del Rey Books in 1984. Its sequels are *The Armlet of the Gods, The Sorceress of Scath,* and *The Scroll of Lucifer.*

7. As of August 1994, all four novels were in their fifth printings.

8. Due to financial problems, Pulphouse discontinued the series before Eshbach's anthology could be published. As of 1994 he was expanding his four-thousand-word story to novel length. In the meantime, his agent was seeking a publisher for the erstwhile Pulphouse anthology.

9. Eshbach's sister died two years later, age ninety-two.

10. Since this conversation, Eshbach finished the first installment of his projected trilogy and sent it to Lester Del Rey. After accepting it, however, he retired from Del Rey Books in the fall of 1991. On May 10, 1993, he died of a massive heart attack at age seventy-seven. Meanwhile, Eshbach's novel has not yet been published, and the other books in the trilogy have not been written.

11. In the summer of 1994 Eshbach gave the work "a necessary and thorough editing" and sent the final results to Advent. It will be published under the title *Have Trench Coat, Will Travel.*

12. "Beyond Thirty" was published in the February 1916 issue of *All Around Magazine;* "The Man Eater" appeared as a six-part serial in *The New York Evening World,* November 15-20, 1915.

13. During the night of March 12-13, 1994, Verna Trestrail died in her sleep at age seventy-three. Eshbach continues to handle Doc Smith's estate.

8.

FROM PRINT TO THE SCREEN

A Conversation with Curt Siodmak

Even a man who is pure in heart
And says his prayers at night,
May become a wolf when the wolfbane blooms
And the autumn moon shines bright.
　　　　　　　　—Curt Siodmak, "The Wolf Man" (1941)

CURT SIODMAK MAY HAVE THE LONGEST PROFESSIONAL career of any writer in the science fiction field. Not counting a fairy tale he published at the age of eight in a children's magazine, he has been writing and publishing for over three-quarters of a century, with his first "professional" sale in 1919. And he is still writing and publishing.

Like that of his older brother, Robert, his career began in Berlin in the days of the Weimar Republic. He has written short stories, novels, and plays, but it is as a Hollywood screenwriter that he made his mark. For twenty years, from 1938 to 1957, he regularly churned out original and adapted screenplays, sometimes two or three per year. In all, including collaborations, he

299

crafted approximately forty-eight screenplays for films in Germany, Great Britain, America, Sweden, France, and Switzerland. Meanwhile, he produced approximately fifteen novels in Germany, America, and France, and his total number of short stories is unknown even to himself. Later in his career, Siodmak also directed a handful of Hollywood films, although it was his brother, Robert, who went on to become celebrated for directing such classics as *The Spiral Staircase* and *The Crimson Pirate*.[1]

Robert and Curt were the sons of a well-to-do Jewish banker in Leipzig, Germany (although Robert was actually born in 1900 in Memphis, Tenn., during a business trip by his father and Curt was born in Dresden two years later). Robert graduated from the University of Marburg and began acting in repertory theater, but the hyperinflation of the Weimar years forced him to give that up and become, first, a bank clerk, and then a failed businessman in a series of unsuccessful ventures. In 1925 he managed to find a job in Berlin as a title writer for imported American films. In 1926 Robert became a film editor. In 1929 Robert and his brother, Curt, collaborated with Billy Wilder and Fred Zinnemann—both of whom later became prominent Hollywood directors—in creating the noted feature documentary *People on Sunday*, marking Robert's directorial and Curt's screenwriting debuts.

Curt had hoped to graduate from a German university, but the inflation of the years immediately after World War I again interfered. When his father was unable to finance his continued education in Germany, Curt went to Zurich, Switzerland, where he obtained his B.A. in engineering in 1924. He was already writing short stories, which appeared in top German magazines. One such story, "The Eggs From Lake Tanganyika," was seen by Hugo Gernsback and reprinted in the fourth issue of his new science fiction magazine, *Amazing Stories* (July 1926).[2] Thus, though he'd never heard of either Gernsback or his magazine, Siodmak became a "Gernsback author," a reputation he has retained ever since.

Upon graduation from the University of Zurich, Curt joined

his brother in Berlin. There, the vagaries of the financial situation made it impossible to pursue his engineering career. Instead, he drifted into his brother's film circle and wrote scripts for several of Robert's films. Both brothers fled the Nazis in the early thirties and eventually ended up in Hollywood. Curt was quickly given a job writing a sarong picture for Dorothy Lamour and a succession of such assignments followed for the next two decades. A number of his assignments for Universal Pictures— *The Wolf Man, House of Frankenstein, Frankenstein Meets the Wolf Man, Son of Dracula,* and others—have since become horror classics. This, as he makes clear in the following conversation, was entirely accidental. He had no particular affection for or interest in either horror or science fiction—indeed, he never read the stuff. It was merely a job.

This unfamiliarity with the field may explain why Siodmak's output—though prodigious—is also so derivative. Siodmak never displayed much feeling for or understanding of the field. Even his most noted novel and film, *Donovan's Brain,* a 1943 story about a disembodied brain kept alive in a vat, was a crude science fiction cliché at the time. The August 1926 issue of *Amazing Stores,* for instance, the very next issue after the one that introduced Siodmak to America, featured a cover of two scientists recoiling in horror from a still-living head in a lab vat.[3]

Nor, though Siodmak claims credit for creating the Wolf Man character in 1941, was his werewolf creation without precedent. *The Wolf Man* was Lon Chaney Jr.'s second horror film and the role for which he is most remembered. Indeed, he was honored with his in-character Wolf Man portrait on a U.S. postage stamp. Werewolves, however, were not new to cinema. As early as 1913 Bison Films had made a silent film, *The Werewolf.* In 1933 Guy Endore's classic novel, *The Werewolf of Paris,* burst upon the world and Endore was quickly snapped up by MGM as a screenwriter to turn his novel into a screenplay. Universal Studios rushed to beat MGM to the screen with their own werewolf story. In 1935 they turned out *The Werewolf of London* with, not one, but *two*

werewolves, one of them an Oriental werewolf played by Warner
Oland, of later Charlie Chan fame. Thus, when Universal Studios
returned to the werewolf theme in 1941 with an assignment to
Siodmak to write a screenplay, the ground was well-trodden—
although now-integral parts of the werewolf legend, such as
Gypsy curses and silver bullets, made their first appearance in this
film and might have been Siodmak's ideas. In addition, the script
was unusually literate for both a B film—and for Siodmak.

In 1943 Siodmak coscripted *I Walked with a Zombie,* a true
horror classic from the team of producer Val Lewton and director
Jacques Tourneur, who also brought us 1942's *Cat People.* This
was perhaps Tourneur's best work, almost poetic, complemented
by the haunting camera work of J. Roy Hunt and the dialogue of
Ardel Wray, based upon an original story by Inez Wallace. Here,
also, however, the film, though nightmarishly beautiful, was
basically the well-known story of *Jane Eyre* transposed to the
West Indies and it is unclear what, or how much, Siodmak contributed to the film.

Even at the time, Siodmak's films were recognized as plod-
ding and predictable, if not outright ridiculous, confirming that
his talents were of the stolid workmanlike variety which welded
worn-out SF conventions onto mundane formulas. For example,
of *Curucu, Beast of the Amazon,* shot on location in Brazil,
Variety said, "Curt Siodmak's screenplay and direction make formula thriller use of the settings."[4] Of Siodmak's *Love Slaves of
the Amazon,* based upon an unpublished short story of his,
Variety said it was:

> a simple-minded, poorly-made adventure film of which
> everyone says, "there must be a market for them somewhere."
> It's being coupled by Universal with *Monolith Monsters,* and,
> as part of such a package, probably will sneak by. If there's
> anything good to be said about it it's that the Eastman color is
> vivid and impressive, picking up some interesting landscapes
> in Brazil, where this was produced by Curt Siodmak....

Siodmak's script is so clumsy, the temptation is great to consider the whole thing a takeoff on jungle pix that have gone before. His direction isn't any much better, judging by the performances. . . . Siodmak should have to answer to someone why nothing better came out.[5]

Meanwhile, Damon Knight has pointed to Siodmak's screenplay for 1954's *Riders to the Stars* as, "a splendid example of all that is silliest and most unscientific in SF cinema."[6]

Nevertheless, Siodmak has had the last laugh—all the way to the bank. His novels are still in print, at least in Europe, he is financially comfortable, and he now "lives like a king" on a sixty-acre ranch in the wilds of the California outback. If nothing else, the long-distance career of Curt Siodmak proves that there is always a lucrative market for formula.

The great virtue of oral history, such as in the following conversation, is that it gives a first-person "eyewitness" account of events by someone who was there. The great flaw of oral history, however, is that memory is exceedingly fallible, especially about events which happened decades past. Oral testimony, therefore, always has to be verified, as much as possible, by comparison with the record. This is true of the following conversation, where both the great virtue and great flaw of oral history are both on display. This conversation with Curt Siodmak took place on June 11, 1991. Siodmak was eighty-eight years old at the time.

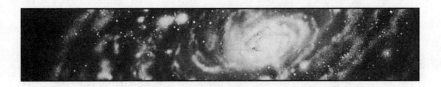

ERIC LEIF DAVIN: *You were born August 10, 1902, correct?*

CURT SIODMAK: Ja, I didn't choose it. I didn't choose my family and I didn't choose Dresden, where I was born. If I'd had a choice, I'd have been born two thousand years ago in Greece during the time of Aristotle, not during the time of Hitler.

Are you Jewish?

My father says so and I am his child.

In Slaughterhouse Five *Kurt Vonnegut described Dresden before the firebombing. Was that an accurate description?*

I don't remember. That was over fifty years ago. In your memory things are so different. I had a lovely big palazzo in Italy with a big staircase. I saw it thirty years later and it was a small house with a small staircase. We're used to big spaces in America. Now I live in California on a ranch. Sometimes we see a jeep on the fire roads and my wife says, "Let's move out, it's getting crowded."

I've been back to Europe a few times. I was invited recently by the head of the film museum in Berlin, who was a house guest here on my ranch a few weeks ago. I'm also a new writer they've just discovered over there. All my books are being republished and I had a new book out two weeks ago entitled *The Riches of Paris*. Only published in France. A historical novel about Louis XIV.

All my books have been continually in print. My book *Donovan's Brain* has been published five or six times in Germany. I was published by Bertelsmann, one of the largest European publishers. I was in Munich about two years ago with a book manuscript. They took it away and gave me cash!

I think the 1953 film version of Donovan's Brain *was the first film I saw based on your work.*

They didn't want me to direct that. I had a contract to direct it, but it didn't happen.

Were you satisfied with what they did?

I don't look at those pictures. They changed too much, especially adding references to God, so I didn't look at it. Another version was called *The Brain,* made by an English company in 1962. They had a cancer cure in it. What is a cancer cure doing in that picture?[7]

But, the book is still in print; sold about five million copies. I just had three of my books come out in one volume. It's written from the shifting viewpoint of a young man in the first story, middle aged in the second, and an old man in the third.

So, you're still active?

What do you mean *still* active? Of course! They just had a big parade for me in Austria. I'm also a lyricist and song writer. I just wrote a play, *The Song of Frankenstein.* It's a comedy. It's huge over there. It's in Vienna, then it goes to Berlin, then it goes to London.

I have also written about five hundred pages of my autobiography, which I've been working on for some time. I threw the first draft away and started from scratch. There was a lady photographer visiting me from Zurich about three years ago. She was interviewing all the people of my circle from the thirties who are still alive. That started me thinking that I should write about my life and about those people, too.[8]

Can we talk about those early days? I think you must have the longest professional career—wasn't your first professional sale in 1909? When you were eight years old you published a fairy tale in a magazine called Kinderwelt, *"Children's World."*

Well, I wrote that fairy tale as a child and I wrote lots of science fiction. I remember one story, it was a long time ago, 1922. I described a telephone booth which would disassemble people into atoms and transmit them to another booth which would reassemble them into people—a matter transmitter.

What would you say your earliest influences were?

I studied engineering in Zurich, Switzerland, and in Stuttgart Hochschule, which was similar to a community college. I developed a car engine in '22, similar to the Wankel engine. I studied lasers in the thirties. My father refused to pay for my education because of the tremendous inflation at that time, so I lost my education. But, I had two friends who invited me to Switzerland, where I met my wife, Henrietta.[9] She was an architect in Zurich. I met her at a fancy dress ball. I was then a student at the University of Zurich, from which I graduated.

Do you credit that engineering education with your ability to think up science fiction ideas?

Not at all. It's like a shoeshine boy asking you if you want a shine. How does he know? He looked at your shoes! I go through life and I see things others don't see because it's my profession. If you have the talent and you do it often enough, it becomes second nature. You don't need an engineering background to do that. And you don't need to read science fiction! I never did read science fiction. I think it's gibberish. I don't understand all the technical words they use.

But, you've written technical stories about outer space like City in the Sky!

City in the Sky is *possible!* But *Star Wars* is *not* possible.

I see. Did you always think science fiction was gibberish?

Of course, it was always gibberish.

You know, the human mind is so limited. We write about societies on other worlds, and they resemble us so much. You look at the paintings of Brueghel or Bosch[10] and all those demons look like men with two eyes and two arms—hard to think of a new shape. The same with societies. You go into outer space and you find fascism or communism or the Roman Empire or feudal Europe. We don't have much in our brains.

I wrote a few books about space, *Skyport* and *City in the Sky*.[11] A friend took me to visit engineers at Lockheed because he thought talking with them would help give me ideas. They got their ideas from reading my books!

For instance, instead of launching rockets from the ground to reach orbit, why not have a huge elevator into space, miles high? Launch things from the top and they save so much on fuel!

Didn't Arthur C. Clarke already write about that in The Fountains of Paradise*?[12]*

Who? I don't know. I never read that.

How did you go from being an engineer to being a reporter and a writer?

I was always a writer. When I went to Berlin in 1924, the inflation made it impossible to make a living as an engineer, so I wrote for the newspapers. My education helped me a lot in my science fiction writing. I didn't know very much, but I knew a little.

But, while my education helped with my science fiction, I also wrote love stories, all kinds of novels. My last one is a historical novel. If the idea is interesting, it doesn't matter if it's science fiction, or not. I'm a writer. I can write about anything.

Was there an active German science fiction community in the twenties?

I wrote a short story called "The Eggs from Tanganyika." It was published in a German magazine and then I got some money from Hugo Gernsback when he republished it. I found an article in *The Smithsonian* about four weeks ago which said he wanted stories which used a lot of scientific research.[13] But, I didn't do any research for that story! I'd never heard of Gernsback before he published my story.

Were there any American science fiction magazines republished in Germany?

It took six weeks for the boat to come over! An exchange didn't exist. Sometimes you got a hardback, but nothing from magazines. How much do you know about German publications? Why should I know what was published in America?

How did you first become interested in film in Germany?

I just got a letter from a friend of mine who's my age. He reminded me that I made my first film in 1926. Then I wrote books. I wrote *Antwortet Nicht*.[14] Then I wrote something called *The Studio Murder Mystery*. In those days, newspapers still published novels in serial form. These were reprinted in smaller and smaller papers, until you got to the village papers, each paying less money. But, you were paid for each publication. The Germans paid very well, not like in America. Here, five weeks after publication your book is forgotten.

Did you have much input into the making of F.P. 1 Does Not Answer?

No, not at all. Someone said, "The writer is the most important person in Hollywood. Don't give him any power!"

And that was true in Germany, too?

No, in Germany a writer had standing.

But, F. P. One was made in Germany!

It was made in Germany, but it was shot simultaneously in three languages. It was the studio's idea. They wanted an international market. The producer for that film had imagination. He worked with Billy Wilder. He protected writers. But I didn't go onto sets. I didn't like actors. My brother, Robert, was the one who did that. He discovered Burt Lancaster, Ava Gardner, Ernest Borgnine, Tony Curtis, he picked them out of the crowd. He was a star-maker. He did *Spiral Staircase* and *The Crimson Pirate,* which was Lancaster's first big film. He wanted me to change my name so there wouldn't be two Siodmaks.

It's strange to hear you say you don't like actors, since you went on to become a director.

I went where the money was. How much money does a writer get? I never made money from my writing. A director made lots more money. Now I live like a king and I own sixty acres in the wilds of California. Not because of my writing!

Is that why you don't like actors? Because they make more money than writers?

What is an actor? Someone found in a drugstore! And if they become successful, they become a son-of-a-bitch! Who are the great actors through the ages? You know only when you know who *directed* them! And how many films do you remember? But, you know Shakespeare, don't you? Who acted in his plays? Books you remember! Books go through the ages. Plays go through the ages. But who remembers the actors of yesterday? Hitchcock was right. Actors should be treated like cattle.

I knew Hitchcock. He came to my office in London and said

to me, "Siodmak, write me a story about a woman who is a deaf and dumb detective." That was a very good idea, but unfortunately, I couldn't do it for him, because I left for America.

What was the first film you worked on?

I worked for a small German newspaper in '26 and was sent to do a story on Fritz Lang's *Metropolis.* He didn't allow reporters on his set, so I and my wife got jobs as extras in the movie. We didn't get much money for it, and we ate up whatever we got.

I never did like that movie. The thing I remember most about it was Brigitte Helm's costume catching fire during one of the disaster scenes. Helm was very pretty and very young. But, she was more hysterical than talented.[15]

In 1929 we made a film, we five young men in Berlin. Robert Siodmak, myself, Billy Wilder, Fred Zinnemann, Edgar Ulmer. We wrote a film called *People on Sunday.* The British stole it and it was made into a film called *Bank Holiday.* This picture is a classic, it's in every film museum, including the county museum here in Los Angeles. It was our first picture. It was the first money I made. We just took people on the street and turned them into actors, very cheap. It was the same style as what the French later called "New Wave," pictures like *The Bicycle Thief.*[16] We did the same kind of film twenty years earlier, but we didn't get the credit. Truffaut got the credit.

If you didn't like Metropolis, *why are you writing a sequel to it?*

A sequel? I'm not writing a sequel to it. Who told you anything as silly as that?

Forrest J. Ackerman said so.

Well, it might be because I have a friend who reads scripts in Hollywood and he mentioned the possibility of a sequel. I wrote him back some ideas of how a sequel might go, but that was all.

Did you know Thea von Harbou, the coauthor with Lang of Metropolis?

I never met her. I saw her once. There was a split between her and Lang. He left Germany in the thirties, while she stayed. They were going to make Lang an "Honorary Aryan" and he said he'd think it over. But, he was out of the country immediately after that.

It was a nightmare time, the thirties. I don't like to think about it. I don't think the Germans have changed in their attitudes toward Jews, even today. In 1985 I went back to Berlin to see how the people behaved, what Germany was like. I stayed in the best hotel in Berlin. I saw what kind of pictures they were showing. My name was still known. It was good for the ego. But the memories made me sick. There I was, standing on the same sidewalk in front of the same theater where I'd stood sixty years before for a screening of my science fiction film *The Invisible Agent*.[17] In the meantime, there'd been a world war, they'd killed my family. It made me feel sick. You Americans don't know what it was like to live through those times.

But every country's the same. Here we had the Vietnam War. But we faced it. We have the Vietnam Memorial, we write books about it, we make pictures about it. But the Germans don't face it. You can't make a picture today in Germany and show the Nazis.

I met so many people who said they were anti-Nazi. I asked, "Was that in 1945 or in 1942?" They don't say anything. But this isn't about politics here.

You left Germany in 1933, correct?

No, I didn't leave Germany. They threw me out! I got a letter from the German writers' union telling me I wasn't permitted to work in Germany anymore because I'm Jewish. In 1936 I received a letter in England from my publisher in Leipzig, Bertelsmann, now framed and hanging on my wall. It says, "Dear Mr. Siodmak: This is to inform you that all your books have been confiscated by the Gestapo. So sorry. Heil Hitler!" This is the same publisher who published my latest book last week!

Why did you leave England in 1937?

My wife wanted to go to America. She couldn't explain what it was. She was afraid of the Nazis coming. We tried moving to Switzerland but came back because she was pregnant and wanted to give birth to a British child. So, we moved to Los Angeles. Now we live in the country because she doesn't like the city anymore. I don't fight it; she's always right.

How did you make contacts so quickly when you moved to Hollywood in '37?

Somebody took me to Paramount. I got a job the first week. My first assignment was writing a picture for Dorothy Lamour, *Jungle Princess*.[18] It was standard in those days for old alcoholic screenwriters to be kept on and they'd assign younger writers to work with them and do the writing. I was given such an assignment of writing *Aloma of the South Seas*.[19] I made twenty-eight pictures for Universal. That was another time when you had to really work! My brother also had no job. So, Preston Sturges said he'd get him a job. He called the head of Paramount and said, "I have the most important director in Europe in my office." So, he was hired.[20]

How long did it take you to write a screenplay when you were working for Universal?

About ten weeks from scratch.

How long for The Invisible Woman, *in 1941, John Barry-more's last picture?*

He was an absolute mess. Couldn't remember one line. So, I was on the set all the time. I wrote his dialog for him as he walked up and down the staircase and he could read it as he walked up and down. You had to be careful or he'd walk out of camera range. I could tell you stories, but this is on tape.

How about The Son of Dracula?[21]

It was an interesting idea. Here was a woman in love with a man who would live forever, a vampire.

Was that your idea?

Of course, of course. The directors had no ideas. Actors have no ideas.

Did you come up with the idea for The House of Franken-stein?

Well, of course. I had a little altar in my room. I'd say to it, "My weekly check, my weekly check," and I'd go back to my typewriter. You have to write a lot of jobs to feed a family. I didn't want to make *art!* By chance the times have caught up with me and some people think the things are interesting. But, it was just a job. You didn't get much money for writing these things, $400 or $500, perhaps $1,000. That was good money in those days, but you had to keep working.

And you originated the idea for Frankenstein Meets the Wolf Man, *didn't you?*

Of course! And I created the character of The Wolf Man. I wish I had the copyright on him, but Universal owns it. Originally it was just entitled *The Wolf Man,* and would have had Boris Karloff in it, but he had to make another picture, so we had Lon Chaney Jr. I had two hours to come up with the idea for *Frankenstein Meets the Wolf Man.* I was told, "Here are your actors: Claude Rains, Ralph Bellamy, Lon Chaney.[22] You'll have a budget of $80,000. You begin shooting in two weeks. Goodbye!" So, I quickly wrote a script and was working on it right up to the last moment. I didn't have the money to hire another writer, so I had to write it myself. There's a book coming out on the classic Universal monster movies and it publishes my original shooting script for *Frankenstein Meets the Wolf Man.*

You know, I never made the big pictures. In those days, there was something called "Block Booking." A theater had to buy three hours of entertainment from the studio, okay? So, most of my films were made just to fill out the block. They've become "horror classics," but that was not of my doing. I was just making a living, that's all. I wrote sixty producible film scripts. I have two which have never been filmed.

Why were so many of your films horror stories?

They were just assignments given to me.

Did you respect the things you were writing, or did you just consider it trash?

I respected it. If you spit at your work, it will spit back at you. In your life, you are merely the echo of your own energies. I put all my energy into every job I had. I took them all seriously. I did a picture in England called *Transatlantic Tunnel.* It was the first time the British engaged American actors. Richard Dix, others. It opened up the whole English film industry. It was based on a famous novel by a German, Bernhard Kellerman, *Der Tunnel.*

Napoleon came up with the idea first, though. I got the job because I could read the original. They asked, "Can you write a script for it in three days?" I said, "Oh, sure." However, it took six months.[23]

What's your method for so much productivity?

I write twenty-four hours a day. When I'm on the phone, walking around, I'm writing in my mind. Basically, you're like a lighthouse keeper; you're married to the thing. Writing becomes the world, and the world becomes a dream. I've never had a problem with ideas, they just come. I have in my garage two hundred books with my stories, and that's only a third of my output. A young man came to me and said, "I want to be a writer. How do I get an agent? How much money can I make?" I took him to the garage and told him, "When you have that many books, come back."

What should I do to reach the age of ninety and still be active, like you?

Be curious. The brain is a muscle. As long as you work with it constantly, it stays young.

NOTES

1. Robert Siodmak died in Switzerland on May 10, 1973.
2. This was the story—with a Frank R. Paul illustration for the magazine's cover showing a giant fly attacking a warship—which captured the young Raymond Z. Gallun's eye and moved him to purchase his very first science fiction magazine. He was an instant convert to the genre. It has been reprinted in Forrest J. Ackerman, ed., *The Gernsback Awards I, 1926* (London: Turret, 1982).
3. Siodmak turned his novel into the original screenplay for the 1953 film of the same name. The film starred Nancy Davis (the future

First Lady, Nancy Reagan) and Lew Ayres, World War II pacifist who briefly served time with pacifist SF editor Charles D. Hornig.

4. *Variety,* Nov. 7, 1956.

5. *Variety,* Dec. 4, 1957.

6. Quoted in Peter Nicholls, ed., *The Encyclopedia of Science Fiction* (New York: Doubleday & Co., 1979), p. 548.

A small selection of other films for which Siodmak wrote the original screenplays include: *House of Frankenstein* (1944), in which all the Universal monsters were thrown together to revive the flagging series; *Bride of the Gorilla* (1951), also directed by Siodmak, in which Raymond Burr is a were-gorilla killed by cops Lon Chaney Jr. and black actor Woody Strode in his debut; and *The Magnetic Monster* (1953), cowritten with Ivan Tors and directed by Siodmak. The latter film starred Richard Carlson, omnipresent actor in 1950s' Grade B science fiction films. Siodmak and Tors wrote the screenplay in hopes of creating a TV series based on Carlson's character, who was an agent of the Office of Scientific Investigations. Sounds like *X-Files.*

Some of Siodmak's adapted screenplays include: *Black Friday* (1940), cowritten with Eric Taylor, in which Boris Karloff performs a brain transplant; *The Invisible Man Returns* (1940), cowritten with Lester Cole and Joe May, who directed it. This was Vincent Price's first starring vehicle; *Tarzan's Magic Fountain* (1949), cowritten with Harry Chandlee. Basically *Lost Horizon* in the jungle, this was the first Tarzan movie to star Lex Barker, who made several sequels; and *Earth vs. the Flying Saucers* (1956), cowritten with George Worthing Yates and Raymond T. Marcus [Bernard Gordon], with special effects by Ray Harryhausen. Based on Maj. Donald E. Keyhoe's 1953 book, *Flying Saucers From Outer Space*, although greatly influenced by George Pal's 1953 film, *War of the Worlds.* Indeed, except for *War of the Worlds, Earth vs. the Flying Saucers* is the only 1950s' SF film to feature a mass invasion of aliens. It contains the famous Harryhausen-engineered scene of a flying saucer crashing into the dome of the U.S. Capitol Building, a scene later spoofed in the TV cartoon series *The Simpsons.*

7. A British–West German production, it is also known as *Vengeance* and *Ein Toter Sucht Seinen Moerder.*

8. Unable to find a publisher, Siodmak self-published his completed autobiography on August 10, 1997, in a signed and boxed edi-

tion. Its title, *Even A Man Who Is Pure in Heart . . .* , comes from the opening lines of *The Wolf Man.* The publication date coincided with the U.S. Post Office release of the commemorative Lon Chaney "Wolf Man" stamp.

9. Henrietta De Perrot, whom he married in 1931. They had one child, a son, Peter, born in Great Britain and now a well-to-do American businessman.

10. Pieter Brueghal (1564?-?1638), Flemish painter known for his paintings of demons and infernal regions. Hieronymus Bosch (1450?–1516), Dutch painter of devils, monstrosities, and other gruesome subjects.

11. *Skyport* (New York: Crown, 1959). Basically Ayn Rand's *Fountainhead*—in the sky. *City in the Sky* (New York: Putnam, 1974). Basically *Grand Hotel*—in the sky.

12. Published in 1979, it won the Hugo in 1980 as Best Novel.

13. Daniel Stashower, "A Dreamer Who Made Us Fall In Love With The Future," *The Smithsonian* 21, no. 5 (August 1990).

14. *F. P. 1 Antwortet Nicht* (Berlin: Keils, 1931). Published in America as *F. P. 1 Does Not Reply* (Boston: Little, Brown, 1933). Filmed in Germany in 1933, for which Siodmak wrote the screenplay. An English version was released in 1938 in Great Britain by Gaumont. It is about floating airports—"Flight Platforms"—in the middle of the ocean.

15. Talented or not, Brigitte Helm—only a teenager when she portrayed *both* the heroine and the evil robot-vamp in Lang's classic silent SF film *Metropolis*—went on to make a string of films in which she almost always had the starring role. She easily made the transition to sound and starred as the Queen of Atlantis in G. W. Pabst's excellent 1932 film, *L' Atlantide.* As with the filming of Siodmak's *F. P. 1,* Pabst's film was shot simultaneously in German, French, and English with different casts, except for Helm, who starred in all three. According to Nicholls, Pabst's film, "is generally regarded as superior, not only because of its visual flair, but also for Brigitte Helm's striking performance as the queen" (p. 49). Brigitte Helm's last film was *Ein Idealer Gatte (An Ideal Spouse),* in 1935. She died in Switzerland on June 11, 1996, at the age of ninety.

16. In fact, this was a 1947 Italian film directed by Vittorio de Sica, which won a special Academy Award before foreign films had their own category.

17. *Invisible Agent* was made in Hollywood in 1942 as an espionage thriller in which the son of the original Invisible Man volunteers to spy on the Nazis and Japanese for the Allies. Highly unlikely that this war propaganda film would have been screened in Berlin anytime before 1945.

18. Actually, *Her Jungle Love,* 1938. Starring Lamour and Ray Milland as her lover, this South Seas sarong-film was essentially a remake of Lamour's sarong-debut, *Jungle Princess,* which paired her with Milland in 1936, before Siodmak left England.

19. 1941, another Dorothy Lamour sarong film.

20. Robert Siodmak settled in Paris after being expelled from Germany in 1933. He left Paris for Hollywood in 1940, just ahead of the German army.

21. Released in 1943, it was cowritten with Eric Taylor and directed by Siodmak's brother, Robert. It starred Lon Chaney Jr. as "Count Alucard" ("Dracula" spelled backward).

22. Actually, these were the actors in *The Wolf Man* (1941). *Frankenstein Meets the Wolf Man* (1943) starred Chaney, Bela Lugosi, Lionel Atwill, Ilona Massey, and Maria Ouspenskaya. Siodmak is obviously thinking about *The Wolf Man* (cowritten with Gordon Kann, which brings into question Siodmak's claim to have created the character) all the while he is talking about *Frankenstein Meets the Wolf Man,* for which he was, indeed, the sole screenwriter.

23. *The Tunnel* (aka *Transatlantic Tunnel*) was actually cowritten with L. Du Garde Peach and Clemence Dane, a well-known British author. It was released in 1935 and told the story of the construction of a tunnel beneath the Atlantic linking Britain and America. There was a previous 1933 German film, *Der Tunnel,* based upon the same novel, which linked America with the Continent, bypassing England. The epic grandeur of the German film was lost in Siodmak's cowritten screenplay, which turned the construction of the Tunnel into a love-story triangle centered around the master engineer, his wife, and a vamp.

Napoleon's idea for a tunnel, which Siodmak mentions, was for an undersea link between England and the rest of Europe—which now exists as the "Chunnel." This is yet another science fiction idea which has become reality!

9.

SECOND GENESIS—
THE BIRTH OF
SCIENCE FICTION CINEMA

Kurt Neumann and
"Rocketship X-M"

APOCALYPSE. THE END OF THE WORLD. NUCLEAR Holocaust. Visions of the end, usually in atomic flames, have become a staple of the science fiction imagination. Indeed, even humanity's oldest story, the Babylonian "Epic of Gilgamesh," c. 2000 B.C.E., contains a story of the end, of a mighty flood which inundates the world, as Noah's flood would later. It seems that such eschatological nightmares have always been with us. The modern counterpart, of course, is nuclear holocaust, a major theme in SF literature that is relatively recent and, in the world of cinema, it is as recent as the 1950s. And Kurt Neumann, an obscure journeyman Hollywood B-movie director, was the first person to put such a vision on the silver screen with his innovative 1950 SF film *Rocketship X-M*. Indeed, that film was also the first "modern" film to introduce the idea of space travel to moviegoers. This combination—space travel and global catastrophe—are the hallmarks of modern science fiction cinema and their appearance marked the emergence of the science fiction film as a distinct genre. After Neumann we were swamped with such films, so much so that we have forgotten where it all began. *But it began with Neumann.* A brief look at Kurt Neumann's career thus helps us trace how science fiction in the fifties exploded suddenly from a genre that was found virtually in written form alone into a genre that also had a vibrant life in film, a life in which space travel and nuclear holocaust were dominant motifs.

Of course, one could argue that science fiction had a film life which began almost simultaneously with the invention of motion pictures themselves. Motion pictures are now over a hundred years old, with France's Lumiere brothers, Louis and August, making the first film—that of workers leaving a plant at the end of their shift—in 1895. The next year, inspired by the Lumiere brothers, Frenchman Georges Melies bought motion picture equipment and began making his own films. Over the next few years, Melies, a former magician, turned out a number of trick films using the new optical illusion techniques that film technology made available. This culminated in 1902 with his famous *Le Voyage dans la Lune* (*The Voyage to the Moon*), one of the first SF films, in which a manned projectile is fired to the Moon out of a huge cannon, à la Jules Verne.

The silent film era saw a number of other notable excursions into science fiction, including a 1906 American version of Verne's *Twenty Thousand Leagues Under the Sea* and a 1907 French version by Melies. Other countries were also quickly producing silent SF films. Two notable examples were the Soviet Union's *Aelita* (1924), in which the Bolshevik Revolution is replayed on Mars, and Germany's *The Woman in the Moon* (1929), by Fritz Lang and Thea von Harbou, featuring yet another trip to the Moon. (This was the film David Lasser obtained for the famous Interplanetary Society event in New York at which G. Edward Pendray was mistaken for a famous French "astronaut.") The team of Lang and von Harbou also gave us perhaps the most famous silent SF film of all, *Metropolis* (1926), a story of class warfare in the year 2000.

The 1930s also had a number of worthy film entries into the SF field, such as *The Tunnel* (1935), with a screenplay cowritten by German Curt Siodmak—based on a popular 1913 German novel by Bernhard Kellerman—about the construction of a trans-Atlantic tunnel from New York to England. The thirties also produced a spate of SF matinee serials, such as Gene Autry's *Phantom Empire* (1935) and Buster Crabbe's familiar Flash Gordon serials (1936–1940). Perhaps the most ambitious and best SF film of the thirties was *Things to Come* (1936), scripted by H.G. Wells from his 1933 novel, *The Shape of Things to Come*. This latter, however, was a major box office flop and perhaps helped convince major studios that science fiction was not a wise investment, for no other SF film for the remainder of the thirties (or even the forties) equalled its budget. Lothar Mendes' *The Man Who Could Work Miracles* (1937), also based on an H.G. Wells novel and already in the pipeline when *Things to Come* was released, was the last of such attempts.

But, while one could certainly add to this list, the SF film was the rare exception in a film world dominated by "mundane" comedies, adventures, war stories, gangster stories, romances, and musicals. The science fiction film *as a distinct genre* did not exist. What changed this was World War II and the nuclear destruction of Hiroshima and Nagasaki. Global war and the realization that a single bomb could destroy an entire city forced the recognition upon everyone that science and technology could now determine the destiny of humanity. Shortly thereafter, the modern science fiction film, with its emphasis on global disaster and space travel, emerged.

In the 1950s we drowned in a deluge of SF films of almost biblical proportions. Some of these films had big budgets and "name" actors, such as Walt Disney's version of Verne's *Twenty Thousand Leagues Under the Sea* (1954), starring Kirk Douglas, Peter Lorre, and James Mason as Captain Nemo. That same year brought George Pal's version of H. G. Wells' *War of the Worlds*. In 1956 we got rewritten Shakespeare with MGM's well-financed *Forbidden Planet*. But SF films had not yet reached the blockbuster proportions of the 1980s and 1990s, when they became the most expensive, yet highest-grossing, films of all time. Most of the films in the tidal wave of the fifties were what are termed "B-movies," low budget and independently made quickies for drive-in double bills. Many of them featured mutated monsters of one kind or another.

One of the most memorable and profitable—so much so that it spawned two sequels in 1959 and 1965 and a remake and another sequel in the 1980s—was *The Fly* (1958). A science fiction horror classic, it was produced by Twentieth Century Fox, starred Vincent Price, and had a relatively big budget for its ilk and subject matter. The George Langelaan short story—about a scientist who invents a matter transmitter, with tragic results— was turned into a screenplay by none other than James Clavell, who went on to write *Shogun*, *Tai-pan*, and *Noble House*. In addition to the gripping story itself, there were some original and compelling special effects and images in the film. There was the use of "dislocated" sound, when an experimentally transported cat yowled simultaneously from everywhere in the room; and there was the multiple vision of the insect-headed scientist watching his wife screaming as she saw him for the first time, her image split into hundreds of small images to give the effect of seeing her through the multi-faceted fly eye. It was a fascinating novelty and impressive by fifties standards. The director responsible for this SF cinema classic was the German director Kurt Neumann.

Kurt Neumann was born in Nuremberg, Germany, on April 5, 1908. He came to America in 1925 at age seventeen and, in an amazingly short time, was in Hollywood directing comedy shorts and foreign versions of American films. From 1932 to 1958, not counting the myriad forgettable quickies he directed before then, Neumann produced, directed, and wrote at least fifty-seven films in all genres, directing at least one film every year except for 1941. In 1944 he codirected and coauthored *Return of the Vam-*

pire for Columbia Pictures, starring Bela Lugosi as he returned to the role of a vampire in London—with a werewolf assistant! The next year he became the regular director of Johnny Weissmuller's Tarzan films.

There had been silent era Tarzan films, but the ones we remember are those launched by MGM in 1932 with *Tarzan the Ape Man,* starring Weissmuller as Tarzan and Maureen O'Sullivan as Jane. With good supporting casts and big budgets, these were major films and MGM produced a dozen between 1932 and 1943, all starring the two principal actors. When MGM lost interest in the series, RKO stepped in. While O'Sullivan dropped out when RKO took over, perhaps because the smaller studio meant smaller budgets, RKO managed to keep Weissmuller and put Neumann in charge of churning out the films. In quick succession Neumann produced and directed Weissmuller in *Tarzan and the Amazons* (1945), *Tarzan and the Leopard Woman* (1946), and *Tarzan and the Huntress* (1947). In 1953 he directed RKO's *Tarzan and the She-Devil,* with Lex Barker as Tarzan and Raymond Burr as the villain.[1]

But as the fifties unrolled, Neumann was also branching out into fantasy and SF films. In 1952, taking a break from Tarzan, he directed *Son of Ali Baba* for Universal. This was standard Arabian Nights fare, but the two young stars—the unknown Tony Curtis and Piper Laurie—were hits and were teamed for two sequels.[2] In 1957 Neumann did double duty with a package deal of two SF films for the small independent studio, Regal Films. The first of these, which he also produced, was *Kronos,* a small $160,000 film which *Variety* called, "a well-made, moderate budget science-fictioner which boasts quality special effects that would do credit to a much higher-budgetted film . . . Neumann's general handling of subject is high-class."[3] The special effects, "which give eerie overtones to pic's unfoldment," were designed and created by Irving A. Block, who also conceived the story and who just the year before had conceived the story (after Shakespeare's *The Tempest)* and designed the special effects for *Forbidden Planet.*

Kronos featured Jeff Morrow, who also starred in *This Island Earth* (1954), and several other SF films of the fifties, such as *The Creature Walks Among Us* (1956). Leonard Maltin, in his comprehensive *Movie and Video Guide: 1995*, gives the film two-and-a-half stars, describing it as, "Diverting science-fiction with unique monster: an enormous metallic walking machine capable of absorbing the Earth's energy, . . . nice touch of mysterioso and convincing performances." Meanwhile, Peter Nicholls, in his *Encyclopedia of Science Fiction*, says that, while the script is average, "Kronos itself is such an original and unusual monster that it stands out among all the giant reptiles, giant insects, and so on of the 1950s sf boom."

The other film Neumann directed as part of this SF double bill for Regal was *She Devil,* based on the story "The Adaptive Ultimate" by "John Jessel," otherwise known as Stanley G. Weinbaum. The story was originally published in the November 1935 issue of *Astounding*. It concerns a dying young woman who is given an experimental serum which enables her to be infinitely "adaptable" to whatever circumstance she encounters. In this case, she "adapted" to her disease and recovered. Then she mutated (Hollywood FX techies would say she "morphed") from a Plain Jane to a gorgeous woman when that proved to be more "adaptable" to her surroundings. She became superstrong, because that was more adaptable. As she could "morph" into anything, she decided to do whatever she wanted. She killed with impunity, and when brought to trial, morphed into an entirely different person no witness could identify. Even her fingerprints, voiceprints, retina prints, DNA sequence were different. She could be stabbed, shot, and she "adapted," closing the wound and going on as if nothing had happened. She could be poisoned and she adapted. Becoming the most seductive vamp in the world, she became engaged to the head of the "World Council," and soon, it seemed, she would be the absolute dictator of the world. She was, indeed, the "ultimate adaptive."

This story is the only Weinbaum tale made into a movie and

there is something about it that seems to attract producers. For instance, there had been a radio version of the story broadcast on March 26, 1949, on the CBS radio network series *Escape*. Then it was aired on the pioneering NBC-TV series *Science Fiction Theater* as "Beyond Return" on December 9, 1955. *Science Fiction Theater,* says Ed Naha in his *Science Fictionary*, was "The great-granddaddy of all sf anthology shows," but lasted only one season, 1955–56 (although Peter Nicholls says it ran until 1957). The story was broadcast live and no known kinescope of it exists. Margaret Weinbaum Kay, Stanley Weinbaum's widow, told me she remembers sitting in the New York studio with her daughters from her second marriage watching the show being produced.

It's quite possible that a producer at Regal Films monitored this anthology series in hopes of finding a good story and saw the production. Certainly Regal moved quickly thereafter to acquire the film rights. Following negotiations, almost a year later to the day, on December 4, 1956, Margaret Kay signed a contract before a notary public in Milwaukee selling all motion picture rights to "The Adaptive Ultimate" to Regal Films "forever" for one dollar, "in hand paid." On the very same day, perhaps by arrangement, Arthur P. Lawler, vice president of Street & Smith Publications—which owned *Astounding* when it originally published the story—signed a contract before a notary public in New York City selling all "right, title, or interest" it had in the motion picture rights to the story to Regal Films for one dollar, "in hand paid." The amount of money might seem absurd today, but Margaret explained to me that no one else had approached her for the film rights and she wanted to do everything in her power to keep Stanley Weinbaum's name alive. Beside this concern, money was, understandably, immaterial.[4]

Regal then handed the story over to Neumann to rewrite for the film version he would also produce and direct. The male lead was Jack Kelly, who would go on to star on television as James Garner's brother in the *Maverick* Western series, while the female lead, the "She Devil," was played by Mari Blanchard (1927–1970). Blanchard never escaped the B-movies, acting in eighteen of them between 1950 and 1963, as well as in a 1960–61 television series entitled *Klondike*. Some of them were fantasy films, such as *The Veils of Baghdad* (1953) and RKO's *Son of Sinbad* (1955). Others were SF, such as the "Doctor Heidegger's Experiment" segment of the Nathaniel Hawthorne-inspired *Twice Told Tales* (1963). In the 1953 film, *Abbott and Costello Go To Mars,* she played Allura, Queen of the Amazons of Venus. (Abbot and Costello never made it to Mars!) Anita Ekberg was one of her Amazons.

Neumann's *She Devil* differs greatly from Weinbaum's story and the whole production was pitiably underfunded by Regal. Nevertheless, *Picturegoer* magazine termed it "slickly made, neatly plotted," and some thought the film was saved by its dedicated cast and crew. Even so, Leonard Maltin terms it a "bomb" in his video guide and it died at the box office.

While both *Kronos* and *She Devil* were produced as a drive-in double bill by Regal Films, they were distributed by Twentieth Century Fox. The next year, Neumann would direct *The Fly* specifically for Fox. But he often worked with small independents, such as Regal. Producer Robert L. Lippert was another such. Lippert was receptive to individual writers and directors and funded a large number of small-budget films at this time, giving some noted directors their big breaks. Such was the case in 1948 when Lippert agreed to fund a script dealing with assassination, which writer Samuel Fuller wanted to sell. However, Lippert mandated that the script had to have a cowboy in it. Fuller agreed, provided Lippert would then let him also direct the film, as well as write it. The result was the 1949 film, *I Shot Jesse James,* with Preston Foster, Barbara Britton, and John Ireland as Bob Ford, the assassin who shot Jesse James in the back. Fuller shot the film in only ten days for $118,000, which included Fuller's $5,000 fee. Lippert was pleased when it turned a nice profit at the box office. Fuller then shot the 1950 Western *The Baron of Arizona,* starring

Vincent Price, in eleven days for $135,000. He shot *The Steel Helmet,* one of the first films about the Korean War, in Los Angeles' Griffith Park during ten days in 1951 with a cast of twenty-five extras, who were local students. In 1953 Fuller made *Pickup on South Street,* starring Richard Widmark. His career culminated with 1980's *The Big Red One,* about the 1st Infantry Division in World War II, starring Lee Marvin. Thus, it was to Robert Lippert that Kurt Neumann also turned when he wanted to scoop George Pal on a particularly interesting project.

In early 1950 Kurt Neumann learned that the Hungarian emigré director George Pal was planning an ambitious SF film for Eagle Lion Films. This was to be the first "modern" space movie, the first film since World War II and its V-1 and V-2 rockets to deal with the subject of space travel by rocketships. Hitler's "V" weapons had shown the feasibility of such science fiction dreams and rocket travel at last seemed actually possible. Pal's film was to be called *Destination Moon,* and was based on the Robert A. Heinlein novel *Rocketship Galileo*, with Heinlein retained as script consultant. Pal's film was to be a scientifically realistic account—given the current state of knowledge—of the first landing on the Moon. The budget was big for the time: $600,000. The technical advisor was Dr. Hermann Oberth, who had also served as technical advisor for Lang and von Harbou's 1929 film *The Woman in the Moon.* Oberth brought instant credibility, for in 1923 he had written and published *The Rocket Into Interplanetary Space*, the first complete theoretical description of how space travel might be accomplished by rockets.

Neumann went to Robert Lippert and proposed that they beat George Pal to the box office. Lippert agreed and came up with $94,000 for the venture, which was to be called *Rocketship X-M.* Other than the money, the film was entirely Neumann's. He wrote the screenplay, assembled his team, and directed it. For special effects, he got Irving A. Block, later to do the special effects on his *Kronos* and MGM's *Forbidden Planet.* The soundtrack was provided by classical composer Ferdé Grofe, best-

known for his "Grand Canyon Suite." *Variety* later said Grofé's
"eerie music . . . builds a mood . . . calculated to thrill." Unable
to afford the likes of renown SF artist Chesley Bonestell, who
was painting the background scenery for *Destination Moon,*
Neumann moved his cast and crew to the barren Red Rock
Canyon in the Mojave Desert outside Los Angeles and had his
rocketship land on Mars instead of the Moon. With red tints in
the otherwise black and white film, the Mojave Desert did a good
job of standing-in for Mars. The film was shot in a fast three
weeks and opened in New York on May 26, 1950, one month
before *Destination Moon* made it into theaters.

Neumann's story for *Rocketship X-M* had pilot Lloyd
Bridges and navigator Noah Beery Jr. heading a crew (which
included Hugh O'Brian, later TV's Wyatt Earp) on the first
rocket to the moon. A meteor shower forces them to land on
Mars instead. (Hey! It's the fifties!) According to Ed Naha's *The
Science Fictionary,* once on Mars they find a "nuked-out civilization and a host of unfriendly humanoid-mutant cave people.
All but two of the landing party meet their Maker courtesy of a
ticket provided by the mutants. The two survivors head back for
Earth but run out of fuel on the way down. BAM!" But not
before they radioed Earth a warning of the atomic holocaust
they'd found on Mars. It was an amazingly somber denouement
for a supposed "exploitation" film.

Although the film is badly dated from the perspective of half
a century later, at the time of its release, *Variety* stated, "The fascinating excitement of space travel has been excellently presented in 'Rocketship X-M'. . . . [Neumann's] writing, production and direction gain potent realism by a matter-of-fact
approach and the restrained playing of the six principals in this
drama of space."[5] Both Neumann's film and George Pal's more
documentary-like *Destination Moon* did very well at the box
office, making about the same amount, despite the huge difference in budgets. Together, says Gregory B. Richards in his *Science Fiction Movies,*[6] "both pictures had the effect of inciting

Hollywood to pump out a number of cheap imitations and films on other science fiction topics to cash in on the boom the two had started." The very next year, for instance, brought George Pal's Paramount production of *When Worlds Collide*, from a novel by Philip Wylie and Edwin Balmer; Robert Wise's Twentieth Century Fox production of *When the Earth Stood Still*; and Howard Hawks's RKO production of *The Thing*, based on John W. Campbell's short novel *Who Goes There?* All of these films had the common element of some world-threatening crisis coupled with space travel.

But Neumann's film should be remembered for more than just unleashing a flood of space travel films. That, after all, was an idea he picked up from George Pal, and only his initiative and energy made it possible for him to beat Pal to the theaters with the first of the fifties' space-travel movies. What is far more important about Neumann's film is something he didn't lift from Pal's project—or any other film project. This was the idea of a nuclear holocaust, which seems to have found its initial cinema presentation in the 1950 *Rocketship X-M* depiction of the Martian civilization devastated by atomic warfare. It was an idea that would become a cinema cliché thereafter, but, in the words of *Variety,* Neumann was the first film maker to "pose an idea of what atomic warfare may mean to this world."

Apocalyptic visions had not always entertained the idea of atomic warfare. Indeed, the earliest such visions were religious ones, such as the Book of Revelations of St. John, also called "The Apocalypse," from whence we get the very term. And before the Apocalypse of St. John we find the Judaic roots of the idea in the Hebrew Bible. These views of the end of the world, however, envisioned the end as being the result of Divine Will.

The eighteenth- and nineteenth-century romantic movement brought scientific romances which posited forces other than divine intervention as responsible for the end. One of the earliest such was Mary Shelley's second SF novel, *The Last Man* (1826), in which a great plague wipes out humanity but for a last man in

Rome. Edgar Allen Poe then introduced the possibility of cosmic disaster in "The Conversation of Eiros and Charmion" (1839). This was followed by French astronomer Camille Flammarion's *Omega*, which in 1893 had a comet smash into the earth. But in all such cases, the end of all things, or at least the end of humanity, was the result of natural causes. Nature had replaced God.

With H. G. Wells, humanity replaced nature. Perhaps the first tale raising the possibility of humanity's *self* destruction was his story "The World Set Free" (1914), which, for the first time, envisioned atomic warfare. Indeed, one might argue that with this story we get the nuclear age.[7] Physicist Leo Szilard is credited with conceiving of the idea of the nuclear chain reaction necessary for the release of atomic energy. But the idea came to him, he says in his autobiography, as he walked down a London street in 1933 trying to figure out exactly how the nuclear energy Wells described in "The World Set Free" might indeed be set free. Life imitated art and the atom was unleashed.

Other than Szilard, however, not many immediately followed Wells's lead, certainly not in the realm of fiction, for it seems few were interested in seriously exploring the possibilities of nuclear power. Even Wells did not envision a nuclear holocaust destroying civilization in his *The Shape of Things to Come*. Rather, it was decades-long conventional warfare, followed by yet another plague, the "Wandering Sickness," which destroyed civilization. One of the few who did seriously explore the possibilities of nuclear energy was John W. Campbell, and, because of his interest, atomic power was a constant theme of stories which he published in the pages of *Astounding* in the 1930s and early 1940s. But outside the pages of *Astounding*, the pickings were meager, despite the plethora of "radium" rays, beams, drills, and so forth.

Then came Hiroshima and Nagasaki. And then came the first Soviet atomic bomb in September 1949, and atomic warfare thereafter became a staple of written science fiction. And, eight months after the Soviets proved that any nuclear war would not be one-sided, came *Rocketship X-M*, and "nuclear holocaust" at last entered cinema's thematic vocabulary. Coupled with the concept of space travel, the modern science fiction film thus began to take shape as a distinct genre.

It would be interesting to ask Kurt Neumann where he got the idea of presenting a nuclear holocaust as a warning to fifties' America so soon after it became clear America no longer had a nuclear monopoly. Unfortunately, Neumann died in Los Angeles on August 21, 1958, at the age of fifty, shortly after finishing *The Fly.* According to the *New York Times* of August 22, 1958, "A coroner's autopsy was ordered to determine the possible presence of carbon tetrachloride in the stomach." Carbon tetrachloride is a clear, colorless, nonflammable, toxic liquid much used in cleaning solvents. His death followed by five weeks that of his beloved wife, Irma.

NOTES

1. Lex Barker debuted as Tarzan in "Tarzan's Magic Fountain" (1949), written by another German expatriate, Curt Siodmak.

2. That same year, in typically productive fashion, Neumann also directed two other films, including an excellent fight movie for United Artists called *The Ring.* This was a film ahead of its time, concerning Chicano boxers in California fighting Anglo discrimination and each other for the American Dream. It starred Rita Moreno, a fine actress who is the first Hispanic woman to win an Oscar and the only performer ever to win the Quadruple Crown of an Oscar, a Tony, an Emmy, and a Grammy.

3. *Variety,* April 10, 1957.

4. On April 12, 1995, a producer at Twentieth Century Fox called me, as executor of the Stanley G. Weinbaum Estate, seeking to purchase the film rights to "The Adaptive Ultimate" for $50,000. Under current copyright laws, all of Weinbaum's stories are copyright protected for seventy-five years from date of original publication. In the case of "The Adaptive Ultimate," published in 1935, the copyright is in force until December 31, 2010.

Additionally, the copyright laws provide a five-year window of opportunity for the creator of any work to reclaim the copyright and all other rights after the "old" copyright provided for under the pre-1978 laws expire. The "old" copyright on this story expired on December 31, 1991. Therefore, Fox assumed the estate had reclaimed all rights in the story from Regal at that time.

Indeed, the literary agent for the Weinbaum Estate, Forrest J. Ackerman, should have written a letter to Regal Films and the U. S. Copyright Office at that time informing both that Regal's rights in the work had been "terminated." This had to be done two years before the five-year window closed, that is, the letter had to be written by December 31, 1994 to give a full two years before the window closed on December 31, 1996. Ackerman neglected to do so. But, Ackerman was ignorant of this option under current copyright law. Indeed, Ackerman did not even realize that this story—or any of Weinbaum's other stories—was still under copyright protection. Thus, when Fox called me in April 1995, the estate had missed reclaiming film rights to this story by less than four months.

The copyright, therefore, remained with Regal and its successive copyright holders. In 1959, Regal sold the copyright to National Telefilm Association (NTA). In January 1985, NTA merged with Republic Films. In 1994, Republic Films became Republic Entertainment, Inc., owned by Aaron Spelling. In early 1997, Fox bought an eighteen-month film option on "The Adaptive Ultimate" from Spelling's Republic Entertainment for $50,000. Thus, almost sixty years after Weinbaum's death, his work continues to generate interest—and big bucks!

5. *Variety,* May 3, 1950.

6. New York: Gallery Books, 1984.

7. That same year, 1914, brought Arthur Train and Robert W. Wood's "The Man Who Rocked the Earth," serialized in the *Saturday Evening Post*. It also featured radioactive fallout and radiation sickness.

10.

THE PRIVATE HISTORY OF A RESCUE THAT FAILED

Laurence Manning and Sam Moskowitz

Atomic motors of huge size were constructed and the entire core of the planet scooped out and its stone transformed into metal. From the center, great rocket tubes flared out to the surface—fifty miles away—and the entire planet was in a few centuries made into a rocket ship. . . . The whole planet was set under motion by earth-shaking blasts from the great rocket chamber and the voyage commenced. . . .

When the grey stretches of intergalactic space were reached, a course was set to avoid all stars and the pace was speeded up to 150,000 miles a second. . . . Four million years were to elapse in this monotonous journey and . . . a few hundred new humans were bred and educated during the first two or three centuries. . . .

It is regrettable that the colonization idea was not thought of until a million years had elapsed. This consisted of breeding a hundred humans and thoroughly educating them, stopping the Humanity *in her course, entering a galaxy and finding a planet, and then leaving the hundred colonists on it to multiply and explore their new universe. This was done . . . more than one*

333

hundred and seventy times in the last three million years of the voyage. Twice during this period, the Humanity *was deserted for a new planet and fresh and improved machines and equipment were set up, the name and purpose in each case being transferred to the new planet-ship, and the old one left with the current quota of colonists in the quickly deserted universe that then held them.*

—Laurence Manning, "The Living Galaxy" (1934)

HARDLY A PERSON IS STILL ALIVE WHO REMEMBERS THE name of Laurence Manning. Even within the science fiction community, he is largely unknown. Yet, Manning was a true pioneer of science fiction and, during the early 1930s, one of the very best writers in the field. For a brief time, he was also very prolific, contributing more stories to Hugo Gernsback's *Wonder Stories* than any other author, fifteen in all between 1932 and 1935 (including one with Fletcher Pratt in 1930), as well as a story to Gernsback's *Science Wonder Stories*. His story "The Man Who Awoke" (*Wonder Stories*, March 1933) was so popular among readers that, not one, but *four* sequels quickly followed. Over forty years later, in 1975, Ballantine Books published all five stories for the first time in a book and, commented Lester Del Rey, "after slight editing, they read well now."[1]

In the story, Norman Winters awakes from suspended animation two thousand years in the future. There he finds a civilization based on strict recycling of scarce natural resources after twentieth century humanity, during "The Age of Waste," had poisoned, polluted, and plundered the Earth. The concept of "ecology" was thus introduced to a Depression-era America which still ravaged the environment and thought natural resources would last forever. Isaac Asimov wrote in 1974:

> In the 1970s, everyone is aware of, and achingly involved in, the energy crisis. Manning was aware of it forty years ago, and

because he was, I was, and so, I'm sure, were many thoughtful young science fiction readers. . . . It was a funny kind of escape literature that had the youngsters who read it concerned about the consequences of the waste of fossil fuels forty years before all the self-styled normal and sensible human beings felt it necessary to become interested.[2]

In "The Living Galaxy," in the September 1934 *Wonder Stories,* Manning also introduced the idea of "generation ships," huge star ships which take hundreds of years to reach another star system, travelling, as physics demands, at less-than-light speed. In the process, generations of humans on board are born, live their lives, and die. This innovative concept was quickly picked up by Murray Leinster in "Proxima Centauri," in the March 1935 *Astounding Stories,* and, most memorably, in Robert A. Heinlein's "Universe," in the May 1941 *Astounding Science Fiction.*

With his "Voyage of the *Asteroid,"* in *Wonder Stories Quarterly* (Summer 1932), and its three-part sequel, "Wreck of the *Asteroid,"* beginning in the December 1932 *Wonder Stories,* Manning broke with the heroic tradition of contemporary science fiction. Instead of concentrating on the glories and successes of space exploration, Manning's moody and somewhat pessimistic story about Martian exploration portrayed the hazards, difficulties, failures, and political maneuvering which was certain to make space exploration much like terrestrial exploration had been. Despite its downbeat perspective, most reader comments praised it as the best story in the magazine and Sam Moskowitz believed it may have inspired Arthur C. Clarke's novel *Sands of Mars.*[3]

Meanwhile, some commentators, including Moskowitz and Mike Ashley, observed that his story of intelligent plants, "Seeds from Space," in the June 1935 *Wonder Stories,* may have given John Wyndham the idea for his better-known novel *The Day of the Triffids.*[4]

Laurence Manning, then, deserves to be remembered. Instead, he is forgotten. This is the story of how I and, more importantly, Sam Moskowitz tried to change that situation—and how we failed. It is also a story that, I think, sheds some light on how Sam came upon ideas for essays, and how he pursued them. That, too, deserves to be remembered.

Laurence Manning was born in 1899 in St. John, New Brunswick, Canada. He was graduated from King's College with a law degree, but never practiced law. During World War I he earned the rank of lieutenant in the Royal Canadian Air Force. In 1920 he relocated to the United States and became a naturalized citizen. For most of his life he ran the Kelsey Nursery Service and his book on gardening became the standard manual for the Garden Clubs of America. While just beginning as a writer at *Wonder Stories,* he became a founding member of editor David Lasser's American Interplanetary Society and served as both treasurer of the society, editor of its publication, *Astronautics,* and the society's fourth president, when it became known as "The American Rocket Society." In 1930 he published his first science fiction story, "The City of the Living Dead," in the May *Science Wonder Stories,* the collaboration with Fletcher Pratt.[5] His other stories soon followed, but—except for two short fantasies in the 1950s—he fell silent after 1935.

Isaac Asimov, a young fan of Manning's, was resentful of Manning's post-1935 silence. After he became a science fiction writer himself, Asimov thought he finally knew why Manning abandoned his successful writing career. "The trouble was, I'm sure, that science fiction in those days paid virtually nothing, and that nothing only after long delays. Naturally, then, people weren't going to spend time at it unless it was truly a labor of love."[6]

My own feeling, based on what I later learned, is that Manning lost a private reason for writing after 1935. Perhaps more than any other writer, Manning was identified with Gernsback's *Wonder Stories*. Beyond that, he was a close personal friend of Gernsback's. At the end of Gernsback's tenure, he wasn't able to pay Manning for his stories—but Manning continued to write for him, anyway. After Gernsback lost *Wonder Stories* to a conglomerate in the summer of 1936 and left the science fiction field, I believe Manning simply lost interest in writing for anyone else. Personal loyalty, I believe, kept Manning writing even after the checks ceased coming—and that was no longer there.

I became interested in finding out what had become of Laurence Manning in the fall of 1985 when I was doing the research that resulted in my essay "The Age of Wonder," which appeared in *Fantasy Commentator* (Fall 1987). The primary focus of my research was David Lasser and I was doing everything possible to track down anyone who'd been associated with him while he was editor at *Wonder Stories*. Laurence Manning was an obvious candidate for investigation and at least the 1979 *Science Fiction Encyclopedia* did not list a death date for him.[7]

One of the people I wrote to for information was long-time science fiction editor and writer Frederik Pohl. On May 21, 1986, Pohl wrote back, saying, "Laurie Manning was a neighbor of mine in Monmouth County, NJ—he lived on Portland Avenue, Highlands, NJ—but I lost touch with him ten years or more ago, and I fear he may have died. . . ."

I immediately turned to the best investigative tool I've yet discovered—the telephone. Using the phone books in the library, I obtained an address for Laurence E. Manning on the indicated street in Highlands, NJ. By this time I'd already interviewed David Lasser. On June 6, I wrote Manning, telling him Lasser had told me they'd been good friends in the early 1930s and that Manning had served as treasurer of the Interplanetary Society. I asked him if I might speak with him about the old days at *Wonder Stories*. "It is my hope," I said, "to document as much history of this almost forgotten era as I can before it is gone forever. If you are at all able to assist me in this effort, it would be a gift from heaven."

I didn't receive a reply. Fearful of the passage of time, two weeks later, on June 21, I called the number I'd gotten from the phone books. I reached Edith Manning, Laurence's widow, who said she'd been expecting and waiting for my call. "Laurie," it seems, had died in 1972 after a long illness following a stroke. However, Edith, then in her eighties, was alive and well, physically and mentally. Edith was very friendly and we spoke for quite some time. Immediately after hanging up, I typed up notes on our conversation, from whence comes the following:

Edith graduated from college on June 3, 1928. She married Laurie two days later. They were happily married for forty-four years. Laurie, she said, was a multitalented man who did many things well. However, he became bored easily, and so didn't stay at one thing for too long. This may be why, she speculated, he abandoned science fiction after 1935. The exception to his boredom seems to have been gardening. He ran the Kelsey Nursery Service for most of his life and wrote fourteen books on gardening.

Edith confirmed that Laurie and David Lasser had been close friends who saw each other frequently. For this reason, there was no need to write and there were no letters extant from Lasser to Manning. Nor, she said, did Manning leave any autobiographical writings. Additionally, he destroyed his original manuscripts after publication because he didn't like the clutter. Indeed, she said, not many documents about Manning of any kind were still around.

Still, I thought perhaps an interview with Edith about Laurie might reveal something and asked if I might visit for that purpose. I also thought a look through what few papers of Manning's remained might reveal something. She invited me to visit at any time. "The latch string is always out," she said. However, I'd have to tolerate a Newfoundland dog of over one hundred pounds and a fierce Bermuda cat. She gave me explicit directions for getting to her house. In the meantime, she was writing up notes in response to my June 6 letter and would shortly send them to me. I then called David Lasser, in California, and told him of my talk with Edith. He was very pleased to learn she was still alive. I gave him her phone number and later learned that he called Edith and they had a long and nostalgic conversation.

Shortly before this, on March 24, I'd written James Gunn asking to write an entry on David Lasser for *The New Encyclopedia of Science Fiction*, which he was editing for Viking Press and which was eventually published in 1988. On July 1, Gunn's assistant, Stephen H. Goldman, replied to my request, saying, "Sorry, we have no plans to include an entry on Lasser."

Inclusion in the encyclopedias of a field is a major way that memories and reputations are preserved. To be excluded from them is one way of being consigned to oblivion. On July 10, I replied to Goldman—with a copy to Gunn—saying:

> I was disturbed that you thought David Lasser did not deserve an entry. This seems to me an egregious miscarriage of judgment. I was also disturbed at the absence of several other well-known SF names from the list of entries you enclosed. At the same time, I noted the inclusion of many who are peripheral to the world of science fiction. While you include Gore Vidal—you plan no entry on pioneer female SF writer Leslie F. Stone. Carl Sagan, who just published his first SF book [*Contact*], is there—but not Raymond Z. Gallun, who started publishing SF in 1929 and whose latest book, *Bioblast,* was published by Berkeley Books last October. You include Doris Lessing—but not Laurence Manning. Editor Forrest J. Ackerman—but not Sam Moskowitz. Editor Terry Carr—but not Charles Hornig. Editor/Author John W. Campbell—but not editor/author Hugo Gernsback. Artist Frank Frazetta—but not Margaret Brundage.
>
> Yes, I'm familiar with all the writings of these . . . authors which would justify their inclusion in an encyclopedia of SF. Nor do I think a single one of them should be dropped. But I marvel at your criteria that you would include authors who have, say, written only one SF novel—like Vidal or Sagan—while excluding others who have had far more influence upon the development of science fiction.

I then asked that Gunn and Goldman reconsider and include entries on Gernsback, Stone, Manning, Moskowitz, Gallun, Hornig, Brundage, and Clark Ashton Smith. "Since it took over three months for you to reply to my previous letter," I wrote, "and since you have a first deadline of August 1, I would appreciate a timely reply. In the meantime, I send you my manuscript on David Lasser ["The Age of Wonder"] and hope you will reconsider your decision to exclude him."

That same day I wrote Edith, as I'd not received the notes she'd said she was making in response to my June 6 letter. I told her that it had been a pleasure to speak with her and that "you mentioned on the phone that you were jotting down some comments about my David Lasser manuscript. I do hope our phone conversation hasn't interrupted that. I would still very much appreciate any comments you may have at all about the relationship between your husband and Mr. Lasser. Any memories at all of that time would be welcome." I also sent her a copy of the letter I'd written that same day to Gunn and Goldman.

Shortly thereafter I received a handwritten note from Edith, mailed on July 14, in which she said, "I'm too lazy to rewrite what I jotted down on your envelope, so I just enclose it for your interest." Enclosed was a large piece of the manila envelope in which I'd mailed her my essay on Lasser. On it, in pencil, she'd indicated a few of Laurie's achievements. He'd published many articles on gardening for *House & Garden, American Forests, Gardener's Chronicle, Horticulture,* and *Organic Gardening.* He'd also written a book, *The How & Why of Better Gardening,* published by Van Nostrand for the Garden Clubs of America. In addition, he was a musician, singer, and actor with the Monmouth Players, as well as a Fellow of the American Rocket Society.

On July 21, I called Edith to thank her for the mailing and to follow up with a few more questions. At my urging, she had looked through the papers left by Laurie at his death. She said that she had thrown nothing away; however she could find no completed manuscripts, nor were there any notes for anticipated stories. She also added that Manning never rewrote any of his stories. He'd stay up all night turning out a first draft, which then would go immediately in the mail. Also, the reason he wrote *The How & Why of Better Gardening* was because Random House pressed him to write a gardening book in the fifties. So he finally turned it out.

On August 1, the preliminary deadline for Gunn's encyclopedia, I got a call from James Gunn himself. We talked about the people I'd mentioned, who were missing from his encyclopedia. I told him I was particularly interested in the group of writers and editors affiliated with *Wonder Stories*. I followed up our conversation with a letter of the same date telling him that I would most particularly be interested in writing entries on David Lasser, Charles Hornig, Laurence Manning, Raymond Z. Gallun, and Sam Moskowitz. Further, if he didn't have anyone doing an entry on Hugo Gernsback, Sam Moskowitz would be the ideal person to write one. "I know Mr. Goldman is in charge of the 'lesser' editors and authors, but since he is on vacation for the next three weeks, a word from you on the above mentioned individuals would be most appreciated."

On August 7, I got a postcard from Gunn in which he said, "All right, you've convinced me. Give me 50 words each on Hornig and Lasser, on speculation. I'll have Steve get back to you on Gallun, Moskowitz, & Manning as soon as he returns from his vacation."

Steve Goldman wrote on August 21, assigning me the entries on Lasser (75 words), Hornig (50 words), Gallun (50 words), and Manning (50 words). He wanted them by January 1, 1987. He said nothing about an entry on Moskowitz.

On September 18, I wrote Goldman thanking him for assigning me the above entries and assuring him he'd have them well before January 1 (and he did). But, I wrote, "I'm also interested in doing the 200-word entry on Sam Moskowitz. . . . I have followed his career extensively and have everything he's published. I think I could do him justice."

I didn't hear back from Goldman or Gunn concerning my entry on Sam, so on December 28, I wrote Goldman again. "I am still interested in doing the entry on Sam Moskowitz," I said, "if that has not already been assigned to someone else."

On February 14, 1987, I wrote to James Gunn: "I'm *still* trying to find out if you will let me write the entry on Sam Moskowitz. You will recall that I wrote you August 1 of last year with this request. . . . Please let me know if I can write the Moskowitz entry. However, if you have already assigned him to another writer, even that information would be welcome."

Gunn finally responded with a postcard on February 18 saying, "Sorry. Your request to write the Moskowitz entry must have slipped between the stools. . . . You are welcome to do 200 words on Sam as editor, scholar, and fan, and collector."

Meanwhile, I'd been in touch with Sam (who *did* end up writing the entry for Gunn on Gernsback). On July 5, 1986, I wrote Sam telling him about my June 21 phone conversation with Edith Manning. I also enclosed a copy of Goldman's July 1 letter and list of entries, expressing my disappointment with it.

Sam wrote back on July 17, saying, "I agree with literally everything you say with no exceptions. This is the first I have seen of the authors and editors that are to be included and it is so heavily weighted in favor of current writers that it is absurd. . . ."

Then Sam introduced a fascinating question about Laurence Manning which occupied our attentions for some time thereafter:

In the February 1936 issue of *Wonder Stories,* on p. 877 where they listed forthcoming stories, they announced, " 'Maze of Creation' by Laurence Manning is the new serial starting next month. You will find this sequel to the well-liked "World of the Mist" far superior to any tale of its kind that you have ever read. We had a very difficult time selecting a suitable title for this new novel, packed with originality of plot, action, and science theory." ["Next month's" issue of *Wonder Stories*, March-April 1936, was also the *last* issue of *Wonder Stories*—and there was no story in it by Manning.] In 1953, when I was editing *Science-Fiction +,* I was very aggressively seeking out authors and stories, so I wrote Manning asking to see that story, which was never published when *Wonder Stories* was sold to Standard Magazines [August 1936]. Manning called me up and promised to whip the story into shape, claiming it needed some revision. He sent me a letter July 1, 1953, saying that he was delayed by bursting a blood vessel in his eye and by heavy seasonal business, but "I went over the mss. and it needs some rewriting—not too bad. I will do it. When done I will send it to you—maybe in a month or two. . . . 70,000 words or less it will be." He also sent me at the time a book on gardening that he had written [*The How & Why of Gardening*]. . . .

Well, the manuscript was never completed before the magazine died, but when Manning died, April 12, 1972, I didn't know it until a friend showed me the obit some months later. I wrote the widow a long, comprehensive letter on June 9, 1972, telling her I was working on historical material, telling of my previous contact with her husband, asking if it might be possible to see his correspondence, since I was doing something on the period in which he was active. She never responded and I took this to mean that she didn't want to be bothered. I live only an hour's drive from her and could easily have noted items of importance historically in his material without ever removing the material, if she was afraid of that. Actually, I probably would have been able to make more of the material than anyone else, because of my long-time previous relationship with Hornig and Gernsback.

However, in view of the fact that he was revising the novel, "Maze of Creation," for me in 1953, I doubt very much that he would have destroyed it. It had been accepted once by *Wonder Stories* and I was ready to buy it, so he knew it was not a lost cause.

On July 22, I replied, discussing my exchange of letters with Gunn and Goldman. I also enclosed a copy of a July 18 letter I'd received from Charles D. Hornig, in which he answered a number of questions I'd put to him concerning his tenure at *Wonder Stories.*

> Hornig does say that Gernsback wrote to Manning because they were friends. It would be interesting to see a couple of those Gernsback-to-Manning letters to know their nature, but Edith Manning has already told me that Manning burned all his correspondence because he didn't like the clutter. Alas, we'll never know.
>
> Regarding Mrs. Manning. . . . Her lack of reply to your letter back in 1972 may not have been a signal that she didn't want to be bothered. I sent her my Lasser material and a request for information and never got a reply, either. So, I . . . called her up. She was very friendly on the phone and we had a long discussion about "Laurie" Manning. . . . So, it may have been lethargy which was responsible for her lack of reply.

I then told Sam that I had asked Edith about "Maze of Creation" in my July 21 phone call to her:

> She said that Manning never actually wrote it. All there were, she said, were notes. Certainly the ms. doesn't exist anymore, if it *was* written. After receiving your letter [of July 17] I called her again and read her the comments from Manning you quoted. She said she would look through the files again, but she doubts there is a ms. I'm to call her again at 8 this evening to learn the results of her new search for the manuscript. Since I want to send this letter off today, I'll drop you a postcard tomorrow letting you know if she has found the "Maze" manuscript.

On August 11, I wrote Sam saying, "I trust you received my letter of July 22 and the following postcard concerning Manning's 'Maze of Creation.' At my behest, Edith Manning went through all the papers Laurence Manning left at his death. She says she threw away absolutely nothing, but could find neither a manuscript nor notes of any kind which might have been the

'Maze of Creation.' " I then reported on the status of my negotiations with Gunn for the entries on Manning and the others,
including Sam. I said I anticipated Gunn would eventually autho-
rize me to write an entry on Sam and I'd appreciate it if he'd send
me some comments on what he considered his most important
achievements/contributions to the SF field. Also, I reported that
Gunn told me the omission of Gernsback was an oversight and
that he'd be allotted a five-hundred-word entry.

Sam replied August 14, on First Fandom stationery:

When I left *Science Fiction +,* I took with me some of the correspondence with authors and filed it separately. In looking
over it before leaving on vacation, I found several very interesting things. First, there was one letter from Manning which
stated that he had reread "Maze of the Enchanter" and found it
"good," needing only a few changes for updating, nothing
major. This makes it even more likely that he would have kept
a copy of the manuscript. Secondly, I found that he had
another unpublished novel which had been rejected, apparently by Lasser. I do not remember the name, but it was something like "Gromphus."

I don't think I would waste any more time before suggesting to Mrs. Manning that she have me come down and look
over Manning's stuff. There is no way of knowing what the
health will be of either her or myself, but more important to her,
it is virtually a last chance to see that the name of Laurence
Manning is remembered or whether permitted to slip into
oblivion. Actually, more important than the unpublished manuscripts are any correspondence regarding either the American
Interplanetary Society or *Wonder Stories.* These would provide
an excuse for a reappraisal of his published works. Right now
his survival as a figure in the history of science fiction rests on
a thread. His "Man Who Awoke" series went into paperback
and that is no longer easy to find; Groff Conklin anthologized
his important short story, possibly the first about space generations in an intergalactic ship, was it "The Prophetic Voice" (?)

[No, it was "The Living Galaxy"] in *The Science Fiction Galaxy* published by Perma Books and an inferior later short story of his from a post-Gernsback Standard/Beacon magazine, did it have "Ilotha" (or some exotic name) in the title? Lowndes did a few of his Stranger Club stories in his weird reprint magazine [*Magazine of Horror* and later in his *Famous Science Fiction*, both in the late 1960s] and when Manning receives a brief mention in something like *Anatomy of Wonder* I find echoes of comments I made in *Seekers of Tomorrow*, which means that his inclusion is only because of my comments and not because they have read the stories themselves. If you talk to Mrs. Manning, tell her I use a speaking device so don't get turned off by the peculiar sound of my voice.

It made sense that Sam, rather than I, should follow up with an in-depth interview of Edith Manning, as I'd originally planned to do. Not only did he live close by, but he knew far more about Manning's situation than did I at that point. Besides, I was up to my neck in many other projects. On August 20, I wrote to Edith suggesting that Sam visit her to talk about Laurie:

He is the most knowledgeable historian of science fiction around and has published 60 books on the subject. He once taught the history of science fiction at the City University of New York and was himself editor of Hugo Gernsback's last science fiction magazine. . . . It was while Sam edited this magazine that he got to know Laurie very well, as Laurie was one of his authors. Sam has always been a great fan and champion of Laurie's and wants to make sure his stories are remembered and valued by today's science fiction community. For that reason, Sam would love to drop by some time just to talk with you about Laurie and perhaps take a look at the notes and papers he left behind. . . . Would this be OK with you? Sam lives in nearby Newark, and you would find him a most pleasant and entertaining visitor.

Edith agreed, Sam got in touch with her, and a visit was arranged. In the meantime, on August 24, Sam sent me a long letter for my use in writing the entry on him in Gunn's encyclopedia. It listed what he thought were his major contributions to science fiction. Until Sam's reputed self-written obituary is found, this is probably the closest we'll get to knowing what Sam felt his own major accomplishments were. For those who are interested, I refer you to my entry on Sam in *The New Encyclopedia of Science Fiction*.

On October 23, I wrote to Charles Hornig, the *Wonder Stories* editor who had written that blurb about Manning's forthcoming new novel, *Maze of Creation*. "You wrote as if you had already read Manning's manuscript," I said. "Is this true? Did you actually see his story? Or was it really something merely *promised* by Manning—and you were blurbing it sight-unseen? If you *did* have the ms. in hand, what was it about? Do you remember any of the plot? What may have happened to the manuscript?"

On October 29, Hornig replied:

I have absolutely no memory of the Laurence Manning story you mention, "Maze of Creation," that should have been published if *Wonder Stories* had continued in 1936. I assume all manuscripts were returned to their authors, including that of Manning. Chances are it was not good enough to be published anywhere else! Remember, we had the bottom of the pile. However, in the case of Manning, we might have had first crack at it.

The Manning story must have been in my hands and read by me, or I could not have written the blurb about how good it was. I never would mention a story that had only been *promised* to me.

It is possible that the title I suggested, "Maze of Creation," had not been placed on the manuscript itself, and it may still be in existence somewhere under Manning's original title, whatever that was. I hope you can solve this mystery!

In the meantime, I'd received Sam's report of his visit with Edith Manning. On October 19, he wrote:

I drove down to Edith Manning's last Wednesday [October 15] and it proved to be about a one and a half hour drive over high-speed highways, but the directions her son gave me were excellent and I did not go out of my way by even a block. The Shrewsbury River is really a long, narrow, very wide bay, or actually an inland penetration of the Atlantic Ocean, made to appear like an inland water by the long, narrow seabreak formed by the action of the ocean through thousands of years, terminating in Sandy Hook. Actually, there are still a large number of shrews in the area (often killed and brought in by Edith Manning's cat), which is probably the reason the waterway was so named.

The house is set down on declining terraces, all planned and landscaped about 100 feet from the road, and the rear of the property, cultivated and landscaped, descends a hundred feet down to a pier which Manning had built many years ago, but which does not appear to be used, though it is in good repair. He designed the house himself and also laid out the grounds and the house looks somewhat like a Dutch ginger-bread structure, one floor with a small apartment in the base-ment (this used to be his office). Nothing in the way of a nursery is on the grounds, Manning was merely set up as a sales organization selling plants by mail and working with a number of nurseries to fill orders.

Mrs. Manning is 80, a bit leathery in appearance, not over-weight, smokes and drinks but seems to be in relatively good shape, is friendly and has all her affairs in order, but is astute and sounded me out. Once convinced of my good intentions she was very cooperative. I interviewed her about Manning and she showed me the papers and manuscripts that were immediately available.

On the matter of things like Manning's birth, baptism, date of entering and leaving schools and colleges, entry into the armed services, the nature of the business he was engaged in, there was as complete a set of papers and certificates as one could wish for. These would be of considerably greater importance if Manning was a major figure in the science fiction and fantasy world, but as it is, they are primarily confirmatory of material about his life already known and add preciseness to generalities of only very minor interest in any appraisal.

From the interview I obtained material about his and her background, the nature of their upbringings, his relationships with his parents, his brothers and sisters and his children, as well as with her. I got information on the personality of the man, the nature of the Kelsey Nurseries, how she met and married him, the nature of his death. Apparently, he was multi-talented as a musician, singer, artist, designer. He came to the United States from Canada as an agent of the Canadian government working in Washington, D.C.

There was a bound volume of the 1926 *Amazing Stories* among his effects, indicating that he was reading science fiction almost from the beginning (it started with the sixth issue). He had joined the American Interplanetary Society and there met Fletcher Pratt, who was never a good story teller (his wife, Inga M. Stephens, collaborated with him for years on his early science fiction), but apparently he was a good editor. That first story of theirs ["City of the Living Dead"] was Manning's concept and almost entirely written by him, despite the collaborative credit to Pratt. Manning wrote out of a need to write and for pleasure. At the end, he wasn't paid by Gernsback, but he didn't care, even though he was in tight circumstances. At this visit, no correspondence with Gernsback came up (though there was a letter from Robert A. W. Lowndes and one from a Doubleday editor).

I found an unpublished, untitled 30,000-word story with a carbon that had been submitted to Lowndes and rejected as being too old-fashioned. She loaned me the carbon and I am reading it, but am only about 7,000 words into it so far. It's about a girl, accidentally dropped overboard from a ship in the Pacific, washed up on an island rock no more than 200 feet across, which has no water and only some seaweed on it. But a young man appears, with a monstrous sort of head covering, who was cast up on the rock with his father 20 or more years previous and apparently the story is going to be about the ingenious methods by which they survived (the father is now dead), how salt water is refined into potable liquid, a diet heavy in fish and though I haven't gotten that far yet, I think there is going to be some sort of underwater habitation; the girl will fight at least one giant octopus and in the end he will swim her to an island where she can be picked up and choose not to return to civilization with her. She will never marry. There may be more substance, which I will impart when I have completed it.

Though the story was submitted to Lowndes in 1968 (at that time Lowndes was reprinting Manning's Stranger Club series in one of his reprint magazines [*Magazine of Horror*]) and may have asked if Manning had anything unpublished or maybe Manning volunteered it. Lowndes, under no circumstances, could have used anything longer.

The story could have been written as early as 1930 and obviously not for a science fiction magazine, possibly for a market like *Argosy* or *Bluebook*. It is very smoothly written and Manning is unquestionably a born storyteller, but to this point none of the advanced social ideas that manifest themselves in "The Man Who Awoke" series (which unquestionably is derived from *Last and First Men* by Olaf Stapledon) have come to the fore. It is also possible that David Lasser encouraged stories with a socialist theme (he had Nathan Schachner and Edmond Hamilton writing such stories).

Manning had copies of the magazines with most of his stories. (Some of the 1934 and 1935 *Wonder Stories* didn't seem to be there, though they may have been sent to Lowndes to reprint The Stranger Club series from and never returned.) Manning had apparently bought or received two additional copies of "The Man Who Awoke" series and pasted them up page-by-page in a large, hardcover scrapbook, so as to make them appear like a hardcover book. The magazines he kept seem to indicate that outside of articles on plant life for flower trade journals (of which a number were in evidence), he wrote for no other fiction magazine. The stories he had in *Fantastic Story* in later years were early rejects exhumed, submitted, and sold.

One other important bit of writing that I found, which may have a relationship to "Maze of Creation," was 60,000 words on non-fiction philosophical and scientific discussion on how life evolved. This was in the form of single-spaced, seemingly first-draft notes and elaborations, typed on different colors and sizes of paper. It had a title, "The Creation," and in some form had been submitted to Doubleday, for there was a one-page letter from Doubleday about it and it almost seemed to be a work in progress. Mrs. Manning was quite evidently tiring and I didn't want to wear out my welcome, so I did not go further into it except that it was definitely non-fiction and that it could easily have been the basis of the plot of "Maze of Creation." In announcing "Maze of Creation," Charles D. Hornig character- ized it as "packed with originality of plot, action, and science- theory," That last bit, and the similarity of titles to "The Cre- ation" seem linked.

One of the reasons I borrowed the manuscript was so that I would have an excuse to return, but she issued that invitation on her own. As it stands, an article on Manning would have to spotlight his work, being a review and analysis of everything he ever had printed, with his life as a background, with no pre- conceived conclusions, presenting what was found. In him Gernsback had found a highly original story teller who was apparently voluntarily exclusive. If Gernsback had been able to pay, he could have kept Weinbaum exclusively, and undoubtedly others, and held on, but there we are in the "Worlds of If."

If you write Hornig at any time, you might ask him what he remembers of "Maze of Creation." I think I asked him once and drew a blank, but you never know. I do know that "Maze of Creation" was 90,000 words long, because I found my let- ters to Manning asking him to cut it from 90,000 to 70,000 *before* submitting it to me, because there was no way at that time we could have used a novel of that length. Though again, in the Worlds of If, since I asked him for it substantially before the first issue appeared, had he got it to me fast and had it been really top-notch, it might have helped save the magazine and created a new reputation for himself!

I thanked Sam for his report on October 22, and said:

I was intrigued by your discovery that Manning wasn't being paid at the end, as Hornig says Manning was a preferred writer and close friend of Gernsback's. Manning got three-fourths cent per word, while the going rate was a half cent. If Manning wasn't being paid, then you know Gernsback was in dire financial straits. . . . If Gernsback *could* have paid, he *would* have! He was caught between a rock and a hard place and couldn't do anything about it. He *liked* Manning and certainly Manning would have been paid if Gernsback had any money at all. I really think Gernsback's reputation as a skinflint should be revised to show how he had no choice. Maybe some *small* article could be written just on Gernsback's finances. . . .

I think that, based on what you've found at the Manning residence, it is appropriate to do a retrospective on Laurence Manning. It may be the last time something important can be written about him, as I doubt anything more substantial will surface in the future. You probably now have access to everything that remains. . . . Whaddya think?

I followed this with a letter on November 3, to A. Langley Searles, the editor of *Fantasy Commentator,* telling him everything I knew about the matter and suggesting that Sam write a piece for *Fantasy Commentator* entitled "The Search for the 'Maze of Creation.' " In the proposed article, I wrote, "Sam tells about this last major piece by Manning, how it was promised to *Wonder Stories*, to *Science Fiction +,* what Hornig says, Sam's visit to Edith, his speculations about what he found. I think this would be a fascinating and exciting interim report on a detective search for a little bit of *Wonder Stories* history and would add a spicy little fillip to the end of 'The Age of Wonder.' . . ." The next day I wrote Sam suggesting the same thing, asking him to please think about it.

On November 6, Langley wrote back, saying, "I think your idea for a coda by Sam covering the lost Manning story is an excellent one, and I intend to write him as soon as I finish this letter to you. . . ."

On November 10, Sam wrote me concerning some of Hornig's comments to me in his October 29 letter:

> It is interesting when Hornig says: "Remember, we had the bottom of the pile," referring to the manuscripts he received. Strangely enough, partially because of their very clean-cut presentation, they read very original and interesting at the time. Every now and then he would have an issue quite as good as *Astounding*.
>
> His comment now lays greater importance on Gernsback's searching out foreign translations. He needed them to try to get better quality material, as well as something novel. Unfortunately, they were not as swift-paced as American material and did not have the same acceptance.

On November 14 and 20, I sent Langley two more long letters dealing with revisions of my conversation with Charles Hornig, then in the pipeline. In passing, I also mentioned that I hoped Sam said yes to doing a short piece on his search for the "Maze of Creation." I never heard anything else about the project.

Nevertheless, I knew Sam had now acquired much material on Manning and I expected to see an article at any moment on the search, either in *Fantasy Commentator* or somewhere else. More than a decade passed and nothing appeared. No doubt Sam had many other projects in the hopper.

Then came the horrible news that Sam had died April 15, 1997, of a sudden and massive heart attack. As the shock faded, I eventually remembered the search for Laurence Manning's faded reputation which Sam and I had briefly shared in the summer and fall of 1986. In late July of 1997, I called Langley and reminded him of Sam's visit to Edith Manning a decade before. Sam had to have a file on Laurence Manning, I told him. There must be extensive notes on his interview with Edith, perhaps a tape of it, as I taped all of my own interviews. Perhaps Langley could visit Sam's widow, Christine, and look for such a file. He then might be able to take Sam's notes and flesh them out into some kind of article on Manning and the long-ago search.

Not likely, Langley told me. He said Sam relied almost entirely on his prodigious memory and, at most, there might be a single page of scrawled and (to us) incoherent words, phrases, and dates which Sam would have used to jog his memory when writing up the piece. There would be no way for anyone but Sam to reconstruct any notes which might exist. No, he said, our best hope is for you, Eric, to get in touch with Edith Manning as fast as possible and do the interview all over.

So, on July 31, 1997, I again called the number I had for Edith Manning in Highlands, New Jersey. It had been disconnected. I called telephone information and was told there was no number, not even unlisted, for a Laurence or Edith Manning anywhere in Highlands or adjacent communities. I'll keep searching, but if Edith is alive, she'll be either ninety-one or ninety-two. The odds seem against me finding her.

And so, it seems, we will never get that last chance to revive the memory and reputation of Laurence Manning. Our attempted rescue had failed. And the essay I'd urged upon Sam Moskowitz a decade ago—"The Search for the 'Maze of Creation' "—ends up being this essay you've just read. Only now it's about more than just the work and memory of Laurence Manning. It's also about the work and memory of Sam Moskowitz.

NOTES

1. Lester Del Rey, *The World of Science Fiction: The History of a Subculture, 1926-1976* (New York: Ballantine Books, 1979), p. 64.

2. Isaac Asimov, ed., *Before the Golden Age: A Science Fiction Anthology of the 1930s* (New York: Doubleday & Co., 1974), p. 373.

3. Sam Moskowitz, *Seekers of Tomorrow: Masters of Modern Science Fiction* (Cleveland & New York: The World Publishing Co., 1966), p. 387.

4. Moskowitz, *Seekers of Tomorrow*, p. 128; Robert Ewald and Mike Ashley in *Science Fiction, Fantasy, and Weird Fiction Magazines*, edited by Marshall B. Tymn and Mike Ashley (Westport, Conn.: Greenwood Press, 1985), p. 751.

5. He must have met Pratt shortly before the founding meeting of the Interplanetary Society at the home of G. Edward Pendray, another *Wonder Stories* author, on April 4, 1930. A dozen people, including *Wonder Stories* editor David Lasser, were present. Intimate contact between the three must have been likely, as the Pratt-Manning collaboration was published in the next month's *Wonder Stories* (May 1930).

6. Asimov, *Before the Golden Age*, p. 373.

7. Peter Nicholls, ed., *The Science Fiction Encyclopedia* (New York: Doubleday & Co., 1979).

11.

THE BIRTH OF
SCIENCE FICTION HISTORY

Sam Moskowitz—
The Immortal Historian

THE LAST TIME I SAW SAM MOSKOWITZ HE WAS WAVING goodbye as Anita Alverio and I roared out of a Pittsburgh hotel parking lot on my motorcycle. We'd rendezvoused with Sam at this hotel when he was attending the 1993 Dum Dum there, and Anita and I lived in Pittsburgh. (Dum Dum is the annual convention of the Edgar Rice Burroughs fan club). It was a convenient place to meet one another at last.

Of course, in a way I'd already met Sam Moskowitz, the science fiction scholar, many decades before. I met him in the late fifties and early sixties while growing up in Phoenix and reading his profiles of SF authors in the various magazines I bought off the newsstand at the local grocery store. Any magazine which carried a Moskowitz profile always seemed to have more heft to it than the myriad lightweight competitors also beckoning me with their garish covers. I usually went for the Moskowitz. And when these profiles were later published as *Seekers of Tomorrow* and *Explorers of the Infinite*, I eagerly bought them, even though I'd already read their contents.

I followed these first essays of Sam's in anthologies edited by him, where he brought to light some unimaginably antique SF treasures. I was interested in history anyway. By reading Sam, I was able to combine two of my greatest pleasures: reading history and reading science fiction. And so Sam remained a name in a magazine or on a book cover to me for many years, a name I enjoyed reading and learning from. I never had any reason to believe he would ever be anything else but that name on a piece of paper.

This changed around 1986 when, for reasons not relevant here, I wrote a long essay, which accompanied a long conversation I taped, on pioneering SF editor David Lasser. I find it difficult to write things to order. Rather, I go where my interest carries me—then later try to find someone to publish it. Such was the case with my Lasser essay and conversation. I had no idea where the piece might be published.

Not knowing what else to do with a piece of SF history, I searched out Sam Moskowitz's address and, on June 13, 1986, mailed it to him. On June 16, Sam replied with an enthusiastic letter telling me how great and original he thought my essay was. He said I should send it to A. Langley Searles at *Fantasy Commentator*, which was "the very best of all the scholarly fantasy magazines" and was where he published most of his essays. Well, I thought, if that's good enough for Sam Moskowitz, it's good enough for me.

After correcting me on a number of points in my essay, Sam wrote one other thing. When I sent it to Searles, because I was an unknown quantity, "tell him I suggested it on reading your manuscript, because he has seen my correspondence with Lasser and would swear you stole it if you didn't mention that I had gone over your piece." I did as Sam instructed. I don't know if Langley discussed my essay with Sam, but I do know that on July 8, Langley wrote me an equally enthusiastic letter saying he very much wanted to publish my essay in the next issue of *Fantasy Commentator*. And so it was.

And that was the beginning of my relationship with both Sam

and Langley. In the dozen years since, I've published a number of essays and conversations with SF pioneers in *Fantasy Commentator*. Each one benefitted from extensive "in-progress" suggestions from Sam. And there were many other projects Sam urged upon me which I just did not have the time to follow through on. Sam accepted me, perhaps not as an equal, but certainly as someone who knew enough and cared enough about our shared objects of affection that he could discuss our unearthing of SF's distant past as a mutual labor of love. I think perhaps the most important success story that grew out of our relationship was the literal rescue of all the business correspondence and story manuscripts of SF giant Stanley G. Weinbaum, a rescue operation that also involved Norm Metcalf, of Boulder, Colorado. This is perhaps not the place to go into detail about that collaborative effort, except to say that it resulted in a special edition of *Fantasy Commentator* devoted to new material on Weinbaum, sixty years after Weinbaum's death

So, when Sam wrote me that he was coming to Pittsburgh for the 1993 Dum Dum and that he wanted to meet me, I was thrilled. At last! The man himself!

It was a beautiful, sunny, summer day when Anita and I rode out to the suburban hotel to see Sam. We met him in the morning and spent the day with him. After all our correspondence, it seemed we already knew each other very well and instantly felt at ease with each other. Other than the meeting itself, no great and wonderful events transpired. We hung out. We talked. We sat outside at an auction of Edgar Rice Burroughs (ERB) memorabilia and marvelled at the enormous prices mundane objects associated with Burroughs brought. Cancelled checks wrote to pay trivial bills commanded amazing sums. Sam laughed at this and joked that he should've saved all of his own cancelled checks, had he only known what prices they might one day bring.

Sam bought nothing at the auction, explaining that he already had everything he wanted. "I have a number of Frank Paul paintings," he said. "The originals for various magazine covers. I've been offered fantastic sums for them, but what would I do with the money? I couldn't buy another Frank Paul with it!"

Growing tired of ERBdom's frantic bidding for pieces of the True Cross, we retired to the hotel's restaurant, where Sam treated me and Anita to an excellent lunch. The lunch stretched into mid-afternoon as Sam talked about new projects he was working on, and asked about my own. Sam had just finished his "autobiography" of John W. Campbell, based upon extensive correspondence he'd recently gained access to. Sam explained how he knew what even the most obscure reference in Campbell's letters referred to because "I was there." And, if he didn't know right away what Campbell was talking about, he could soon enough ferret out the context from his unparalleled personal working library back home, which surely contained every SF fanzine produced from the olden days.

Eventually, it was time to go. We were all tired from hours of excited conversation and a long ride lay before me and Anita. Nor was the day over for Sam. He was scheduled to participate in some up-coming panel.

Instead of bidding us farewell in the hotel lobby, Sam insisted on walking out to the parking lot with us. For reasons unknown to me, he was fascinated by the fact that I drove a motorcycle and wanted to watch us roar off on it. So, in the lot we all gathered around my bike. He smiled broadly as Anita and I buckled on our helmets and pulled on our leather gloves. We shook hands and hugged a final time. Then Anita and I climbed on the bike, fired it up, and took off. As we pulled out into traffic, Anita waved. Sam waved back, still grinning like the Cheshire Cat. I kept my hands on the handlebars.

I understand from Langley that Sam told him all about my motorcycle when he got back. His fascination surprised me at the time. Since then, I've settled upon the idea that he was just very curious about something unfamiliar to him. That would be so characteristic of Sam. He was always curious—about every- thing. That's what made him such a fine scholar of science fiction. He wanted to know everything there was to know about science fiction. And I think he did.

That's why science fiction lost its greatest historian and most dedicated fan when Sam Moskowitz died at the age of seventy-six. A leading editor and critic, he was also the foremost expert on science fiction's pulp magazine origins and the author or editor of sixty hardcover and paperback books. He was a recipient of the Pilgrim Award from the Science Fiction Research Association (1981) and a member of the Science Fiction Hall of Fame (1972). No one knew more about the early years of science fiction, or had done so much to document this largely unheralded literary genre. No one devoted so much time and energy to tracking down every nugget of information, from the origins of the words "science fiction" and "fanzine" themselves, to who wrote the first twists on now-standard SF clichés. Though others have worked diligently to shed light on various forgotten corners, for more than half a century Sam Moskowitz was the main searchlight cutting through the night.

Sam Moskowitz died on Tuesday, April 15, 1997, after suffering a massive heart attack in the early morning hours of Tuesday, April 8, at his home in Newark, N.J. He had just returned from a weekend SF con in St. Louis. The day before, he'd attended the funeral for a member of the local chapter of "New Voices," of which Sam was the president. "New Voices" is a medical self-help group for people who have lost their larynxes due to throat cancer, an illness Sam had already fought and survived. He retired about midnight on the eighth. A few hours later he woke his wife in an agitated state. A medical doctor herself, she recognized the signs of a heart attack and quickly rushed him to the intensive care unit of the local hospital. Though he lingered for a week, he never regained consciousness.

Sam Moskowitz began his self-appointed task of documenting the history of science fiction in the early 1940s. After working at hard manual labor all day, he would come home and put in another full "day" of research and writing about the field.

Until his retirement, he had worked for many years as the editor of a frozen-food industry magazine. Much of his work appeared in *Fantasy Commentator*, a "fanzine" begun by A. Langley Searles in 1943 and which continues publication to this day. Indeed, Sam Moskowitz was originally best-known in the genre for *The Immortal Storm* (1954), a history of the science fiction fan movement from its beginnings up to World War II, which appeared first as a series in the pages of *Fantasy Commentator* between 1946 and 1952 before the Atlanta Science Fiction Organization Press published it as a book in 1954. Searles, who had urged Sam to write the series, had recently urged him to continue with his fan history. This Sam was doing, and Searles was publishing, at the time of his death. This continuation will remain forever incomplete, as no one other than Sam Moskowitz has the intimate knowledge needed to write such a history.

Other works for which Sam is noted include: *Explorers of the Infinite* (1963) and *Seekers of Tomorrow* (1966), both collections of author profiles which had appeared in various SF magazines over the years; *Science Fiction by Gaslight* (1968); *The Man Who Called Himself Poe* (1969); *Under the Moons of Mars* (1970); *Strange Horizons* (1976), another collection of author profiles; *Science Fiction in Old San Francisco* (1980); and *A. Merritt: Reflections in the Moon Pool* (1985). Sam also recently discovered that the version of *The Black Flame*, by early SF giant Stanley Weinbaum, with which the world was long familiar, was a greatly truncated version. Thus, almost sixty years after its original 1939 publication, Sam made possible the first complete edition of this SF classic from Tachyon Press (1995), for which Sam wrote the introduction.

Sam was consulting editor for *The Pulps* (1970), an anthology of pulp magazine fiction, and general editor of the two important reprints of the Hyperion Press Science Fiction Classics series (1974, 1976). Among the dozens of other anthologies he edited are *A Martian Odyssey & Other Classics of Science Fiction by Stanley G. Weinbaum* (1962), for which Sam wrote a biographical introduction; *Masterpieces of Science Fiction* (1967); *Ghostly by Gaslight* (with Alden H. Norton, 1970); *When Women Rule* (1972); and *Out of the Storm* (1975) by William Hope Hodgson, containing a twenty-five-thousand-word critical biography of the noted author written by Sam.

Sam Moskowitz also organized the first World Science Fiction Convention (1939), taught the world's first college-level course in science fiction (1953-1955), and edited both Hugo Gernsback's last magazine, *Science Fiction Plus* (1952-1954) and a brief revival of that greatest of all fantasy magazines, *Weird Tales* (1973-1974).

Sam also possessed what is no doubt the most comprehensive science fiction collection in the world, which he insisted was a "working library," out of which grew his writing. This personal library (and his own phenomenal memory) is what made possible his massive "autobiography" of the legendary science fiction editor John W. Campbell, which is awaiting publication. Based entirely upon Campbell's voluminous correspondence, no one else could have envisioned such an imaginative undertaking, much less had the personal and documentary resources to carry it through to completion. There will be no other such masterpieces of historical reconstruction. There will be no other Sam Moskowitz.

For many, Sam's first effort, *The Immortal Storm*, remains the work by which he is best remembered. It is truly a history book to me, in the same category as Damon Knight's *The Futurians* and Fred Pohl's *The Way the Future Was*, which, in their early sections, cover some of the same territory. Indeed, it is instructive to read these three as a unit, for they represent the opposing sides of the major fan feud which dominates the last part of Moskowitz's book. That was the feud between New Fandom, of which Sam was a leader, and The Futurians, of which Knight and Pohl were members. This feud is presented as a matter of almost earth-shaking consequence by Sam as, in fact, he seemed to consider all fan activities at the time. In a way, this provides a form of novelistic conflict.

In his desire to tell all, however, Sam goes a little further than some readers may prefer. For example, were this book in fact to have been written with "the narrative drive of a fine novel", as the Hyperion Press publicity kit claims, it should perhaps have ended with the first World Science Fiction Convention, the Worldcon, of July 1939. In retrospect, that was the real climax of the New Fandom-Futurian conflict.

There is no need to recount that convention and the events that led up to it except in the barest outline: Against great odds, Sam, William Sykora, and James Taurasi created the New Fandom organization and organized the unprecedented first Worldcon within an amazingly short period of time. This was done in the face of incessant sniping from The Futurians, the other major fan organization of the time. Then, at the New York convention, there was a dramatic show-down between the rival groups. Sam and Taurasi literally stood in the door to bar entrance to the major Futurian leaders, whom they were convinced were bent on disrupting, perhaps destroying, all that New Fandom had labored so hard to achieve. (Many years later, one of the Futurians publicly admitted that this was, indeed, the game plan.) Those Futurians who gave their word of honor not to disrupt the proceedings—such as Isaac Asimov—were allowed in. Those who refused to so swear were turned away. The convention went on to make history as the first of a successful half-century-long tradition of SF conventions, which continues to the present. That makes a satisfying climax, and, if this were indeed a "fine novel," that's where the story would have ended.

However, let us admit that, foremost science fiction historian though he was, Sam was not a fine novelist. One of the major reasons for this was because he violated Voltaire's warning to writers *not* to tell everything they know. Sam couldn't help doing so. More, he didn't even *want* to do so. Therefore, his everything-including-the-kitchen-sink approach to history compelled him to carry his story on for another four anti-climactic months, to November 1939. In an Epilogue he states that he wanted to continue his chronicle, "in *detail*" (his emphasis) up to Pearl Harbor "with the same detail, research and thoroughness which has characterized it to this point," with "no important omissions that might cause knowledgeable parties to question its authenticity or careless errors that might be seized upon to discredit the entire work." Decades later, Sam returned to that task once more with three further installments in the same pages of *Fantasy Commentator*. Alas, he never realized his stated ambition, however. Perhaps due to venturing far afield to chronicle fan activities overseas and in Los Angeles, Sam had still not reached Pearl Harbor at the time of his death.

As it is (and more so with the three later installments), the work is perhaps the most comprehensive history of science fiction fandom in the 1930s we are ever likely to get. But Sam's tendency—in all of his work—to tell everything he knows, regardless of importance or perceived relevance, does make it difficult for many readers to appreciate his accomplishments. Indeed, I think this is one reason academics have had such a seemingly hard time accepting his work.

In addition, Sam courted academic disdain when he sometimes allowed himself to get carried away. It is easy, especially for academics, to ridicule Sam's purple prose and suspect that no one, not even Sam, took seriously the importance he attached to the activities of the minuscule group of science fiction fans. For instance, he writes, "But again stark drama was preparing her lines for recitation. . . . Ragnarok had caught the entire fan world napping!" (p. 77). Now, how many of these Asgardians are we actually talking about here? For the most part, we're dealing with about forty or fifty active teenage fans. Sam accepts as reasonably comprehensive the 1937 fan polls conducted by fan Jack Speer and his Oklahoma Institute of Private Opinion, which usually mailed out only forty ballots nationwide (p. 122). At the same time, Sam himself admits that "Active fans then numbered less than fifty" (p. 114). Likewise, in discussing the circulation of major fan magazines in the summer of 1938, such as *The Sci-*

ence Fiction Collector and his own *Helios*, Sam says, "None of the journals named above had a circulation of more than fifty" (p. 151). Possibly this number could be pushed up to around one hundred, for in late 1938 Sam records a fan poll in *The Science Fiction Fan* in which ninety-one ballots were cast (p. 188) and he notes that at the same period several important fanzines "had a paid circulation list of over a hundred," (p. 200). Even so, we are talking about a very small number of people out of the entire American population.

I believe, however, that Sam was quite sincere about the significance he saw in their poorly reproduced publications, their living room gatherings, their tempest-in-a-teapot feuds. Already in the thirties Sam was writing fan history (he claims he was "obsessed" with it) and took umbrage when fellow fans made fun of his efforts. "Moskowitz realized," he says of himself, "that when people laughed *at* something they would no longer take it seriously; and to him, these articles on fan history were serious things indeed," (p. 203). Such being the case with his first efforts in this direction, how much more so must he have felt about his *magnum opus* on fan history?

And perhaps Sam was quite right in doing so. Historical importance, after all, is not necessarily measured by numbers. In some cases, *influence* is the significant factor to be weighed. Christianity, for instance, was started by twelve men. Out of the fifty to a hundred active teenage fans Sam mentions came a disproportionate number of authors, editors, and publishers who have shaped (and continue to shape) sixty years of science fiction into the most vital literary genre now in existence. Indeed, it is almost the *only* literary genre left. Only the mystery genre can yet boast of mass-circulation fiction magazines on the newsstands. Science fiction flourishes while all the other pulp genres that glutted the newsstands of the thirties—Westerns, South Sea adventures, air war stories, boxing stories—have long-since disappeared. In the book stores, the science fiction and fantasy paperback sections dominate the floor space. Science fiction novels now regularly appear on the *New York Times* best-seller list. The biggest Hollywood money-makers in history are science fiction epics such as *Star Wars, Star Trek, E.T., Independence Day, The Terminator, Alien*, and their clones. These facts tell us that this literature—despised and ridiculed, spurned and rejected—was different from all the others. Something about it made it live long and prosper, while other literary fields withered and died.

Additionally, many of the pioneering efforts of 1930s fandom have flourished and borne fruit over the past sixty years. Fanzines—virtually unique to the field—continue to proliferate. The Worldcon, launched by New Fandom in the thirties, is now sixty years old and has spawned imitators by the score. Not a weekend exists without some science fiction convention taking place somewhere in the country. Indeed, even gatherings of sub-divisions of the field, such as *Star Trek* conventions, teem in such number and size as to dwarf the dreams of First Fandom back in the thirties.

And we also have the persevering example of journals such as *Fantasy Commentator* (which is older than I am and is still publishing!) and, indeed, of Sam himself, who was still documenting the history of the field up to the end, just as he was sixty years ago. David G. Hartwell has said that, "The Golden Age of Science Fiction is twelve," meaning that is the age at which most of us were hooked on the field. I suspect that remains as true today as it was in the 1930s. Yet A. Langley Searles is long past the age of twelve and is still publishing his journal. Sam was long past twelve and yet was still "obsessed" with the field. Even I am now old enough to have a son or daughter of twelve, yet I, too, remain in love with the field. What is it about science fiction that has made it and its adherents so persevering, so influential upon American (indeed, world) culture, so—*different*?

Perhaps it is because, in its own way, science fiction, unlike all the other literary genres, is a secular religion, a secular millennialism, which shares with other millenarian movements the basic belief in a future age of human perfection. Central to bringing about this future Edenic age is Science, with a capital "S." I used to live in Boston and many times visited the Boston Museum of Science which, like Chicago's Museum of Science and Technology, was built in an earlier time when science was itself a secular religion and these were the temples of the new religion. They were inspired by the same unambiguous belief in continuous human progress, which we identify so closely with eminent Victorians such as Thomas Huxley and his student, science fiction writer H. G. Wells. This is the same belief in the unending triumphs of science Frank R. Paul glorified by his magazine covers and Hugo Gernsback proselytized with his publications. It is the same all-consuming faith in "The Shape of Things To Come" that seduced the twelve-year-olds of 1939 and will continue to seduce the twelve-year-olds of 1999.

But what is so different about this particular millennialism is that the Millennium actually seems to be arriving! The wild fantasies of the thirties, laughed at and derided by the "realistic" multitudes, have come true. Nuclear weapons ended World War II. The Falklands War and the Persian Gulf War were fought with missiles. Human organ transplantation is a mundane surgical procedure. We have produced test-tube babies. We have cloned sheep. Humans have walked on the surface of the Moon. Robot probes have landed on and mapped the entire surface of Venus. Other robots have landed on and rolled over the surface of Mars. A space station is in orbit around Earth. Space shuttle launchings are routine events. Remote controlled spacecraft have flown into the heart of Halley's Comet and out beyond the Solar System. The Galileo spacecraft in orbit around Jupiter explored that planet and the Jovian moons. The Cassini spacecraft is now en route to Saturn, where it will spend four years in orbit exploring the ringed planet and its icy moons, especially the biggest, Titan. Worldwide telephone and television communication is instantaneous because of a network of geosynchronous satellites circling the earth twenty-seven thousand miles up—a possibility first conceived by Arthur C. Clarke, *a science fiction writer!* Even the millennial (and science fictional!) date of the year 2000 is just around the corner. The "Class of 2000" is already in high school and college! *We are now living in the science fiction future prophesied in the 1930s!*

Is it any wonder, then, that Sam Moskowitz took so seriously his task—and almost his task alone!—of documenting the genesis of that small band of spurned seers who foresaw the Millennium and created their own literature to describe it? Of course he wasn't writing novels! He was recording for the ages, while the data could yet be retrieved! That's why he felt compelled to throw in everything (including the kitchen sink!)—because, as with the *New York Times*, which sees itself as the newspaper of record, Sam Moskowitz saw himself as the science fiction historian of record. Others can and will build upon what he unearthed (as, indeed, I have myself), but at least he made sure the informational building blocks were salvaged from the oblivion of history. Sam was there, blazing the path that others must follow. He wrote what should not be forgotten. Nor is it any wonder that Sam approached his task with such an elevated view of the importance of the events he was documenting. *He was revealing the origins of a prophetic new literary genre.* Time for the naysayers to stop nitpicking, I think, and appreciate what a priceless legacy Sam Moskowitz left us—and the world.

Conclusion

LOOK BACK IN WONDER

The Discovery/Birth of a Genre

WHEN I WAS SIX SCIENCE FICTION WAS A MONSTER THAT came out of Hollywood. It was 1953 and producer George Pal released his version of H. G. Wells's *War of the Worlds*. Gene Barry starred in it, but what burned itself into my impressionable young mind was how the invading Martian ships—floating slowly over the landscape like abstract giant sting rays—turned artillery pieces and their crews into instant smoking ash with their heat rays. And—*quick!*—there goes an actual Martian scurrying through the ruined house! Gosh! Wow!

I wanted more, and Hollywood cooperated by unleashing a horde of Grade-B science fiction films upon the land. By chance I was growing into intellectual consciousness just as the "Second Genesis" of science fiction—its rebirth as a distinct cinematic category—was taking place. A flood of low-budget SF films raced across the American landscape in the fifties, sweeping me along in the torrent. In 1954 director Jack Arnold enthralled me with *The Creature from the Black Lagoon*, starring omnipresent fifties

371

SF actor Richard Carlson. The Creature was a humanoid amphibian, a living fossil which had somehow crawled out of time's abyss and was splashing around the Amazon. The Creature had to compete for my rapture with *Them!*—giant ants created as radioactive mutations by atomic-bomb testing in the Western deserts. The next year, 1955, Jack Arnold returned with *Revenge of the Creature*, in which Clint Eastwood made his movie debut as a lab technician. That same year Arnold also turned out one of the best giant insect flicks of the fifties, *Tarantula*. This time the humongous arachnid was created by Leo J. Carroll, a "mad scientist" whose experiments went awry. Clint Eastwood was one of the jet fighter pilots who blasted it into oblivion at the end.

But science fiction's Second Genesis as a cinematic category was not just about big bugs. Walt Disney also introduced me to Jules Verne in 1954 with *20,000 Leagues Under the Sea*. Kirk Douglas became one of my favorite actors and I yearned for a model of Captain Nemo's "Nautilus." I was introduced to Shakespeare (though I didn't know it at the time) in 1956 by *Forbidden Planet*, the SF classic based on *The Tempest*. It starred Leslie Nielsen, Ann Francis, Walter Pidgeon, Jack Kelly (later, with James Garner, a "Maverick" in the TV series), and, most memorably for me, Robbie the Robot. "Monsters from the Id!" What a concept! Just what was the "Id," anyway?

At this point, my exposure to science fiction resembled *everyone's* exposure to such fiction before 1926, when Hugo Gernsback launched the first science fiction magazine. It was haphazard and I had no idea that what I was enjoying was a distinct type of story-telling. I had no label for what I had found. I did not yet know it was called "science fiction." I just knew these types of stories excited me—and I searched everywhere for more of the same. One of the places I found them was in the pages of the now unfortunately defunct *Classics Illustrated* comic books. I don't know how I stumbled upon this wonderful series, perhaps in the racks of comic books at the local grocery store, as specialty comic book stores did not exist at that time. In any case, I was soon ordering issues through the mail and I was filled with joy when I found the small rolled-up tube of brown paper in our mailbox, which told me another issue had arrived. In this way I discovered such amazing stories as Stevenson's "Dr. Jekyll and Mr. Hyde," Verne's "From the Earth to the Moon," and Wells's "The Time Machine," "The First Men in the Moon," and "War of the Worlds." To this day, the definitive *Classics Illustrated* image of the Martian war machines—gigantic walking tripods supporting gun-barrel-sprouting cowls—dominates my imagination, so much more powerfully than George Pal's floating sting rays.

And then I discovered Edgar Rice Burroughs! I was raised on the outskirts of Phoenix, Arizona, where the city met the desert. Our "neighbor" in one direction was an incredibly ancient woman, Mrs. Herald, who had homesteaded the entire tract of land where our home and many others stood. This was back in the days before 1912 when Arizona was still a pioneer territory. Over the years she had sold off acre after acre, but she still retained a vast amount of desert wilderness upon which she raised goats, chickens, and a male peacock named "Geronimo." In the mid-fifties I spent many a long summer afternoon sitting in her living room listening to her stories of pioneer days—or tales of the German and Italian POWs incarcerated during World War II across the street from us at Papago Park.[1]

Sometimes Mrs. Herald loaned me books which she thought might interest me from her library. Among these were first editions of the Tarzan tales, which her deceased husband had bought her back in the teens of the twentieth century. Along with Tarzan, however, were other books by Burroughs, which interested me far more. These were the first three John Carter of Barsoom (Mars, if you need to know) novels: *A Princess of Mars, The Gods of Mars*, and *The Warlord of Mars*. God! *When* is Hollywood going to make a movie of *Princess of Mars*? I'm *still* in love with Dejah Thoris! That *has* to be the most beautiful name of any heroine in all of science fiction!

For a brief period while reading these novels, the line

between fiction and fact blurred. I wanted so hard for Barsoom to exist that I almost believed it actually *did*! I almost believed that, through an act of will, I, too, could wake up on the Red Planet. Here, indeed, I experienced that "Sense of Wonder" that Robert Silverberg also felt upon reading his first SF books:

> Their impact on me was overwhelming. I can still taste and feel the extraordinary sensations they awakened in me: it was a physiological thing, a distinct excitement, a certain metabolic quickening at the mere thought of handling them, let alone reading them. It must be like that for every new reader— apocalyptic thunderbolts and eerie unfamiliar music accompanying you as you lurch and stagger, awed and shaken, into a bewildering new world of images and ideas, which is exactly the place you've been hoping to find all your life.[2]

Yessss!

When, soon thereafter, I attempted my own first science fiction story, it was a blatant imitation of Burroughs, filled with one chase and escape sequence after another. I thought it was so horrible I never showed it to anyone (or even told anyone about it!). Instead, I clambered into a deep irrigation ditch surrounded by high weeds and knelt in the bottom where no one could see me. There I tore my story into teensy bits, piled the fragments into a cone, and set fire to them with a match. I just can't write fiction, I concluded.[3]

When I was nine I discovered science fiction books. Sometime in 1956 my parents took the family to visit a woman friend in one of the new cinder block subdivisions sprouting in the desert around Phoenix. I've forgotten her name and even what she looked like. All I remember is that she gave me a new paperback anthology of stories she thought I might be interested in. It was *S-F: The Year's Greatest Science-Fiction and Fantasy*, edited by Judith Merril and published by Dell. Merril, who died in 1997 at age seventy-four, had (according to the back-cover blurb) chosen the best tales "culled from more than a thousand stories published in books and magazines during the past year [1955]." With an introduction by Orson Welles, it was the first volume in what became a long and influential series of "best of" anthologies, and what stories! Merril's choice for the best stories of 1955 included works by writers I soon came to realize were giants in the field: Isaac Asimov, Theodore Sturgeon, Damon Knight, Jack Finney, Zenna Henderson, James Gunn, Henry Kuttner and C. L. Moore, Mildred Clingerman, Avram Davidson, Shirley Jackson, Algis Budrys, and Walter M. Miller Jr. "The sky's no limit," the back cover blurb continued, "to the adventure and excitement, the sheer reading pleasure, you will find in this selection of the very best of science-fantasy."

More than forty years later I still have that very book (it is here beside my keyboard as I type). On the cover is an abstract painting popular on SF paperbacks in the mid-fifties. The top left corner says, "Dell First Edition." The top right corner has the price: 35 cents. It is falling apart, the pages are loose and tattered, the binding is gone, and it smells musty. But I treasure it still, because this book was my conscious gateway to the literature. It was with this book that I at last discovered the name of what I was reading: "Science-Fiction and Fantasy"!

Curiously, although the copyright page of Merril's anthology clearly listed the magazines in which the stories first appeared— *Astounding, Galaxy, The Magazine of Fantasy and Science Fiction*—I still did not realize science fiction magazines existed. Perhaps I didn't pay attention to copyright pages at age nine. But, now that I knew my stories had a name, I searched out the SF section of my grade school library. There I discovered further gems, not least among them the fantastic juvenile fiction of Robert A. Heinlein.

In 1947 Heinlein began publishing a string of well-written SF novels aimed at the juvenile audience. The first in this series was that year's *Rocket Ship Galileo*. Over the next dozen years his juvenile SF brought to "children's literature" the same "adult" characteristics of strong narrative lines, crisp dialog, believable characters, and authentic scientific detail, which John W. Campbell had already made mandatory in the pages of *Astounding*. Although I retained my fondness for Burroughs, Heinlein became, for a time, my favorite author and I read everything of his in my school library. I thought one of the best of Heinlein's juvenile SF novels was 1958's *Have Spacesuit, Will Travel*.[4] As with all these novels, it featured a juvenile hero. In this case, the hero won a used spacesuit in some kind of contest and, through an unexpected chain of events, soon had to put it to use in space.

After that I was searching for Heinlein paperbacks in the drug stores. In 1959 I came across his impressive *Starship Troopers*, which was made into a big-budget Hollywood movie of the same name in 1997. Originally written as a juvenile SF novel, it was rejected by his publisher, Scribners, because of the violence. It is also a heavily didactic novel in which Heinlein's political views are given full rein. It projects a militarized future society in which only those who serve in the military are allowed full citizenship. Over the course of the novel a young pacifist learns the errors of his ways, goes through boot camp, and emerges to become a heroic warrior in Earth's war against alien aggressors. While it gave rise to Heinlein's reputation as a fascist, it was also powerfully written and won the 1960 Hugo for best novel of the year. I was under its spell for quite a while.

Also in 1960, at age thirteen, I belatedly discovered science fiction magazines. I was in our local grocery store perusing the magazine racks. I saw what I thought was a science magazine— it had a cover featuring giant test tubes and hypodermic needles and promised "science fact"—and I bought it for 50 cents. It was the March 1960 issue of Campbell's *Astounding Science Fact & Fiction* and the cover illustration was for "Immortality for Some," a short story by little-known Scottish SF writer "J. T. McIntosh." (I also have this issue and I'm looking at the cover as I write.) McIntosh's story turned out to be forgettable, but I was captivated by everything else I found in the magazine. I sacrificed (you wouldn't believe how I sacrificed!) to get the five dollars needed for a year's subscription and never missed an issue for the next six years. After a long, circuitous route, I'd at last found the Mother Lode, the Holy Grail, the Promised Land. I'd found the source of the literary genre which had come to obsess me.

And, indeed, magazines *were* the source of the genre, for science fiction came into existence as a distinct and self-conscious literary genre between 1926 and 1938 in the pages of the science fiction *magazines* launched at that time. "Science fiction" *elements* and *precursors*, to which advocates can and do point, existed since time immemorial, a fact I do not dispute—but only after 1926 was the literature *conscious* of itself as a distinct literary genre.

Partly this was because several revolutionary developments were necessary before the genre could be born. Not least among these was the Industrial Revolution (in itself a product of the earlier scientific revolution), which began in England around 1780 and spread to America around 1830.

Both primitive and advanced societies of the ancient past viewed life as an eternal present. "There is nothing new under the sun," the Book of Ecclesiastes tells us. The ancient Greeks, the Romans, and the medieval Europeans assumed that their surroundings would persist largely unchanged—*forever*. "Progress" was an alien concept. The Industrial Revolution, however, changed that. It revolutionized not only material life, it also revolutionized world-views, it revolutionized how people viewed time and society. For the first time in human existence, the material world changed—and continued to change—dramatically within the space of a single human lifetime. Individuals could look back to their youth and see that they lived differently *now* than they had in the past. Thus, for the first time, people became *conscious of change*. The present, they discovered, was *different* from the past. That being the case, no doubt the *future* will be *different* from the *present*! And what might that future bring? For the first time in human existence, the future was unknown—for the future would be vastly different from everything around us. In what manner it might be different, we could only speculate. And thus a tremendous mental revolution—one of those "paradigm shifts" in human intellectual history—took place.

Over time this awareness of progress—inescapable in the ways it changed everyone's lives—also began to enter literary consciousness through the work of such apostles of the future as Jules Verne and, later, H. G. Wells. These, however, are just the most well-remembered names from the period. Between 1870 and 1900 hundreds of novels and short stories appeared from a number of authors which we might rightly term "science fiction" in nature. Coupled with the new mass literacy and the rise of mass-circulation magazines (made possible by both the Industrial Revolution and widespread literacy), the ground was thus prepared for the birth of specialty magazines and, eventually, the science fiction genre.

In broad outline we can see the gestation of the genre as the mass-circulation magazines evolved. By the 1850s industrial production of reading material made possible the "story newspapers" and eventually the weekly tabloid "dime novels" which featured the endless adventures of Buffalo Bill, Ned Buntline, and their ilk. By the 1880s inexpensive magazines of all kinds flourished. It was the decade of the 1890s, however, that brought on the era of the "pulp magazines," the most cheaply produced of all such magazines, printed on inexpensive pulp paper. Fiction of all kinds was hungrily devoured by the new magazine-reading audience thus created and in October 1896, Frank Munsey launched *The Argosy*, the world's first all-fiction magazine and also, incidentally, the very first "pulp."[5] Circulation sky-rocketed instantly and within a decade, by 1907, *The Argosy* had the unheard-of circulation of half a million.

In 1904 Street & Smith produced their *Popular Magazine*, Munsey's first competitor. In 1905 William Randolph Hearst bought *Cosmopolitan* and converted it to a venue for popular fiction which, however, also featured many popular science articles. In 1906 Munsey's *The Rail-Road Man's Magazine* appeared, the very first magazine of specialized (genre) fiction. The next year, 1907, Munsey published *The Ocean*, the first sea-fiction magazine. A year later, in 1908, media entrepreneur Hugo Gernsback launched the nonfiction *Modern Electrics*. Between 1911 and 1912, Gernsback experimented with teaching science through fiction by serializing his science fiction novel, *Ralph 124C 41+*,[6] in his *Modern Electrics*. Between 1915 and 1917, Gernsback returned to his task by publishing his series of updated Baron Munchausen pastiches in *Modern Electrics*, now renamed *Electrical Experimenter*.

History was almost made in 1919 when *Thrill Book* appeared. It *almost* became the first fantasy and science fiction magazine, but its publishers were not convinced there was a large enough audience to support such a specialty magazine, and so it mixed such stories with general fiction. The next year H. L. Mencken launched *Black Mask*, which specialized in horror, supernatural, and crime fiction. Not until the late 1920s would it begin to focus on crime fiction and come into its own as the home of the hard-boiled detective story by the likes of Dashiell Hammet and Raymond Chandler.

Love Story Magazine, the first pulp specializing in romance fiction, appeared in 1921. Then, in 1923, the legendary *Weird Tales* was launched as the first all-fantasy fiction magazine. That same year brought a favorable reception to Gernsback's all-"Scientific Fiction Number"—the August issue of his nonfiction magazine, *Science & Invention*. Encouraged, the next year, 1924, Gernsback began soliciting subscriptions for a proposed all-"Scientific Fiction" magazine. In April 1926, Hugo Gernsback introduced *Amazing Stories*, the world's first specialty science fiction magazine—and a genre was born. Others would imitate him and, after 1929, there would be a flood of specialized genre pulp magazines of all kinds, a flood that would continue to rise throughout the 1930s.

In retrospect, the appearance of a specialty science fiction magazine seems almost inevitable. Genre pulps for every taste were being produced. In this context, the "science fiction" niche would have been filled sooner or later, by this person or that. Hearst was mixing popular science articles with fiction in *Cosmopolitan*. Bernarr MacFadden was interested in science fiction and was actually publishing such stories in his magazines prior to 1926. Indeed, he eventually forced Gernsback into bankruptcy in order to acquire *Amazing Stories*. Due to a confluence of socio-cultural factors, then, it was simply *time* for such a magazine to appear. If Gernsback had not given birth to such a magazine, some other equally enterprising media mogul—Hearst, MacFadden, William M. Clayton, Louis Silberkleit, or Street & Smith—would shortly have done so. But, Hugo Gernsback is the "Great Man" who got there first (perhaps because of his desire to teach science through fiction), thus laying claim to his place in history. And once it had a room of its own in the pages of Gernsback's magazine, science fiction quickly jelled into a self-conscious literary genre.

But, unlike all the other niche genres around it, science fiction was vastly *different*. Harlan Ellison claims the difference lies in the fact that science fiction is the only *optimistic* genre. It is optimistic because it is about *tomorrow*. Thus it presupposes *there will be a tomorrow*! We may be living like maggots, he says, but at least there will be a tomorrow. No doubt this is part of science fiction's appeal. But I don't think this is science fiction's major difference. Rather, the distinguishing characteristic of science fiction—and the reason it outlasted all the other niche genres which cluttered the magazine racks around it in the 1930s—is that *this new literary genre generated a feeling of awe, a "Sense of Wonder," which turned readers into fanatics.*

This "Sense of Wonder" was not dependent upon the quality of the writing (indeed, I now recognize Burroughs to be a rather poor writer). Rather, it was and is dependent upon the presence of new ideas, novel ways of looking at humans and our place in the universe, unexpected and creative ways of looking around us at the cosmos. Science fiction alone has the power to unlock the doors of perception through which we step into a twilight zone of the imagination in which all things are possible. Indeed, this is perhaps the very touchstone of science fiction, as all other forms of fiction—even fantasy—present us with worlds, societies, and ideas already familiar. It is no accident that science fiction fans refer to nonfans as "mundanes" (from the Latin *mundus*, "world," and meaning those who see only the ordinary work-a-day world), for the essence of science fiction is that which is *not known*, the *unfamiliar*. Science fiction sees a newer world than the mundane one around us. It sees the rare, the extraordinary. Time and again the pioneers we spoke with in these pages testified to the light that went on in their minds when they first discovered science fiction. It was the classic "Aha!" experience, the revelation that humanity—*that life*—did not always have to be as they had been led to believe!

Science fiction *is* the only optimistic genre. It is also the only literary genre which teaches us that there are *no limits to the possible*. Thus, it answers a hunger of the human soul which always aches for what is *beyond*. And, through the memories of these Pioneers in Wonder, we have been privileged to have been present at the Creation of this "wonderful" literary genre.

NOTES

1. Indeed, the largest escape of German POWs in America during WW II (some of the 425,000 held in American prisons) happened at Papago Park—but this German "Great Escape" is another story.

2. Robert Silverberg, "The Making of a Science-Fiction Writer," in *Reflections and Refractions: Thoughts on Science-Fiction, Science, and Other Matters* (Grass Valley, Calif.: Underwood Books, 1997), pp. 145–46.

3. Perhaps my self-assessment was premature. Since then I have

published twenty-five science fiction and fantasy short stories in one professional venue and various small press magazines and won an international science fiction short story contest.

4. For those too young to remember, the title was a take-off on a popular television Western which ran from 1957 to 1963, *Have Gun, Will Travel*. It made a star out of Richard Boone, who played a hired gun named "Paladin." Our hero lived a dandified life in San Francisco. Once called into the field—which could be anywhere in the West—he dressed entirely in black. However, like the Magnificent Seven, he was a *good* mercenary who fought for the oppressed. "'Have Gun, Will Travel' read the [business] card of a man," sang the theme song. "A knight without honor in a savage land." Richard Boone died of cancer in 1981.

5. This issue was actually dated "April, 1894/1896."

6. "One to foresee for one."

INDEX

383

Notes

Notes

Notes

Notes

Notes

Notes

Notes

Notes